SHENANDOAH UNIVERSITY LIBRARY
WINCHESTER, VA 22601
WITHDRAWN

D0072625

*The Foundations of
American Citizenship*

The Foundations of American Citizenship

LIBERALISM, THE CONSTITUTION, AND CIVIC VIRTUE

Richard C. Sinopoli

New York   Oxford
OXFORD UNIVERSITY PRESS
1992

4.2

*This work is dedicated
to the memory of my parents.*

Oxford University Press

Oxford New York Toronto
Delhi Bombay Calcutta Madras Karachi
Kuala Lumpur Singapore Hong Kong Tokyo
Nairobi Dar es Salaam Cape Town
Melbourne Auckland

and associated companies in
Berlin Ibadan

Copyright © 1992 by Oxford University Press, Inc.

Published by Oxford University Press, Inc.,
200 Madison Avenue, New York, New York 10016

Oxford is a registered trademark of Oxford University Press

All rights reserved. No part of this publication may be reproduced,
stored in a retrieval system, or transmitted, in any form or by any means,
electronic, mechanical, photocopying, recording, or otherwise,
without prior permission of Oxford University Press.

Library of Congress Cataloging-in-Publication Data
Sinopoli, Richard C.
The foundations of American citizenship : liberalism,
the Constitution, and civic virtue / Richard C. Sinopoli.
p. cm. Includes index.
ISBN 0-19-507067-4

1. Political science—United States—History—18th century.
2. Citizenship—United States—History—18th century.
3. Liberalism—United States—History—18th century. I. Title.
JA84.U5S555 1992 320.5'1'0973—dc20   91-25505

135798642

JA   Sinopoli, Richard C.
84
.U5   The foundations of
S555   American citizenship
1992
320.51 Si67f

Acknowledgments

A great many people have been generous with time, suggestions, and criticism in the course of writing this book. It seems ages ago when this project started as a dissertation under the guidance of a great professor and dear friend, H. Mark Roelofs. Mark's love of scholarship and generosity of spirit are unparalleled and his contribution to this endeavor has been invaluable. Ron Replogle was also an especially valuable source of ideas and inspiration. Louis Koenig, Lawrence Mead, David Richards, and Irving Kristol also offered valuable suggestions at this stage. More recently, I have been aided by numerous friends, colleagues, conference panelists, and anonymous reviewers. Of these, several colleagues at the University of California at Davis must be mentioned. Larry Peterman, John Gates, Edmond Costantini, and Donald Rothchild commented generously on chapters and offered useful advice. In addition, Monte Freidig, Scott Hill, David Lewis, Roger Rose, and John Zawiski provided able research assistance. Finally, I am grateful to James Kloppenburg, who generously waived anonymity as a reviewer for Oxford, to Valerie Aubry for supporting the project, and to the other anonymous reviewers who made the book longer but hopefully better. Though my debts of gratitude are extensive and deep, errors of fact and interpretation are, alas, mine alone.

Contents

The Foundations of
American Citizenship

1

Introduction:
The Constitutional Founders'
Liberalism and Civic Virtue

Jean-Jacques Rousseau wrote in his first published discourse that "we have physicists, geometers, chemists, astronomers, poets . . . [but] we no longer have citizens."[1] In so doing, he pointed to a long-standing, probably eternal, problem of political life. How does an individual reconcile private capacities and goals with the duties—and opportunities—of public life? Rousseau's solution, by and large, consists of a campaign of education and socialization, reminiscent of the Spartans, to remind each and every member of the political community that the good of the community takes precedence over that of any of its members. If you are a poet, Rousseau suggests, your poetry should laud the country that enabled you to develop your gifts. If you are a chemist, your life's work should be put at the service of the community. Each person, is in a sense, public property. Whatever your particular gifts, you are first and foremost a *citizen* and, as such, you should not only serve the state in your particular occupation but should take an active part in its governance.

The vast majority of Americans of the founding generation—or our own—would not accept a Rousseauian solution to this tension between the demands of public and private life. The founders examined in this study, opponents in the debates over the ratification of the Constitution of 1787, were too committed to the liberal individualism Rousseau often criticizes for this to be the case.[2] Jefferson perhaps best sums up the liberal response to Rousseau's republican vision. It is "indeed ridiculous," he wrote, "to suppose a man ha[s] less right in himself than one of his neighbors or all of them put together."[3]

Jefferson neither denies nor denigrates the duties members of even a liberal commonwealth owe their peers. He does deny, however, that the community has the legitimate authority to direct the activities of individuals, whether in religious worship or choice of occupation, for the good of the whole or for that of some other citizen. The claims the state can make on the individual are restricted by that person's rights.

Yet the problem itself—why be a virtuous citizen if one can avoid the costs associated with doing one's duty?—is one the constitutional founders recognized and considered in great depth. This study examines notions of

3

citizenship as they were developed and used in the debates over the ratification of the 1787 American Constitution. The ratification of the Constitution led to wide-ranging debates not only in state conventions convened to decide on the proposed Constitution's fate but in newspapers and pamphlets around the nation. *The Federalist*, coauthored by Alexander Hamilton, James Madison, and John Jay under the pseudonym Publius, is the best-known example of this pamphlet literature, which began to appear in great quantity shortly after the adjournment of the Constitutional Convention in Philadelphia in September 1787. Yet the Constitution's opponents had their say as well. There is an enormous range in the quality, comprehensiveness, and concerns of the Anti-Federalist literature that is certain to confound any student of the political thought of the Constitution's opponents.

It is no easy task to describe an "Anti-Federalist position" on key issues, or to differentiate Anti-Federalists *tout court* from Federalists. Yet an examination of the debates between them will provide a clear sense of the diversity of American views on core political values and conceptions of citizenship. It will also enable us to assess the gulf that currently exists between two canonical interpretations of the founders' thought: liberalism and republicanism. What is the relation of these two interpretations to the Constitution?

It seems plain enough that neither the Federalist nor the Anti-Federalist antagonists in this debate thought it practical or desirable for Americans to be citizens in Rousseau's elevated sense of the term. It is less obvious, however, what they *did* expect citizens to think and feel about their country and how they intend them to act. In fact, until recently it was widely assumed that the issue of civic dispositions was not a question, at least for the authors of *The Federalist*. Publius presumed—we were told—that man is selfish and his politics factious. Moreover, stability of the regime is assured only through "mechanical devices" aimed at pitting "ambition against ambition" within government and faction against faction in society.[4] Such a view of governance was taken as proof that the constitutional founders subscribed to a Lockean liberal political philosophy that emphasizes the selfish interests of the individual over the "common good."

It can no longer be taken for granted, however, that the American constitutional founders—even the authors of *The Federalist*—can be described as Lockean liberals. A body of interpretation has emerged that places civic concerns at the forefront of the founders' understanding of politics. "Republican-revisionist" readings of the founding have focused on the founders' debt to classical republican political thought, which stresses the importance of promoting "civic virtue" among citizens who deliberate on political issues based on their conceptions of the common good. The fullest realization of the self, in the classical republican tradition beginning with Aristotle, results from actively participating as a member of a political community, taking part in ruling and being ruled.[5]

I shall argue that the revisionists were right in asserting that the constitutional founders were more civic-minded, more concerned about the dispositions of citizens to undertake public duties, than the "possessive individualist" or pluralist readings of classical liberalism would have us expect. Indeed, once we focus attention on this concern, we cannot fail to be impressed by the extent and rigor with which this issue was addressed in the ratification debates. Thus, I take republican revisionism very seriously in evaluating the founders' thought, even though it is argued that this interpretation is misleading in several major respects. I reject what I see as a tendency in the revisionist literature to assume that where civic virtue is discussed—and practiced— liberalism must be absent. It is more fruitful to alter our picture of what liberal political commitments are all about than to reject an ascription of liberalism to the constitutional founders because they do not fit a rather poor (and fading) twentieth-century definition.[6]

Debates over ratification of the Constitution revolved, to a considerable extent, around the capacity of the proposed government to engender the un- coerced allegiance of its citizens. Yet Louis Hartz was closer to the truth on core political commitments; the debate over ratification took place within the framework of a broad consensus on basic liberal values.[7] Hartz, however, said too little about what it means to be a liberal and I will take up that problem in presenting what can be called a *modified consensualist* thesis that builds on Hartz's work. Hartz also understated the importance of nonliberal influen- ces—religious as well as republican—on early American political thought.

Consensus need not and, I suggest, does not in this case mean a complete agreement on core political values. By no means do I aim to read republicanism out of the American founding nor to overstate the ideological consensus of a period that, after all, produced the best debates in American political history. Federalists and Anti-Federalists differed—often profound- ly—over the proper role of citizens in a just state. Much of this difference hinged on empirical arguments, for example, supposed relations between the size of government and one's loyalty to it. But some of its elements were more theoretical, and the Anti-Federalists did indeed call upon republican values even if not to the degree or in so robust a form as revisionists would lead us to expect. There are frequent expressions in the Anti-Federalist litera- ture of what might be called republican regret, a sense that economic expan- sion was harming the social bases of equality and, hence, broad-based republican participation in government. But there was an equally strong sense that little can or even should be done to arrest these changes if doing so in- hibits the exercise of "natural rights" to life, liberty, and property. Put another way, republican goods are constrained by liberal rights. Indeed, what the his- torical antagonists hardly contested at all were those criteria by which a state can be defined as just. On this point a liberal consensus held the day. In sum, despite all that we learn from Hartz, we should not understate the virtues of his critics. I will attempt to do justice to this divergence within consensus, which is largely represented by the republican revisionist literature.

The question then becomes: How were problems of citizenship and civic virtue conceived by major Federalist and Anti-Federalist spokesmen? Both Federalists and Anti-Federalists understood that a liberal polity, like virtually any other, required a "virtuous" citizenry if it was to endure. In essence, they realized that institutional and/or social checks and balances were insufficient though necessary guarantors of stability. A stable polity also requires that a substantial portion of its members undertake civic duties and in doing so, bear avoidable costs, including the possible loss of life in defending the commonwealth. They were also aware that a liberalism that emphasizes personal freedoms and often attributes acquisitive motives to individuals is hard-pressed to provide rational grounds for undertaking civic duties that are convincing and effective in practice. There was ample reason for Federalists and Anti-Federalists to believe that citizens are inclined to be free-riders and rulers are inclined to be tyrants.

Leaving the differences aside for the moment, I suggest that both Federalists and Anti-Federalists were concerned with the problem of fostering a *sentiment* of allegiance from which a disposition to undertake civic duties would emerge. Moreover, the debate over the Constitution was based more on empirical hypotheses regarding the capacity of a large federal republic to engender citizen affection and allegiance than on deep philosophical differences concerning the nature of the good or just state. This empirical approach to issues of citizenship owes much to eighteenth-century moral-sense thinking as expounded by Francis Hutcheson and developed and amended by Adam Smith and David Hume, though the Federalists accepted a much "purer" Humean solution to the allegiance problem than did their opponents. These constitutional founders were well aware of the narrowly selfish and narrowly benevolent motives impelling people to neglect civic duties. They were also aware that a liberal political order *could* encourage such motives, as Madison suggests in his famous analogy, "liberty is to faction what air is to fire."[8] Moreover, they doubted the efficacy of reasoned argument alone to counteract these more selfish tendencies.

Yet if it is questionable that men can be *convinced* to be good citizens, they may at least feel disposed and have reinforcing, self-interested motives to be so. The ratification debates consisted, in large measure, of a controversy over which institutional, social, and psychological conditions were best able to promote a sentiment of allegiance and, hence, the disinterestedness and willingness to abide by the laws of one's state, which can fairly be described as civic virtue. In so doing, both the authors of *The Federalist* and the major Anti-Federalist pamphleteers developed provocative and compelling conceptions of the psychological ties that bind a people to their government and rulers to their constitutional and legal duties. Uncovering the political psychological assumptions often implicit in the constitutional controversies will be one of this study's central tasks.

At stake in this controversy between supporters and opponents of the Constitution are basic questions about the founders' conceptions of person and citizen. Given the important role the "framers' intents" continue to play in our legal and political cultures, these questions are still with us. For the many Americans who regret the state of American citizenship (Do we vote enough? Are we too litigious? Do we have a conception of national community?), my reading of the founding era offers a mixed report. On the negative side, word

of the republican tradition in America—at least at the time of the constitu-
tional-ratification debates—has been exaggerated. This will not be welcome
news to communitarian and participatory democratic critics of contemporary
politics, who have sought an American republican pedigree for their views in
this critical stage of the founding era.[9]

One is hard-pressed to find either a significant defense or criticism of the
Constitution on strong civic republican grounds. Even the Anti-Federalists—
who championed the powers of local government and the enhancement of
democratic participation through such policies as rotation in office, recall, and
short terms of office—were liberals when it came to defining first principles.
Indeed, as chapter 7 will show, even their defenses of these devices were developed largely on liberal grounds. They served first and foremost to check the
power lust and acquisitive desires of rulers. The argument that the participation
these practices permitted was good for the type of character it fostered is present
but surprisingly underdeveloped, given what republican revisionism would lead
us to expect. The essential purpose of government for most Anti-Federalists,
as much as for Publius, was the preservation of rights conceived as natural
rights. The justification for the exercise of political power was developed
almost exclusively in terms of the social contract. Moreover, their contractarianism invoked presocial, natural rights and a conception of the state of
nature that owed far more to Locke than to Rousseau.

On the positive side, is the discovery that liberalism is much less inimical to community and active citizenship than its republican critics make
it out to be. Even the authors of *The Federalist*—who are often viewed as
the prototypical liberal pluralists who see politics as a contest between
purely self-interested parties—expect the majority of citizens and, even
more so, most rulers to be "virtuous" most of the time. Their conception
of virtue is, to be sure, more passive than many of us consider desirable
today and it is a conception I seek to describe, not to defend. Richer notions
of community and civic virtue than those conceived by Madison or, certainly, Hamilton are compatible with—even demanded by—liberal political
values. We need not cede to the framers the final word on how best to
balance the demands of competing political goods. Madison and Hamilton
(as Publius) pose one answer to the proper balance of individual and community, governmental efficiency and participation, liberty and equality in
public life. I believe that fuller conceptions of community can be developed
without abandoning what is best in liberalism. If we want to do so—and
avoid the decidedly antiliberal consequences of a Rousseauian republic—
we must look less to the founders and more within ourselves. This normative concern and its implication for contemporary politics will be discussed
in the concluding chapter of this book.

Thinking About Liberalism and Republicanism

Thomas Hobbes observed that truth consists in "the right ordering of names,"
so that the seeker of truth should remember "what every name he uses stands

for, and to place it accordingly, or else he will find himself entangled in words, as a bird in lime twigs, the more he struggles the more belimed."[10] Few of us have had Hobbes's success in heeding this warning. All too often, like Hobbes's "bird belimed," we flutter about in word traps of our own making and only add to the confusion we seek to clarify.

We rarely achieve Hobbes's longed for clarity of expression in the course of our daily lives, perhaps least of all when discussing our political beliefs and commitments. There is no reason why we as citizens should. The languages used to discuss politics are rich and complex. Our commitments frequently demand that we balance a number of competing goods and our moral and political language often reflects this complexity. A way of speaking perhaps appropriate to philosophers or lawyers is not necessarily appropriate to citizens and legislators exchanging views in the public square.

Much of the richness of early American political language is captured in the following excerpt from the state of Virginia's declaration commissioning representatives to attend the 1787 Constitutional Convention in Philadelphia.

> [The] Crisis is arrived at which the good People of America are to decide the solemn question whether they will by wise and magnanimous Efforts reap the just fruits of that Independence which they have so gloriously acquired and the Union which they have cemented with so much of their common Blood, or whether by giving way to unmanly Jealousies and Prejudices or to partial and transitory Interests they will renounce the auspicious blessings prepared for them by the Revolution and furnish to its enemies an eventual Triumph over those by whose virtue and valor it has been accomplished. And Whereas the same noble and extended policy and the same fraternal and affectionate Sentiments which originally determined the Citizens of this Commonwealth to unite with their Brethren of the other States in establishing a Federal Government cannot but be Felt with equal force now as motives to lay aside every inferior consideration and to concur in such further . . . Provisions as may be necessary to secure the great Objects for which that Government was instituted and to render the United States as happy in peace as they have been glorious in War.[11]

Notions of manhood, justice, glory, and fraternity all contribute to the rhetorical force of this piece. Together they represent a plea to Virginians to put aside petty interests and jealousies (as they had done once before) and to harvest the hard-earned fruits of the Revolution. Separately they evoke vastly different political visions. Glory, as Tocqueville and Montesquieu remind us, is a virtue more at home in aristocratic societies than democratic ones. The call for wisdom, magnanimity, and virtue evokes classical republican virtues, while the appeal to fraternal bonds has a decidedly Christian ring.

Yet, however citizens draw upon a wide range of political traditions and ways of speech in discussing their beliefs, it is the scholar's task to press them on their ways of talking—to separate the chaff of rhetoric from the wheat of meaning. Karl Marx reminds us of the difficulty of this task when he observes that it is often just when people seem to be engaged in the greatest revolutions that they conjure up the past and dress themselves in its cloak. For Marx "the tradition of all the dead generations weighs like a nightmare on the brains of the living." For others Marx's nightmare is a sweet dream. In either case, during such epochs people "anxiously conjure up the spirits of the past . . . and borrow from their names, battle slogans and costumes in order to present the new scene of world history in this time-honored disguise and this borrowed language."[12]

It is no easy task to distinguish the historical actor from the role. People do not say all they mean nor mean all they say, least of all politicians trying to persuade others of the worth of their cause. We dissemble in any number of ways not only when we don historic costumes but when, for instance, we invoke the common good to argue for our own selfish interest. Yet we cannot even begin to accomplish this scholarly housecleaning unless we first clarify terms. Specifically, if we want to judge the validity of ascribing a "republican" ideology to the founders, we must state with some specificity what being a republican means. Whether particular members of the founding generation fit this description is another—and later—question.

It is surprising how often the "republican commitments" of the founders are described in the haziest terms. One writer, who seeks to move American politics in a participatory democratic direction, describes the founders' commitments in the following terms. "They all shared a republican concern for a government of excellence, a citizen body of virtue, a public order defined by fundamental law . . . and conducive to well-being, and a community of moderation in which the governed would neither be abused nor be permitted to abuse themselves."[13]

If we accept these standards as defining republicanism (or even describing it), we are likely to find far more of it than we know how to manage. A crude way to suggest this is to imagine a counter claim to this characterization. The author would not want to suggest, one suspects, that there are many proponents of an imperfect government with a fundamental law ill-suited to well-being that permits blatant abuses of public and private power. Perhaps the safest generalization is that people want to think better of themselves, and no more so than when they are trying to convince others that they are right. Of course, he may then want to argue that though, like the founders, later American politicians *claim* to be embodying all these good things, unlike the founders, they are not actually doing so. But an argument like this would require greater specificity of terms in the context of a broader political theory, which seems here to be lacking.

The terms used in the preceding passage lack *differentiating content*. The goods described are too important to virtually any well-ordered polity to be taken as giving concrete instances of any particular political ideology, certainly not liberalism or republicanism.[14] Much the same point can be made for those who set the republican "language of virtue" against the liberal "language of rights," who define republicanism in terms of its stress on "political equality," and "public deliberation," or by citing discussions of "civic virtue" or "common good."[15] There can be a wide variety of *conceptions* that fit under the rubric of such general *concepts*.[16]

If holding to a particular political ideology means anything, it means that there is a certain coherence in one's views so that a view of, say, distributive justice includes or excludes some sets of political and/or economic institutions.[17] Thus, no one who holds to the tenets of liberal capitalism could consistently evoke the distributive principle, "from each according to his ability to each according to his needs." And no one who endorses Aristotle's notion of the virtues could take pure market principles of distributive justice as the best standard. "Economic man" is simply anathema to Aristotle's notion of a well-rounded person, whose development and perfection is the principle task of the polis. This is not to say that if you declare yourself a liberal, or a republican, that I can then deduce your preferred plan of distributive justice. Both ideologies are too variegated for that to be the case. Nonetheless, your choice would be at least somewhat restricted if your ideological commitment means anything. Republican revisionism has been plagued by language too weak to rule out anything and, hence, to mean anything.

A strong statement of the republican, or civic humanist, thesis that avoids the problem of indeterminacy is offered by John Pocock: "Civic humanism denotes a style of thought . . . in which it is contended that the development of the individual toward self-fulfillment is possible *only when the individual acts as a citizen*, that is, as a conscious and autonomous participant in an autonomous decision-taking political community, the polis or republic [emphasis added]."[18] In this view, civic humanism is, above all, a theory of citizenship, but in a specifically Aristotelian sense of the term. Pocock's understanding holds that the moral and rational faculties of individuals are developed fully only if individuals act as citizens. That is, only by actively taking part in the political life of one's community, by undertaking civic duties in it, can one become a virtuous, well-rounded person. The autonomy of citizens is founded in property, ownership of which enables freeholders to participate in politics independent of others' wills. Threats to autonomy, described as "corruption," are a central concern in this tradition, since they undermine the moral personality of the citizen by removing his capacity to act "virtuously," or in light of the common good as opposed to particular private interests.[19] Thus, Pocock refers to "a civic and patriot ideal in which the personality was founded in property, *perfected in citizenship* but perpetually threatened by corruption [emphasis added]."[20]

I describe this as the strong republican thesis because it presents a clear, coherent conception of citizenship and its place in a comprehensive and familiar political theory. There is no great problem in identifying what this ideology *is*, however problematic its attribution to a particular political figure may be. As Pocock's definition makes clear, civic participation is an authoritative good in the context of this theory, that is, a good every individual ought to desire, or, conversely, an individual who does not desire it suffers a fundamental defect of personality.[21] The definition holds that any individual with insight into her own well-being would seek the development, or perfection, of her most essentially human faculties. These moral and rational faculties are perfected, for Pocock, *only* by civic participation. Thus, one's moral identity is inextricably bound with one's civic identity such that one's disinterested performance of civic activities is both an indication of and a necessary means to self-fulfillment. And if a person is disinclined toward civic activity or undertakes it only to promote private ends, not only is his character in question but we are led to doubt that he understands what it means to be fully human.

Republican interpreters of the founding, including Pocock, have held that this core idea survives transformations of republicanism from its Aristotelian origins through its incorporation into eighteenth century Anglo-American political controversies including the debates over the ratification of the 1787 Constitution. Indeed, historians have found in the ratification debates a type of language used by pamphleteers calling themselves Brutus, Cato, Publius, and Republicus that stresses such apparently classical republican themes as civic virtue and corruption, civic education and the merits of small republics. Revisionists are divided over the degree to which the Federalists break with this paradigm, though it is widely held that Anti-Federalist criticisms of the Constitution emerged largely from this tradition of political discourse.

Thus, in *The Creation of the American Republic* Gordon S. Wood characterized the Anti-Federalists essentially as backward-looking republicans. Though his theoretical understanding of republicanism is harder to pin down than that of Pocock, he sees the American political controversies of the 1780s as marking a radical break between a "classical and medieval world of political discussion" into a modern one with the Anti-Federalists clinging to the old worldview. Elements of this earlier worldview include a notion of society as an organic, hierarchically ordered whole in which each order contributes to the common good in a functionally unique way. Republicanism in the American context incorporates an egalitarian element that is at odds with the stress on hierarchy in classical theory. Thus, Wood differentiates American republicanism from mixed government theory although the latter is essential to the classical republicanism of Aristotle or Polybius and also plays a role in American constitutional development. American republicans, for Wood, tend to take men as equals in terms of their capacities to exercise public liberty as *citizens*. Wood is in accord with Pocock on the value and centrality to the good life of civic participation in light of the common good.[22]

There is a weak version of the republican thesis that can, I think, be more reasonably attributed to many early Americans, including the Anti-Federalist pamphleteers examined here. It is more difficult to describe than the strong thesis and it is correspondingly more difficult to understand what institutional and conceptual consequences flow from a commitment to it. However, adherents of weak republicanism would place a value on civic participation for its own sake and not merely as a means of promoting interests and protecting rights. They would also prefer to see civic participation spread over a broad segment of the civic population and, possibly, to expand the size of this population (by incorporating previously excluded groups) and expand the range of its activities beyond minimal acts such as voting.

Weak republicanism is not an ideology in the manner of liberalism or Marxism or Aristotelian republicanism. There is nothing, in other words, in an ideology such as liberalism or Marxism that would compel a believer to reject weak-republican preferences in the way that a classical liberal must reject the idea of proportionate equality since not rejecting it leaves her open to the charge of incoherence. In the context of the founding, I will suggest that the constitutional founders were almost at one in a commitment to liberal ideology, though there was considerable debate over the virtues of weak republicanism. This debate can be divided largely, though not exclusively, along Federalist and Anti-Federalist lines.

Thus, liberals can and have had sharp debates about the advantages and dangers of broad-based political participation. But they cannot consistently endorse the civic-humanism thesis in the strong sense defined by Pocock. The relation between liberalism, community, and participation will be discussed in chapter 2. Here we note only that central to the liberal tradition has been the idea that each person should be free to pursue his or her own conception of the good while granting like freedom to others. Such a view emerges from a world-weary sense of the insolubility of the problem of arriving at a conception of the good that can gain the assent of all members of the political community. The liberal state, which enables its members to pursue their conceptions of the good, provides a useful means of living together with our differences, and it is morally defended for respecting the dignity of each individual. It is a denigration of this dignity to coerce some to conform to the majority's conception of the good—whether religious or political—despite their deepest convictions.

It is incompatible with this core belief to assert that civic participation is the "privileged locus of the good life," as does the civic humanist position according to Pocock.[23] There is a very real sense, therefore, in which establishing the liberal commitments of a constitutional founder is incompatible with attributing strong-republican ideology to him, unless he is quite inconsistent in his basic premises. We shall rarely encounter such inconsistency in the texts explored in the following chapters.

The Constitutional Founders' Liberalism and Civic Virtue

In the early days of republican revisionism, John Pocock asserted that it seems there was "no alternative tradition" to classical republicanism for Americans of the founding generation to be schooled in.[24] Not only did Pocock offer a strong version of republicanism, he claimed that it was the exclusive influence on early Americans. Gordon Wood, on whose primary research Pocock relies, also claimed that "in 1787, classical republicanism was the basic premise of American thinking—the central presupposition behind all other ideas."[25] In more recent works, however, Pocock has claimed that his seminal work, *The Machiavellian Moment*, was a "tunnel history" pursuing a "single theme" to the "partial exclusion of parallel phenomena."[26] And Wood has altogether denied his earlier view in stating that "for early Americans there never was a stark dictionary of traditions, whether liberal or republican."[27]

Now this ascription of many different modes of political thought to the founders makes a lot of sense, much more than the early exclusive republican claims. As much as I think the republican reading of the founding has been overstated, I make no pretence of capturing the full texture of early American political thought given both the temporal restrictions and topic of this work. I do argue that the Anti-Federalists conjoin liberal and weak republican political concerns in an uneasy harmony. Nonetheless, as suggested above, we should resist a tendency in recent readings of the founding to define liberalism in such a way that, whenever such terms as "civic virtue," "public good," and "public deliberation" are encountered, republican commitments are ascribed to their users. This view more presupposes than argues that such goods are somehow inimical to the liberal tradition.

The historian Lance Banning offers an example this reasoning. Liberalism, he argues, "is comfortable with economic man, with the individual who is intent on maximizing private satisfactions and who needs to do no more in order to serve the general good." Classical republicanism, he argues (correctly in my view) "regards . . . merely economic man as less than fully human." He adds that classical republicanism "will identify the unrestrained pursuit of purely private interests as incompatible with the preservation of the commonwealth."[28] If liberalism is identified with the purely selfish maximizer who need do no more (because he is not morally required to do more? or because the commonwealth can be preserved without his doing more) than pursue his selfish ends, it is no wonder we find other than liberal influences among the founders. Any reference to public good or civic virtue must, by definition, derive from some nonliberal tradition of political discourse.[29]

I reject a definition of liberalism that forces the *a priori* conclusion that where virtue exists, liberalism is absent. On the other hand, it would be equally invalid to claim that where rights and interests are mentioned, liberalism is present or predominant. These terms too are general concepts capable of supporting a variety of conceptions and the notion of interest plays an important role in classical republican theory as well as in liberalism. We will not get at the conceptions of such terms without situating them in the context of political arguments developed in the Constitutional texts and debates. Prior to our exegetical task, however, is an analytical one. We must first consider what conception(s) of civic virtue are compatible with, if not required by, liberal first principles. Not all readers will be persuaded by my ascription of particular ideological commitments to given founders. This domain is too contested and too many able scholars have spoken on various sides for one to expect to have the final word on the matter. I do hope to offer some clarification of the conceptual links between core liberal commitments and particular *conceptions* of civic virtue.

Toward that end, civic virtue can be defined formally as a disposition among citizens to engage in activities that support and maintain a just political order. This is a formal definition in that it assumes no particular plan of justice for the citizen to support—whether Platonic, liberal, democratic—and presupposes no particular conception of the term. Second, it makes possible the resolution of what Pocock and others have come to see as the central theoretical problem of early American political thought; How did the languages of virtue and interests relate to one another in the minds of the founders?

The constitutional founders were indeed by and large ideologically liberal. Moreover, "possessive individualist" assumptions about human nature, society, and government abound in their writings. Yet, the relevant question is not whether they were concerned with citizenship and civic virtue but what their conceptions of these terms were. A further question is how their use of the conceptions was consistent with or constrained by their core ideology and what room this ideological commitment left for the political goods associated with republicanism. It is perhaps just because the founders were so keenly aware of the darker motives for human conduct that they considered issues of civic virtue and participation in such depth.

Before I turn to the debates surrounding adoption of the Constitution, I will contend that well-developed considerations of the ways in which liberal states can and do inspire allegiance in citizens were available to the constitutional founders in the writings of Locke and several major figures of the Scottish Enlightenment from Francis Hutcheson through Adam Smith and David Hume.[30] Indeed, this book is devoted as much to a neglected problem in liberal political thought as to the thought of the constitutional founders. The analytical chapter as well as the study of Locke and the Scots are preconditions for the study of the founders given that the very understanding of liberalism is as contested today as is its ascription to particular founders.

Considering how liberals can and have thought about civic virtue and political community can, I believe, help us avoid some of the easy oppositions—public virtues versus self-interest, or individual rights versus the common good—that have lent more heat than light to controversies over the founders' political thought. The analytical second chapter is followed by a third chapter devoted to Locke which focuses on the connections in Locke's thought between his liberal conception of justice and his understanding of the motivations for acting on liberal principles. This theme is developed further in chapter 4, which analyzes the relevant political ideas of the Scottish Enlightenment thinkers, who offer the richest development of an empirical political psychology prior to the American founding. I discuss extensively the ideas of the liberal precursors to the American founders both because I believe that there is a direct influence in some cases (Hume on Madison and Hamilton) and because their philosophical writings help us to better understand the more practical writings of the Americans. The latter clarifying function is more important to me, and I try to be clear throughout when I am claiming that there has been a direct influence.[31]

Chapters 5 and 6 address the political thought of *The Federalist* to get at the core ideological presumptions of that thought and to relate these to the particular understanding of allegiance and civic virtue the authors of *The Federalist* present. Chapter 5 focuses on the former theme and argues not only the relatively uncontroversial point that the authors of *The Federalist* were liberals but, more important, that their liberalism took roughly the form I sketched out in chapter 2. In Chapter 6, we shall see that the authors of *The Federalist* developed an understanding of allegiance and fidelity to office based on a complex moral psychology that is largely Humean in inspiration. It employs notions of interest, duty, and habit to explain how loyalties will crystallize around the new national government and its laws. My goal here is to show how a particularly important group of liberal statesmen regarded civic virtue in a liberal regime, making no claim that this is either the only or the best conception that liberals can offer.

Chapter 7 deals with both aspects of Anti-Federalist thought, focusing on several of what are, by common consent, the best pamphlets in the Anti-Federalist literature. Anti-Federalist conceptions of civic virtue and the sources of allegiance also resided in a complex moral and political psychology, one that relied on ties of personal acquaintance and the bonds of benevolence to explain political loyalties and to argue for the inevitable weaknesses of such loyalties in a large, extended republic. Such arguments are "Hutchesonian" in spirit, if not in origin, and, as I suggest, ultimately less plausible than the political psychology Publius develops. I also evaluate the commitments to weak republicanism, (in one exceptional case, even strong republicanism), found in this literature.

The final chapter assesses the relevance of the constitutional-founding debates for the present and returns to the normative concerns raised in chapter 2. I suggest that we continue to hear echoes of the constitutional controversies in current debates over the proper role of the citizen in the just state. Normatively, I conclude with at least two cheers for a conception of liberalism that recognizes the value of community and participation even if it is not one such liberals as Madison and Hamilton themselves would have endorsed. I thus evaluate both how the constitutional founders discuss what have been taken to be largely republican concerns and what hold these ideas still exert on us today.

I

PROBLEMS AND PREDECESSORS

2

Liberal Community and Civic Virtue: An Analysis

Among James Madison's more frequently quoted remarks was offered on the floor of the Virginia ratification convention: "Is there no virtue among us? If there be not, we are in a wretched situation. No theoretical checks—no form of government can render us secure. To suppose that any form of government will secure liberty or happiness without any virtue in the people is a chimerical idea."[1]

The source of interest in this remark no doubt derives from its apparent inconsistency with the Madison of the best known numbers of *The Federalist*. In *The Federalist*, as well as in the ratification debates, Madison asserts that the purpose of government is to secure liberty—the independence of each from others' wills—and happiness, the prosperity brought about by industry. Yet in *Federalist* 10 and 51 virtue plays little or no role in bringing about or maintaining this desirable condition. There, in fact, Madison emphasizes the tendency of men to "vex and oppress" each other for even the most trivial reasons and to pursue courses of action with like-minded people that are inimical to others' rights and to the common good. He seems to suggest in these essays that a combination of institutional and social checks and balances is necessary and sufficient for a stable polity able to secure liberty and promote happiness.

Madison's remarks in the Virginia debates would indeed be inconsistent with his arguments in *Federalist* 10 if the essay's emphasis on the generally selfish nature of man precluded altogether a capacity for virtuous actions. But to interpret him in this way is not only to slight Madison's more complex understanding of human psychology and motivation but also to lose sight of the purpose of *The Federalist*, which was to defend and justify a plan of government. Madison believes, following Hume, that it is best to assume the worst about human nature in designing such a plan. Yet he is not so foolish as to think that any plan of government could be stable if the sole motive for conduct was for each to vex and oppress the other. Nor does he believe that he is presenting a complete description of the vagaries of human conduct in the categorical statements he makes on the factious nature of man in these two key passages. His task here is political, not descriptive or metaphysical.

The confusion that arises from trying to reconcile these sides of Madison's thought is represented at a more general level in contemporary discussions of the nature of liberalism and its perceived conflict with community. It has become common to portray liberalism as a selfish philosophy destructive of community. Many critics of liberalism today—including a considerable number of writers who seek to revise our understanding of the American founders by emphasizing their nonliberal, classical republican roots—argue that liberalism undermines community by emphasizing the rights of the individual over the ends and values people create as citizens who share and act upon a conception of the common good.[2]

Considering the disagreement about the moral status of liberalism today is useful only insofar as it helps clarify what was at stake in the debates over the ratification of the 1787 Constitution and in sorting through the scholarly commentary on these debates. We all approach texts with some conceptual framework that focuses our attention on some points and leads us to neglect others. It is easier to see how a conceptual framework affects interpretation in other people's work than it is in our own. This is particularly clear in the dispute over the American founders' ideology, in which accusations that interpretations of the founders' thought are determined by the present, normative goals of the interpreter have become commonplace.[3] I hope that this philosophical prelude will alert readers to my assessment of liberal theory and its role for community and civic virtue, a question contested both at the founding and at present though in different forms.

Substantively, this prelude aims to serve as a corrective to a theoretical reading of liberalism employed by many revisionists that leaves, by definition, little or no room for civic virtue. Much of the contemporary literature on the founding portrays the Anti-Federalists as old-style republicans who emphasizing the good of a homogeneous community with a shared conception of the good life and rich notions of active citizenship, while it sees the Federalists as representing a more individualist, more selfish politics within which individuals do not so much come to a consensus based on deliberation about the common good as bargain to maximize personal or group gains and minimize losses.[4]

In subsequent chapters I challenge the historical accuracy of this view. Federalists and Anti-Federalists share deep liberal commitments with regard to the nature of society, the role of government, and the centrality of individual rights to a conception of just politics. Both also recognize the importance of "civic virtue" and develop a conception of it. The theoretical claim about how these two concerns—individual rights and civic virtue—can coexist is important here. Specifically, liberalism is much less inimical to community and to civic virtue than its critics, including many interpreters of the American founding, suppose. Thus, the inconsistency between these two "Madisons" is more apparent than real. The Madison of *The Federalist*, commonly perceived as the designer of a politics built on self-interest, is not contradicted by the Madison of the Virginia debates, the extoller of civic virtue.

Stated more categorically, a concern with the *disposition* of citizens to act justly has always and necessarily been internal to liberal discourse. Acting justly refers minimally to accepting governmental decisions concerning the arbitration of rights as legitimate and to the disinterested performance of the duties of public office. None of these undertakings can be justified adequately on prudential grounds, while avoidance of the costs associated with public duties frequently can. Nor can heroic actions, including risking one's own life to defend the commonwealth, be so justified.

The limits of rational prudence in promoting the stability of political regimes have been well understood in the liberal tradition. Hobbes, as in so much else, led the way in this regard and perhaps still provides the clearest understanding of the logic of social cooperation. Yet, if an understanding of these limits has been more or less constant in liberal thought, there is more historical variation in the notions of how self-interest is restrained, and how it avoids and is kept from lapsing into a narrow selfishness.

The goal of this chapter is to provide some understanding of liberalism in a general way and to evaluate some of the more common critiques of it made by its republican and communitarian critics. The chapter will then consider some of the theoretical limits of rational prudence in assuring stability and what moral, or at least less narrowly self-interested, motives appear in its stead. How particular thinkers prior to the founding saw the relation of liberty to community and to civic virtue will be the concern of later chapters.

Liberal Dialogue: Justifying Political Power

What it means to hold to a liberal political philosophy is a highly contentious question. There is not a single understanding of what classical liberalism entails that can gain the assent of all contemporaries much less the assent of the founders and their intellectual predecessors, who were not even familiar with the term. Nonetheless, it is useful to provide some bare-bones definition at the outset. The degrees to which the founders subscribe to it and the significance of their variations on its theme must come later.

Michael Sandel provides a useful starting point in a recent work. In his discussion, "deontological," or rights-based, liberalism is a mode of political argument culminating in Kant but whose essential elements are anticipated by Hobbes, Locke, and even Rousseau. Its core thesis can be stated as follows:

> Society being composed of a plurality of persons, each with his own aims, interests, and conceptions of the good, is best arranged when it is governed by principles that do not *themselves* presuppose any particular conception of the good; what justifies these regulative principles above all is not that they maximize the social welfare or otherwise promote the good, but rather that they conform to the conception of *right*, a moral category given prior to the good and independent of it.[5]

Sandel is correct in identifying this argument as the essence of the liberal social-contract tradition. It would be unreasonable for us to expect the same theoretical purity in defining liberalism from the founders. Sandel's definition does not, therefore, provide a full description of anyone's political thought. It does, however, aid us in isolating a set of core liberal beliefs.

The justification for persons' voluntarily surrendering their natural liberty in the state of nature is that only through some plan of cooperation can they be assured the security and independence to pursue aims of their own choosing. The priority given the right over the good in classical liberalism rules out any principle of social cooperation that restricts each individual's pursuit of her own conception of the good beyond the extent required to grant equal freedom to all. Thus, justifications of political authority based on "perfectionist" principles, which have required historically that some members of society forego their own development so that others can better pursue theirs, would be rejected because they do not respect the dignity of persons.

More important, a liberal would also criticize perfectionist theories of justice for their implicit belief that one conception of the good can be found rationally acceptable by all (educated and virtuous) persons.[6] That reasonable people may well disagree over fundamental conceptions of the good life even after considerable deliberation is a fundamental premise of liberal thought. Classical republicans as well as medieval theorists were more sanguine about the possibilities that the "best" men could discover the good by the exercise of right reason.[7]

Contractarian liberals also would reject any cooperative principle that would maximize the aggregate happiness of the society at the cost of violating the rights of some individuals in that society. Historically, liberals have disagreed over the class of individuals who count as persons in given societies. The dividing line between persons with rights and obligations in the liberal polity and "nonpersons" has most frequently been based on property qualifications. However, among the class who count politically, respect for individuals, based on a radically egalitarian conception of the capacities of each to select and act on a rational life plan, has been at the heart of the liberal tradition of political discourse.

Liberalism requires a justification of political power from the standpoint of each individual. It recognizes that no single conception of the good, whether religious or secular, is likely to gain full adherence in a political community and that compelling reasons of state interest are required before any individual may be asked to restrict her pursuit of the good for reasons of public utility. Each individual must be shown equal concern and respect in determining the sacrifices that must be made to support the public order. To do anything less is to treat some as the means for the advancement of others.

Could it not be argued that liberalism presupposes a particular conception of the good even though liberals may claim to be "neutral" about such conceptions? Yes and no. The basic presumptions of liberal theory—notions of the moral equality of persons and justification of power through rational dialogue—are clearly moral imperatives. Liberalism is not, therefore, neutral toward morality itself. Nor are the enforcement functions of the liberal state neutral with respect to *all* conceptions of the good life. Actions allowed on behalf of particular conceptions of the good life are constrained by the rights of individuals. Finally, that rights constrain people's pursuit of the good tells us that liberals are not neutral with respect to the criteria defining the public good. If this were the case, liberalism would simply be incoherent and not worthy of serious attention as a political philosophy.

Yet the two points of liberal justice—moral equality and rational dialogue—constitute a rather minimal conception of morality, and one that may become the object of consensus in a society even if there exists considerable disagreement over religious and cultural beliefs that offer richer but more controversial moral theories and conceptions of value.[8] There is no assurance, of course, that even this minimal theory of morality will take hold in particular societies or among all persons in those societies. There is at present no liberal solution to be offered for the problem of governance in Lebanon, for example. Even in the United States, there are a great many persons who find liberal morality offensive in given cases. Thus, a right of free speech or, more in dispute, a right to abortion, allows words or actions that many believe incompatible with a morally decent society. It is not enough for such persons that they do not speak forbidden words or terminate a pregnancy; That others do so causes offense, even revulsion.

Liberal societies offer forums for discussing, if not settling, such disputes. Thus, whether speech in the form of pornography that degrades women ought to be protected in the name of "equal respect" is a reasonable question, as is whether the fetus should be accorded the status of a person. Rights must be determined, not simply discovered, and this determination is ultimately a political process. However, once such a process has been completed authoritatively, the state must protect rights-bearers against those who would prefer not to see particular rights exercised by others. This may restrict the capacity of a minority to live in a society ordered according to its conception of the good, as was the case in the enforcement of desegregation orders, for example.

The justification for state actions should be based not on a "better" theory of value than the one suppressed, but on a collective agreement about the demands of equal respect as defined through rational dialogue in specific cases. The liberal state's exercise of power to enforce rights is not best described as neutral. It is less elegant but more accurate to say that liberals seek to keep enforced moral consensus to a minimum, even though this minimum may not be universally assented to by all rational persons.

The centrality of providing justifying reasons for the exercise of power makes political dialogue an essential ingredient of liberal politics.[9] It is not an overstatement, in fact, to define liberalism as a dialogue about political power asking which acts of power can be justified to free, equal, rational beings. In the United States, this debate takes place largely in the courts and in terms of an interpretation of the rights authorized by the Constitution.

As Ronald Dworkin has argued, this dialogue does not presume that there is a right to liberty as such.[10] If this were the case, *any* law, even one as sensible and harmless as declaring that we drive on the right side of the street, would be suspect since it clearly inhibits the liberty to drive on the left side of the street. Rather, the core value of liberal dialogue is the treatment of all legal persons with equal concern and respect. It is wildly implausible that the right-side driving law violates this stricture. It is almost certain, on the other hand, that a law establishing a religion would. The individual's autonomous pursuit of the good (which could, of course, take place in communion with like-minded souls) is clearly implicated by the second law and not, by any argument I can imagine, by the first. Thus, the exercise of political power replete with the sanction of law is justifiable in the first instance and not in the second.

These examples of liberal justifications of power are not meant to deny that there are indeed hard cases. Liberal dialogue, like any other, can at times turn into a shouting match. Questions about the scope of rights and conflicts among them are, of course, rife in liberal polities. Does, for example, the right to free speech deny the state the power to regulate pornography? Does such regulation presuppose a conception of the good life that inhibits the free development and autonomous choice of the pornography-loving person? The decision of the Supreme Court leaving such regulation up to local communities where the alleged smut has "no redeeming social value" suggests that this is not seen to be the case. The Court, consistent with liberal principles, is not terribly demanding in defining a rigorous test for "social value," but it has insisted that some connection between the contested practice and a rational plan for a good life of at least some members of the political community is required to exclude that practice from state regulation.[11] Liberal dialogue cuts both ways.

Exegetical evidence must be introduced to support the contention that the American founders held to something like this conception of liberalism. There is less disagreement that the preceeding outline captures the essentials of the liberal social-contract tradition. Communitarian and republican critics stress that there are a number of ways in which this tradition can be considered inimical to community and to civic virtue. There are also a number of ways, generally neglected by such critics, in which liberals can claim to further those ends. The communitarian and republican criticisms are best seen through examples drawn from the American context.

Republican-Inspired Critiques of Liberalism

It has become commonplace to contend that nonliberal values that stress common citizenship and civic virtue play a role in early American political culture largely through the influence of classical republican influences on the American founders. Republican revisionism's latest conquest appears to be the field of American jurisprudence including, of course, Constitutional interpretation. It is, as one legal scholar, Kathryn Abrams, put it, "our latest find" and its implications for constitutional interpretation are just beginning to be explored.[12] Another legal scholar, Cass R. Sunstein, sums up the revisionist contribution and gives a sense of how the historical question of the role of republicanism informs the current issue of constitutional interpretation:

> One of the largest accomplishments of modern historical scholarship has been the illumination of the role of republican thought in the period before, during, and after the ratification of the American Constitution. It is no longer possible to see a Lockean consensus in the founding period, or to treat the framers as modern pluralists believing that self-interest is the inevitable motivating force behind political behavior. Republican thought played a central role in the framing period, and it offers a powerful conception of politics and of the functions of constitutionalism.[13]

The Lockean consensus thesis cannot be sustained, that is, if Locke (and presumably "Lockean liberalism") are understood "in the familiar fashion."[14] Republicanism is, he concludes, "now firmly in place, in legal scholarship if not in legal doctrine."[15]

It is curious that a challenge to Lockeanism "as familiarly understood" leads so directly to an endorsement of a republican reading of the founding. There is at least a logical alternative in seeing the founders as Lockean liberals unfamiliarly understood. Such a view might challenge either the description of Locke as a pluralist or the obscure claim that self-interest is the "inevitable motivating force behind political behavior." (Is it the *sole* motivating force? Where does Locke say so? If it is, what exactly is inevitable? Certainly not its victory over other motivations, since these are ruled out by definition.)

Sunstein proceeds to argue that there are four essential features of republicanism that differentiate it from liberalism. These are commitments to (1) deliberation in government; (2) political equality; (3) universality, or "agreement as a regulative ideal";[16] and (4) citizenship. None of these attributes seems on the face of it the least bit incompatible with common sense understandings of liberal politics. Indeed, Sunstein concedes that they are not.[17] Yet, there may be incompatibilities in the particular conceptions of these terms as this particular author employs them, incompatibilities that lead him to consider them distinguishing features of republicanism.

Why is it then that public deliberation is taken to be more at home in a republican than a liberal framework? Because liberalism takes "individual preferences . . . [as] exogenous to politics," while republicanism is "unlikely to take existing preferences or entitlements as fixed." For example, republicans are likely to see the distribution of wealth as a matter for "political disposition." Thus, "understandings that point to prepolitical or natural rights are entirely foreign to republicanism."[18] Wealth is distributed to promote the good of the community, not according to some preexisting notion such as a natural right to property. In fact, because the republican view stresses public deliberation so centrally, it displays a natural tendency toward political equality and, hence, a natural tendency to equalize wealth so as to equalize political influence.

I will indicate in the exegetical chapters that both Federalists and Anti-Federalists rely consistently on just such preexisting, natural rights in their defense of or opposition to the Constitution and do so at such central points in their arguments that these references cannot be taken as mere window dressing. Moreover, there is no imperative, even among the supposedly more republican Anti-Federalists, for redistribution on republican or any other grounds even though the more perspicacious among them recognize that the voluntary exchanges among rights-bearing individuals will lead to social changes potentially harmful to the generation of civic virtue. There is some indication of republican regret over these changes, but not, I think, republican action. The republican revisionist's dilemma is that insofar as one can derive a distinguishable republican practice from his principles, the founders did not engage in such a practice. There are a number of goods mentioned, on the other hand, that do not seem to contravene liberal values, and hence, to offer an instant of an antiliberal, or republican, political ideology.

On the conceptual distinction itself, Sunstein suggests that liberalism restricts public deliberation, or reduces it to interest group bargaining because "individual preferences" are not initially shaped by political discussion. For example, a republican discourse over the distribution of wealth would begin with the question, what sort of community are we? If we value political equality over luxury, we may well decide to tax back or initially restrict the accumulation of wealth in a few hands. The good of the community decided upon by public discussion that generates a consensus takes precedence over the "preferences" of any individual member.

Now, public deliberation that takes this form, that is, stresses the good of the community over the claims of its members, can indeed be described as a republican dialogue. The rights of individuals do not place constraints on actions that can be undertaken to advance the public good. Rather, those rights are determined by the currently dominant conception of the good. It is not the case, however, that such a discussion is the *only* form public deliberation can take. If one accepts my understanding of liberalism as entailing a justification of power from the standpoint of each individual, one is led to conclude that a liberal public deliberation is no contradiction in terms. The essential conception of liberal political theory is dialogic. Moreover, I would suggest that it is empirically true that public deliberation thrives in liberal democratic regimes as perhaps in no other regime currently existing.

Take again the debate over the redistribution of wealth. While such a debate in a liberal context will not begin by asking What kind of community are we? (and may not occur at all), it may well begin by asking, What do our principles require? A full and wide-ranging public discussion can—and has— begun from this premise. Thus, what we might call left liberals have asked whether extensive inequality of income distribution makes a mockery of liberalism's claim to treat persons with "equal concern and respect." "Right" liberals (Reaganite conservatives and libertarians) ask whether taking a rich person's wealth to make a poor person richer is not merely using that rich person as a means to some "socially useful" end.[19] This, many argue, is a violation of rights and also of the claim to treat all persons as ends only. This uncertainty over what our principles require in no way diminishes, and perhaps enhances, the debate that can take place purely within the context of liberal premises.[20]

Examples of this sort of discussion abound in liberal polities, whether the topic is the rights of gun ownership, treatment of animals, abortion, or any other public issue. It is hard to see, therefore, that public deliberation in and of itself is lacking in liberal polities. It is also hard to sustain the claim that such polities take individual preferences as exogenous to politics. Sunstein suggests in this connection that people decide what they want and enter politics in order to get it. Politics is business negotiation by other means. Republicans, on the other hand, allow public deliberation to determine their preferences. In their hearts, they (come to) know the general will is right.

There is, I think, a certain romanticism in this view of republicanism. It is fine where fundamental conceptions of the good are not contested; hence the stress within republican discourse on the importance of culturally homogeneous communities. Yet even within such communities, there comes a time when all the consensus building that is going to take place has taken place and matters must simply come to a vote.[21] At that point, there will be a majority and a minority, and the minority, one suspects, will begin to ask liberal questions pertaining to restraints on the majority's powers.

The attractiveness of these ideologies aside, it is only true in a rather restricted sense that liberalism takes individual preferences to be exogenous to politics and therefore limits the terms of public debate. Preferences are, of course, not all of one kind. It is true that liberal politics does not demand a justification of very deep-seated preferences (more accurately, commitments) about religious beliefs, for example. No one is asked to explain before a board of citizens why she is Catholic or Jewish or anything else. Increasingly, much the same can be said about sexual preferences as they become less and less perceived as choices and more as unchosen attributes.[22] Yet, more ordinary preferences such as those over whether to build a swimming pool or an art museum in one's hometown, or whether to increase taxes to pay for better health care, do require justification in a full-throated political debate. Proponents of the art museum may be attacked on the grounds that their choice will tax working and poor people for something that benefits primarily the better-off members of the community. Or, it may be argued that more people prefer swimming than art and that the government should not seek to "educate" people for their own good instead of simply providing what more people want.

There is no guarantee, of course, that such debates will lead to a consensus. But there is no more of a guarantee when debates focus on the republican question, What kind of community are we? Liberals differ over what their principles require just as members of any community may differ over what their conception of the good is. But that right answers about what principles require are hard to come by—as much as it may indicate that public debates may be never ending—hardly indicates that there is a lack of such debates. Moreover, these debates help us define and amend our principles of justice.

The extent to which people alter their preferences based on this sort of dialogue is impossible to ascertain in advance. It will depend in large part on how deeply they are moved by moral principles. Optimists and pessimists regarding human nature can long debate this point. Both Federalists and Anti-Federalists express a good bit of pessimism. There is no compelling reason to believe, however, that liberalism is a necessary or sufficient cause of such pessimism, the roots of which are undoubtedly quite complex and in no small part Calvinist in origins.[23] In any case, there is no a priori reason to assume that preferences will not be altered by political participation in liberal regimes or will be altered less than in other political systems.

Even if one concedes that public deliberation of the above sort is quite at home in liberal polities, it is still arguable that liberalism fosters selfishness and denigrates community on other grounds. Republican and communitarian critics have suggested a number of ways in which liberalism's rights-based morality does so. The most fundamental is that liberalism in the social-contract tradition fosters an atomistic view of social relations. We are encouraged, it is alleged, to minimize the extent to which we see ourselves as social—indeed, political—beings who are fully shaped by our interactions with others.

Contractors are asked to imagine themselves first in a "state of nature" or behind a "veil of ignorance" and then to choose a form of political association. Such a view, it is charged, makes social attachments appear as detachable, as not constituting the very core of our being. As liberalism encourages the viewpoint of this "unencumbered self," whose ties to family, community, and country can be shed as easily as clothes, it gives rise to an individualistic bias in our thinking. Rather than asking what is the good for myself as a member of a broader community (as son, brother, friend or neighbor), I conceive of myself as detached from these relations and thus ignore the extent to which the very constitution of my being is social.[24]

Certain political relations follow from this view of the self. Central among these is that "relationships with one another are viewed not as in themselves constituting the good of their endeavors but as a means toward private goods independently identified."[25] What should be valued intrinsically becomes valued instrumentally. Moreover, the state is to be neutral with regard to competing conceptions of the good life and, therefore, political forums are denied the role so essential for them in classical republican conceptions: to address the essential question, How are we to live?[26]

There are a number of reasons to doubt this characterization of the liberal self and interaction among selves. First and most important, it neglects an important distinction between social and political relations. The liberal thesis can recognize that humans are social beings and maintain at the same time that social relations flourish only when not coerced—not brought within the purview of state power. One commentator, Will Kymlicka, makes this point most cogently.

> Liberals supposedly think that society rests on an artificial social contract, and that a coercive state apparatus is needed to keep naturally asocial people together in society. But there is a sense in which the opposite is true—liberals

believe that people naturally form and join social relations and forums in which they come to understand and pursue the good. The state is not needed to provide that communal context and is likely to distort the normal processes of collective deliberations and cultural development. It is communitarians who seem to think that individuals drift into anomic and detached isolation without the state actively bringing them together to collectively evaluate and pursue the good.[27]

As Kymlicka concludes, the issue is not whether "individuals' values and autonomy need to be situated in social relations" but whether these relations must or should be political ones.[28]

One can easily think of cases in which liberal polities foster community precisely because communal activities are protected by and shielded from state power. Thus, freedom of association has long held place among those rights essential to any conception of ordered liberty. The liberal state can restrict this freedom if its exercise denies certain citizens equal access to, say, housing or schools and therefore fails to treat persons as equals. There is nonetheless a strong presumption that persons should be left free to pursue their conceptions of the good in conjunction with whomever they choose. That liberalism has traditionally placed such a high value on association is hard to reconcile with the charge that it encourages an asocial view of persons.[29]

Thus, we are led also to see the "unencumbered self" in a different light. A liberal would stress that the very point of a philosophy built around the notion of a social contract is that people recognize themselves as fully social beings. That is, they know that they are the sorts of beings who favor certain ways of life over others and want protection in pursuing these ways against interference from others with different and, perhaps, competing conceptions of the good. To be sure, there is a sense in which people abstract themselves from their particular commitments in taking this self-awareness to liberal-contractarian conclusions. Without this abstraction they could not generalize from their position to that of others. They could not accept that there are other people with similar goals whom they should not interfere with. Such people would simply be dangerous, foolhardy, or self-destructive and might even have to be helped to see the light, perhaps by burning them, perhaps by educating them.

Finally, no matter how much my life is bound up with the life of a broader community, there is an irreducible sense in which it is *my* life and not that of the community. It is, I think, a virtue of liberalism to stress the distinctness of persons and doing so need not have consequences harmful to community. The fact, for instance, that my medical training could not have occurred without considerable state support does not give the state an unlimited authority to direct me to practice where and as much as it pleases. I do not want to suggest that *all* obligations of public service are unreasonable under these conditions, but only that I am not merely an object of the state's action; rather I am a person whose own goals and values ought to be respected to the maximum extent possible. I am an "I" who is not reducible to the social attributes I receive from interaction with others. Any political philosophy that sacrifices this sense of the self existing behind its social roles runs the risk of also losing sight of the "distinctness" of persons and the constraints (which liberalism stresses) on using persons as a means for another or for society as a whole.

It is at least arguable that members of a political community will feel a stronger sense of allegiance to that community if it is one that recognizes the dignity and respect which is to be accorded to each person. Societies organized on classical Aristotelian republican, or utilitarian, grounds require sacrifices from individuals to advance the good of others. Surely that my vital interests can legitimately be sacrificed to produce what may well be a lesser good for others may mitigate the attachment I can feel for the political regime.

Moreover, we have seen in the civil rights struggle, for example, that quests for political and civil liberties essential to the liberal tradition can foster a sense of community among those engaged in them. Community is, in a sense, a by-product of the quest. This explains why efforts to produce community for its own sake often fail. For readers who doubt this, think of those times when the sense of being engaged in a shared purpose has been strongest in one's own life. Such moments will be found for many, I suspect, when they were engaged in a sporting event, or building a float for a high school parade, or protesting a nuclear power plant. In each case, the sense of community is fostered in the pursuit of an extraneous goal. Efforts to organize the community because it might be nice to get together often fail to generate this sense of sharing just because they are so forced.

Struggles for the extension of rights to new classes of persons, as in the civil rights movement, or against the perceived denial of "natural rights" to life, liberty, and estate have been marvelously effective vehicles for generating social solidarity.[30] Unforced cooperation in such causes, indeed in a wide range of pursuits protected under the rubric of freedom of association, demonstrates the capacity of liberal societies to generate community not as a goal but as a by-product.[31]

Does Liberalism Denigrate Community?
The Germ of Truth in Republican-Inspired Claims

Though the more categorical claims of the necessary connections between liberalism and the denigration of community made by communitarian and republican critics are suspect, there are ways in which rights-based liberalism can give rise to selfish dispositions and have this harmful effect. Three of these, though not to my knowledge developed by communitarian critics, bear mention. The first can be described as a "rights illusion." Because rights are such an essential aspect of a liberal political morality, they may be taken to represent the whole of morality. Second, in some cases, knowledge of having a right to do x may generate a desire to do x regardless of the consequences on others. Third, a political philosophy that places such stress on self-reliance and individual achievement risks encouraging a false pride in its achievers.

We often fail to acknowledge the contribution others make to our own successes.

While the first error is, I think, not an uncommon one in our political culture, I cannot think of any major liberal theorist who makes it. Certainly, Locke does not. He recognizes natural duties toward others, such as parents toward children, which precede specified rights.[32] Nonetheless, the following sort of reasoning exemplifying this error will not be alien to most readers. The suburban home owner may reason that he has a right to do with his own property as he chooses. Such a right permits him to install a barbecue pit at the eastern end of his lot. His neighbor's complaint about the smoke wilting his roses, he may conclude, counts for very little. He has not violated any contractual right by his actions, therefore, there are no legitimate grounds for complaint against them and all his moral obligations are met.

We may agree with the barbecuer that he has violated no rights and, further, even that he has not ignored any natural duty toward his neighbor. Yet, we still might want to say that his action is deleterious in a way that he ought to consider because it is destructive of community for him to pay so little heed to his neighbor's wishes. It is, quite simply, unneighborly and makes mutual accommodation more difficult for everyone else (the rose grower is less inclined to lend a third neighbor his hedge clippers). Surely, it is within bounds to remind the barbecuer that his actions are harmful even if no violation of rights has occurred.

A tendency to pose complicated moral problems only in terms of rights runs the risk of limiting moral discourse and even of leading to a dialogic stalemate. The abortion debate in America today is a case in point. The woman's right to control her own body is set against the right of the fetus and proponents of each view see these rights as generating absolute, and contradictory, moral claims.

For liberals, rights-based arguments are essential on such a critical issue. Moreover, the rights-based arguments in common currency are not necessarily the best that could be made.[33] It nonetheless appears that using the vocabulary of rights has bogged down the abortion debate in the United States, keeping it from being set in a broader context of child care issues generally or of public health concerns.[34] It may even encourage a certain callousness. To some right-to-lifers, the pregnant woman is treated as little more than a temporary holding pen for a fetus. To some pro-choice advocates defending a woman's right to control her own body, the fetus is apparently regarded as no different from a wart or a mole. I do not know that "republican" approaches to such a question are more humane. In fact, insofar as they are simply majoritarian, depending on the state of public opinion at the moment, one doubts that they would be. This does not obscure the fact, however, that treating rights as the whole of morality exacts a price both in terms of public deliberation and in terms of community.

The second way in which a rights-based morality can plausibly be claimed to generate selfish dispositions, and thus to be destructive of community, is in generating desires for the good to which one has a right. For example, John dislikes the smell of cigarette smoke and does not want to sit in the smoking section on his airplane flight to New York. He has recently learned, moreover, that airlines must by law find nonsmokers seats in nonsmoking sections. Appealing to this right, he *demands* such a seat even if it means that another airplane will be called into service with only himself as passenger. It is conceivable that absent this right John may have borne the inconvenience of sitting in the smoking section stoically. It is also possible that he would have asked other passengers if they were willing to switch seats, if not for the whole flight, at least temporarily.

Many will no doubt feel that it is a great advance in health consciousness that John have the right granted to him. Whether this is so or not, the right creates in John a certain degree of intransigence which he would not display in its absence. It is certainly the case that John's earlier pliability results largely from powerlessness; he simply has no choice but to smell smoke or make other accommodations at his own inconvenience or expense. Yet, it is at least possible that absent the right, John would have attempted to resolve his dilemma through dialogue and reliance on the good will of his fellow passengers.

That John's right generates intransigence in this instance does not mean that rights claims in general have this effect—or at least not for the same reasons. It is wildly implausible, for example, to believe that a right to an abortion generates a desire to have an abortion that would not exist in the right's absence. The right opens up another choice for the pregnant woman, but we cannot imagine her saying "I am entitled to an abortion and, by God, that's what I want." It is also worth pointing out that this problem is not unique to liberal polities. All positive laws create rights. The right-side driving rule creates the right to drive on the right side just as it forbids driving on the left. Any society, regardless of its core political principles, will run into John's intransigence as it specifies rights through legislation. If it is more common in rights-based liberalism, this is because we tend to formulate a greater number of issues in terms of rights than do other societies.

Third, the language of rights can generate a kind of pride in rights bearers about their own accomplishments and obscure the extent to which their achievements have been dependent on the cooperation of others. Tocqueville had something like this in mind when he observed the tendency of democratic citizens to "[think] of themselves in isolation and imagine that their whole destiny is in their own hands."[35] This is especially common where property rights are concerned. No one captures this concern better than John Locke: "He that travels the road now, applauds his own strength and legs that have carried him in such a scantling of time, and ascribes all to his own vigor; little considering how much he owes to their pains, who cleared the woods, drained the bogs, built the bridges, and made the way passable; without which he may have toiled much with little progress."[36] The hubris Locke describes is not unique to liberal regimes. The story of pride as man's downfall is literally as old as Adam. Indeed, liberal theorists from the progenitor Hobbes on have warned of its dangers. It is nonetheless plausible that a form of political and social organization that rewards individual achievement over ascription and that places at the heart of its canon the right of the person over the fruits of her own labor, fosters a certain willful forgetting of the cooperation that made one's own successes possible. As Tocqueville observed, the organic view of feudal (or classical republican) society recognizes the contribution of all social orders to the common good, indeed, the social conditions of prosperity generally. "Aristocracy links everybody, from peasant to king, in one long chain," he wrote while, "democracy breaks the chain and frees each link."[37]

The relation between liberalism and community cuts in several different directions. The more categorical claims of an inherent opposition between rights-based liberalism and community are not sustainable. In fact, liberalism can claim as one of its virtues a profound recognition of the centrality of community to virtually any conception of the good; further, a recognition of the inviolability of each person can enhance community by assuring each member of the polity that her vital interests will not be sacrificed for the sake of others. Yet, if there is no inherent opposition, it is at least empirically plausible to contend that liberalism can be destructive of community in some instances.

More needs to be done to map the relation between liberalism and community, and hence, the value of liberal and republican institutions, than is attempted in this book. And, though I have avoided exegetical controversies in this sketch of the relationship, the best liberal theorists, including Madison, have recognized and attempted to navigate these crosscurrents. Liberal community *is* different from republican community, just as liberal civic virtue is different from republican civic virtue. The challenge for liberals is to weaken the centrifugal forces that are embedded in liberal ideology and to strengthen those that tend toward community and civic virtue.

One must search out extremes to find a liberal theorist who has contended that polities are sustained if all people seek to maximize private interests at all times.[38] This position would be anathema to the American founders. Nor did the authors of *The Federalist* believe that either institutional or social checks and balances would suffice to stabilize the constitutional regime they proposed if dispositions toward preserving the regime were lacking. How these dispositions arise, and can be brought about, is a topic the founders and their liberal predecessors consider in some depth.

Liberal Obligations and Civic Virtue

Liberal political theorists have long been aware that the pull of self-interest, which liberal philosophy in some sense legitimizes, can lead citizens toward injustice. The question of motivation to act upon liberal principles of justice (an analytically distinct question from that of the derivation of these principles) has been taken up by a range of thinkers from Locke through Madison and beyond. Indeed, liberals have consistently drawn a distinction between the *principles* on which persons ought to act and the *motivation* to act on these principles, as is indicated in the following remarks; the first from John Locke, the second from John Rawls:

> [There are] two parts of Ethics, the one is the rule[s] which men are generally in the right in though perhaps they have not deduced them as they should from their true principles. The other is the true motives to practice them and the ways to bring men to observe them and these are generally not well known or Rightly applied.[39]

> However attractive a conception of justice might be on other grounds, it is seriously defective if the principles of moral psychology are such that it fails to engender in human beings the requisite desire to act upon it.[40]

For both Locke and Rawls the obligations to contribute to the maintenance of the liberal polity are conceived as the rational choices of a free agent. The liberal social contract is legitimized from the standpoint of each individual if and only if he has *consented* to its adoption and *benefits* by its institution. Consent to the terms of the contract is the only legitimate ground for being bound by those terms as it alone is compatible with the equality of all in the state of nature. Each individual, insofar as he is rational, would consent to a cooperative plan only if he were better off with it than without it. Under liberal contractarian assumptions, all are better off by cooperating since only through a publicly enforced legal framework are their security and independence assured. These two aspects—consent and benefit—form the liberal theory of political obligation: one ought to contribute to the maintenance of the public order if one has agreed to receive the benefits provided by it.

The liberal theory of obligation is grounded in a theory of rational agency. It is based on the ideas that all persons are capable of (1) developing a concept of the good on which they would choose to act over time; (2) realizing that the ability to act on one's rational life plan requires social cooperation; and consequently (3) recognizing the need to act in ways that support an established system of justice. Each member of the liberal state ought to recognize, as an intrinsic aspect of his own good, the maintenance of the plan of cooperation that makes the pursuit of self-defined goods over time possible.

Though this notion of obligation is compelling in theory, it is wrought with practical problems. In the first quotation, Locke suggests that principles of justice are understood intuitively by most persons. It is no less true, however, that application of these principles in one's civic associations calls for a degree of disinterestedness and, in fact, virtue that does not emerge spontaneously. That this is so is stressed by Rawls to such an extent that he offers as a criterion for accepting a plan of justice its capacity to engender motivations to support it. Principles of justice may be discovered by reason, or by moral intuition, but motivation to act on these principles compete as bases for action with other, purely prudential inclinations or those arising from what Hume described as limited benevolence. In terms familiar to the founders, these inclinations are provided by passions or interests. Virtue, in the liberal context (though not exclusively in that context), refers generally to the disposition to act justly even when rational prudence dictates against doing so.

That dispositions toward justice and rational prudence frequently motivate different actions is an endemic feature of social life. There are ample reasons to suggest that, despite the condition of unanimity of the social contract and the commonality of interests it presumes, conflicts over scarce resources will be rife in liberal polities. This is so for two main reasons. First, even when the rules of cooperation are mutually agreeable, it is possible for persons in constituted polities to bring about better results for themselves by ignoring the constraints the rules impose. Second, it will rarely be evident in large societies that any individual's defection from support for the public order will pose an immanent threat to it. It is likely to appear to each, therefore, that he can take advantage of the benefits of cooperation without sharing their costs. It rarely will be evident that doing so will jeopardize the plan that provides those benefits. This is the essence of the free-rider problem described in contemporary economic theories of collective action.[41]

It may be that principles of justice are discoverable by reason if we accept as premises a few fairly noncontentious claims defining persons and an initial choice situation. This is, at least, the claim of social contract theory. It cannot be the case, however, that motives for acting on principles are similarly deducible, at least for those living in large, complex societies. It is possible to imagine a society where noncooperative dispositions could be considered both imprudent and immoral. The limiting case would be a society of two in which noncooperation by one party would effectively dissolve the society. Think, for example, of the case of two rowers in a boat in which, if party x were to stop rowing, the boat could not get back to shore regardless of party y's actions.[42] In such a situation, prudential and moral reasoning would coincide. Each would induce one to row and the free rider problem would thereby be eliminated.

Merely to state this exceptional situation is to call attention to the more frequent situation in which moral and prudential motivations can and do pull in opposite directions. That they do so explains the existence of the free rider as a stock figure in liberal political discourse and also exposes the implausibility of an idea frequently attributed to the authors of *The Federalist*. That is the notion that the goal of a stable, liberal society could be realized simply by balancing the self-interested pursuits of individuals and factions against each other in a carefully designed institutional framework. Recognizing the cross-pull of moral and prudential motivations also points to the need, within liberalism, to provide *other than prudential* responses to those who would choose to act as free riders rather than as citizens, as tyrants rather than as legitimate rulers.[43]

Liberal responses to free-rider reasoning are a central concern if one is to establish the relationship between core liberal assumptions and civic virtue. Thus, it is worth examining the formulation and response to the free-rider problem in liberal thought in some depth. To do so will enable us in later chapters to untangle the complex relationship between the language of rights and interests and the language of civic virtue found in the American founding debates.

The free-rider problem is summarized by Hobbes in the following terms. Hobbes's fool argues that "there is no such thing as justice; and . . . every man's conservation being committed to his own care, there could be no reason, why every man might not do what he thought conduced thereunto: and therefore also to make or not make; keep, or not keep covenants was not against reason, when it conduced to one's benefit."[44] One possible though limited response to reasoning of this sort is to suggest that the fool is misreading the counsels of rational prudence. The benefits accruing to him as a result of his disregard for the law, this line of argument would suggest, are not worth the risks. Hobbes seems to have an argument of this sort in mind when he writes: "He therefore that breaketh his covenant, and consequently declareth that he thinks he may with reason do so, cannot be received into any society that unite themselves for peace and defence, but by the error of them that receive him . . . which errors a man cannot reckon on as a means to his security."[45] Hobbes suggests that the rational person fully aware of his own interests will choose the safest course in protecting his life and assets. The fool, by failing to abide by the law, places himself in unnecessary jeopardy. The fool does so because the sole source of his standing as a member of the political community, with full rights and protections in it, is other members' ignorance of his conduct.

This prudentially based response to the fool is, however, riddled with weaknesses, as Hobbes himself is aware. The overriding weakness is that crime may pay. The response can, at best, be stated in terms of probability that the fool will be deprived of his liberty if he breaks the law. This being so, the willingness to put one's liberty at risk to attain some other good would be a matter over which individuals reasonably could differ. The safest course cannot, therefore, be considered a dictate of rational prudence as such. Moreover, since the least risk-averse members of the polity will be the ones most likely to act as free riders, and since this group is, by definition, the least receptive to Hobbes's prudential argument, the practical weight of this argument is seriously diminished.

The prudential argument is also weakened when one considers that risk-averting strategies are not equally prudent for all members of a polity whenever substantial differences in wealth and power exist among them since wealth and power can be used to minimize the negative consequences of risk taking. It may be, for example, that, if I can afford a highly skilled lawyer to advise me on how to evade the law, or, in the worst case, reduce the likelihood and/or severity of my punishment if I do get caught, it makes sense for me to take greater risks than if I must rely on the public defender. Hence, the prudential argument is doubly diminished. It is likely to be found most convincing by those with least inclination and least means to act as successful free riders in the first place.

Hobbes's explicit recognition of the weakness of prudential responses to the fool is witnessed in his reliance on moral ones. These are developed in his discussion of the laws of nature. Natural laws are described as rules discovered by reason that forbid actions destructive of one's own life. Hobbes's description of the state of nature makes clear that noncooperative actions, if they are the general rule, bring about conditions that make each person worse off than she would be by cooperating. He further shows that the willingness to abide by these necessary rules of cooperation cannot arise solely from motivations of self-interest in constituted polities. Hobbes's response to the fool, therefore, is to try to convince him that, at least on occasion, prudential consideration must be set aside as a motive for action.

Central to this moral argument is Hobbes's injunction against *pride*. Pride is the failure of a man to acknowledge every other person as his equal by nature. It leads directly to arrogance, which is the reservation of some right to oneself that one would have others surrender. These vices result from the presumption that one is entitled to some right or good that others ought to be denied based on some intrinsic quality they do not possess.[46] The proud man takes those attributes, such as wealth, learning, or political power, that he believes he possesses in greater degrees than do others as signs of intrinsic superiority. Hobbes's response to him is to argue that his attributes are *themselves the product of social cooperation*. In his own words, "the inequality that now is, has been introduced by the laws civil."[47] One's privileged position in a community cannot justify one's exemption from its laws, but is all the more reason to be bound by them.

Pride is a principle vice because it legitimizes to oneself violations of law and because all are subject to pride. It is quite natural, in Hobbes's view, for men to value themselves more highly than they value others. And this is the major impediment to their taking the laws of nature as maxims for their actions. All men know, he says "that the obstruction to this kind of doctrine, proceed not so much from the difficulty of the matter, as from the interest of them that are to learn. Potent men, digest hardly anything that setteth up a power to bridle their affections; and learned men, anything that discovereth their errors, and thereby lesseneth their authority."[48]

The laws of nature themselves need no great act of reasoning to be discovered. They are also the dictates of scripture and are summarized in the maxim "Do not that to another, which thou wouldest not have done to thyself."[49] To abide by them, however, and thus to act in a just manner, requires a *willingness* "when weighing the actions of other men with his own," to see that "his own passions and self-love, may add nothing to the weight."[50] To be sure, this willingness is only actuated when a sovereign is in place since, though the laws of nature bind in conscience always, they oblige "in effect" only when there is assurance that others will act in a like manner. In one of the delicious ironies of Hobbes's thought, the sovereign becomes the necessary condition for people to lead moral lives. That they do so, at least in part, reinforces the authority of the sovereign and the stability of the political order.

This argument on the limits of rational prudence leaves open many empirical and theoretical questions. How much virtue is required to stabilize liberal polities, and By how many people must it be practiced are examples of the former. The problem of how moral dispositions in general and dispositions toward justice in particular arise raises questions of both types. For now at least the following point seems clear enough. If one accepts the preservation of liberal freedoms as a worthy end, and if one sees that a "virtuous citizenry" is required to realize and maintain that end, then a consideration of the conditions that foster this sense of justice becomes a critical step in justifying a liberal form of government. Such a consideration does no more than inquire into the social and psychological bases of the popular acceptance of liberal norms.

The purpose of considering the bases of legitimacy is to establish that the proposed liberal plan of government can actually exist. The plan can be shown to be viable only if the virtues that must be practiced for the polity to be sustained will, in fact, be practiced. This consideration entails an evaluation not only of how people *ought* to act, but also of how they are *likely* to act given our understanding of human motivations. Thus, we would question the practicality of a polity that could be sustained only by making civic demands that our understanding of moral psychology would lead us to consider overly rigorous. Similarly, we would question a society constituted according to a plan of cooperation that fostered noncooperative dispositions, however unintentionally. The first flaw would be evidenced if the plan required a degree of self-sacrifice or benevolence toward fellow citizens so beyond customary bounds as to be considered heroic or saintly.[51] The second flaw is more relevant to our concerns since it is endemic to classical liberalism.

What, then, is the relation between political obligations and the motives to act on them? The answer to this question depends on beliefs about the cognitive and emotional makeup of human beings, about their relations with others, and about their relations with God. These answers take an increasingly psychological form as we move from the seventeenth to the late eighteenth century. We can begin to see how this comes about by examining, if in a somewhat sketchy way, the thought of John Locke.

3

John Locke: Acting on Natural Law Duties and the Problem of Civic Motivations

What is it that motivates people in liberal societies to act morally and citizens to obey the laws of their states? We have, after all, goals and desires for ourselves and our immediate loved ones that could be furthered much of the time by passing the costs of citizenship on to others. Surely the state's coercive powers play a part in our motivations. Yet, there must be more to civic motivation than coercion. A liberal polity could not survive, given the wide scope it grants to personal freedoms, if most people did not display sufficient allegiance to the regime and obedience to its laws most of the time.

It is not surprising that as quintessential a liberal thinker as John Locke—a thinker who is central in providing the language of natural rights and government by consent, and the call for religious toleration to Anglo-American political discourse—spent considerable time thinking about moral and civic motives (which I take to be moral motives pertaining specifically to justice) and how they arise both as a theological and a political problem. As a Christian thinker, Locke asks how it is that human conduct conforms to conceptions of right embodied in natural and divine law. As a citizen—and one who wrote extensive letters to gentlemen friends on the proper ways to raise their children *for liberty*—Locke asks how it is that children, born with a natural love of dominating others, can learn to curb that urge and conform themselves to the conduct required to sustain a just state.[1] In both cases, he comes to rely on a rather crude hedonistic psychology. Locke, like the American constitution founders, conceived fostering motives for citizenship largely as a molding of the passions through unobtrusive means consistent with liberal principles.

Our present interest in Locke centers on his understanding of the wellsprings of allegiance to political regimes and of a disposition toward justice that can fairly be called civic virtue. The purpose of exploring Locke's thought on this issue is threefold. First, it is worth noting the large role the inculcation of virtues essential to a well-run and reasonably just commonwealth plays in the work of an important thinker whose liberal credentials cannot be denied. Doing so serves as a corrective to some—by no means all—republicanist revisions of Anglo-American political thought that reserve such terms as *virtue* and *corruption* for writers in a civic humanist tradition. Second, even if it is assumed that liberals care about virtue, the question remains what they mean by the term. I suggest that Locke offers a decidedly modern conception of it and its origins, one that would be quite alien to classical republicans. He conceives of public virtue by and large as a restraint on primary, acquisitive dispositions and as a necessary instrument for preserving social order. He does not understand virtue in classical terms (or those adopted by J. G. A. Pocock in interpreting eighteenth century Anglo-American thought that retain Aristotelian traces), as representing perfection of character in pursuit of the good life.[2]

Finally, Locke is a progenitor of a way of thinking about civic virtue that is rooted in the passions and developed through a "liberal" education and socialization. Locke treats the child, that is, the future citizen, as a reasonable being whose conduct can be changed through the strategic use of psychic rewards and punishments, especially the desire for esteem. His approach is both empirical and normative; it explores how civic dispositions that assure stability of the regime emerge and how they can be molded and shaped to further this end. I do not claim that Locke exercised a great direct influence over the constitutional founders on this subject, although we can be confident that their fundamental principles of political right are to a considerable extent "Lockean."[3] Rather, he offers an approach to public virtue grounded in the passions and conceived as a necessary restraint on primary, selfish dispositions. Moreover, he offers a characteristically liberal understanding of fostering the virtues of citizenship. The state plays a very minor role in the shaping of these virtues. They emerge instead from a by and large private and noncoercive channeling of the passions. This approach was developed and refined by Hume and Smith and most directly relied upon in practical politics by the American constitutional founders.

Locke's thoughts on the question of civic virtue and allegiance are not found in one chapter or book, but are scattered throughout his work. Moreover, in order to understand Locke—and liberalism as an evolving political idea and practice—correctly, we must understand them in the context of his broader conceptions of natural law, the obligations it imposes, and the will to act on them. The first two issues are essential to Locke's entire body of work, from his early (unpublished) *Essays on the Law of Nature* through the *Two Treatises of Government*. The third is discussed most extensively in his widely circulated writings on education for gentlemen.[4]

Acting on Duties: From Natural Law to Human Action

Recent scholarship on Locke has stressed the largely theological perspective that informs his politics and philosophy. Such findings should come as no revelation to those who have tried to grasp Locke's entire corpus. Well over half of his *oeuvre* deals directly with such themes as religious toleration, the relation between reason and revelation, and Christianity as an ethics for everyday life. Indeed, a recent work by Richard Ashcraft leads us to question the tenability of even such a division of Locke's work into primarily religious and primarily secular categories.[5] Debates about religious dissent, Ashcraft suggests, called forth from Locke and his fellow dissenters a degree of philosophical explicitness that suffused all aspects of his thought from the most narrowly epistemological to the most political and polemical.

The centrality of natural law to Locke's political arguments whether on property or on obligations to the state have been amply demonstrated in recent works by John Dunn, James Tully, and others. Tully isolates essential features of natural law theorizing and shows that Locke meets the test in each case. Natural law views rest on the belief that there is a lawmaker who makes laws with respect to things to be done by us. Such laws are, therefore, normative propositions and are promulgated by the lawmaker insofar as they are rationally discoverable. Finally, in order to be laws proper they must be and are backed by rewards and punishments.[6]

Locke's *Essay Concerning Human Understanding* includes an argument from design to establish the existence of the lawmaker, whose being is elsewhere a premise of Locke's philosophy. That the law of nature imposes obligations on persons and the manner in which it is promulgated are best expressed in Locke's own words. He writes in the *Second Treatise* that the law of nature "obliges every one" and reason "teaches all Mankind . . . that being all the Workmanship of one Omnipotent and infinitely wise Maker, . . . there cannot be supposed any *Subordination* among us, that may Authorize us to destroy one another, as if we were made for another's uses."[7] The duty not to harm others, or oneself, derives directly from the fact that we are all equally the workmanship of a Divine Creator who maintains in us the right a maker has in his own product.

Locke's reliance on reason to discern our natural law duties is not inconsistent with the empiricist psychology developed in the *Essay* although this was not always apparent even in his own day.[8] The theological significance of this empiricism was not lost on Locke's friendly but somewhat vertiginous reader, James Tyrrell, who wrote that he "find[s] the divines much scandalized that so sweet and easy a part of their sermons as that of the law written in the heart is rendered false and useless."[9] Tyrrell was correct in noting Locke's rejection of even such pleasing innate ideas as those pertaining to our natural duties. He is also correct in noting that the demands of Locke's rationalism are indeed less "easy" to arrive at, and hence preach, than are appeals to men's hearts. However, a close reading of Locke discloses little reason for Tyrrell's divines to be scandalized by his intentions.

"God," Locke argues, "made Man and the World . . . [and] directed him by his Senses and Reason, as he did the inferior animals by their Sense, and Instinct."[10] Man is uniquely able to reflect on his sensory experiences, so that natural law is promulgated to man alone. His reflections lead him not only to discern the existence of the Creator from his own being but to discern at least some of the content of what the Creator requires of him as a moral agent as well. Thus, for example, it is absurd to think that God made man and endowed him with rational and creative faculties for those faculties to lie fallow. Hence men labor not only out of necessity but are indeed obliged to do so given God's discernible intentions.[11] Further, by reflecting upon his instinct of self-preservation, each person can deduce the intention that he and, ceteris paribus, others are to be preserved.

> For the desire, strong desire of Preserving his Life and Being having been Planted in him, as a Principle of Action by God himself, Reason, which was the Voice of God in him, could not but teach him and assure him, that pursuing that natural Inclination . . . he had to preserve his Being, he followed the Will of his Maker, and therefore had a right to make use of those Creatures, which by his Reason or Senses he could discover would be serviceable thereunto. And thus Man's Property in the Creatures, was founded upon the right he had, to make use of those things, that were necessary or useful to his Being.[12]

We reflect on our natures as creatures of sense and instinct in order to ascertain our place in the world in relation to other humans and to nature. Such reflection must be reflection *on* something, hence the centrality of sense experience as a starting point. But, its aim is to define our duties as beings dependent upon the will of our Maker.

Locke remained committed throughout his life's work to this notion of man as God's workmanship and uses it to undergird his moral and political philosophy. Locke made, however, one major alteration in his use of natural law theory from his earlier to late writings that concerns us directly. Locke comes to rely increasingly on a hedonistic psychology of motivation and, therefore, pays more attention in the later works to the actual wellsprings of human conduct as exhibited in our actions and less to the intrinsic goodness or badness of our conduct.

Locke relied much more heavily on a Thomistic notion of the binding force of natural law in his earliest work on moral philosophy. He argues in his *Essays on the Law of Nature* (written shortly after 1660 and some thirty years before he published his major philosophical work, *the Essay Concerning Human Understanding*) that divine law obliges the conscience, "so that men are not bound by a fear of punishment but by a rational apprehension of what is right."[13] He also maintains that fear of punishment is not the grounds of obligation, however powerful a psychological incentive it provides. The obligatory force of natural law derives from its being an expression of God's will. "We are bound to show ourselves obedient to the Authority of His will," Locke argues, "because both our being and our work depend on His will."[14] Though Locke remains committed to this "workmanship" model throughout his works, he comes to rely less on the power of rational apprehension of natural right to determine conduct and places a hedonistic psychology and fears of divine punishment at the center of his thinking about motivation.

Locke's shift in emphasis from early attempts to demonstrate moral postulates deduced from natural law to considering more deeply the ways in which our conduct could be brought into conformity with such law is witnessed in part in his reluctance to publish his early *Essays on the Law of*

Nature. There he considers the grounding of natural law more fully than in later works. Locke also failed to fulfill promises made in drafts of the *Essay* to provide a full consideration of natural law in that work.

The reasons for this failure are subject to debate. W. von Leyden speculates that Locke's abandonment of this project derives from a deeper skepticism about the demonstrative character of morality.[15] It is difficult to give full credit to this view, however, as Locke does not express such doubts directly. Further, Locke engages in the practice whose efficacy he is alleged to question when, for example, he offering such specific moral arguments as in the derivation of property rights in the *Second Treatise*.[16] It is more likely that Locke's hedonism along with the increasingly empirical cast of his philosophy lead him to deal more directly with the problem "of how men can be brought to *practice* the moral principles they perceive as rational."[17] Certainly, the *Essay* and *Reasonableness of Christianity* offer evidence of this focus, as do the writings on education from a more secular standpoint.

Locke's decreasing reliance on "rational apprehension" of right and his increased stress on reward and punishment to motivate good or just conduct call into question his commitment to natural law theory. As Leyden has argued, these two strains of thought "are not easily assimilated to one another."[18] Leyden comes close to suggesting a complete incompatibility when he asserts that Locke comes to conceives of "moral goodness or badness *as* reward and punishment, i.e., the pleasure or pain, following the observation or breach of a law made by God."[19]

Though Locke's arguments on this theme are not altogether clear, there is reason to believe that Leyden's view suggests a more radical break with natural law premises than Locke wishes to make. Eternal rewards and punishments are good or bad because God has chosen them as means to sanction His laws, not because they produce pleasure or pain. Moreover, there are implications to this construction that Locke wants to reject, the most obvious being that the power to inflict pain can function as a grounds for morality. Such a view could be used to legitimize tyrants. Second, this construction identifies morality with the self-interest of the pleasure-maximizer, and, while Locke does not believe that God intended men for a life of misery, neither does he associate the goods they seek with their permanent moral interests, however much the latter might coincide with their pleasure.

Locke does come to adopt a subjectivist theory of the good but he continues to distinguish the good for man from "moral rectitude." This is indicated in his discussion of the relation of good and evil to the will. Locke formulates the problem in an unpublished work on ethics written three years after the *Essay*:

> The pleasure that a man takes in any action or expects as a consequence of it is indeed a good in the self able and proper to move the will. But the moral rectitude of it considered barely in itself is not good or evil nor any way moves the will, but as pleasure and pain either accompanies the action itself or is looked on to be a consequence of it. Which is evident from the punishments and rewards which God has annexed to moral rectitude or pravity as proper

motives to the will, which would be needless if moral rectitude were in itself good and moral pravity evil.[20]

Locke's version of this motivational thesis is as strong in the *Essay* itself. There he claims that "because pleasure and pain are produced in us by the operation of certain objects either on our minds or our bodies . . . what has an aptness to produce pleasure in us is that we call *good* and what is apt to produce pain in us we call *evil*."[21] Under either construction, good or evil have, by definition, a capacity to move the will. They have such a capacity because they are essentially identical to the production of pleasure or pain and men by nature seek pleasure and avoid pain.

Locke expresses here the view, usually associated with Hume, that reason is inert and therefore not a cause of action. In his own words, "Let a man be never so well persuaded of the advantages of virtue . . . yet till he *hungers* and *thirsts* after *righteousness*, till he feels an *uneasiness* in the want of it, his *will* will not be determined to any action in pursuit of this confessed greater good."[22] Locke does not deny in these remarks that "moral rectitude" can, indeed must, be conceived of apart from rewards and punishments. He does claim, however, that, without the appropriate desire, it is indifferent to us. We would not care about moral rectitude per se if it were not connected in our minds with our desires.

As strange as this separation of notions of good and evil from "moral rectitude" are if one accepts Thomistic natural law assumptions, Locke's reliance on a hedonistic psychology occurs fully within a Christian perspective. He has no doubt that an unclouded hedonistic calculation would lead one to tend one's soul as best one could as no pleasures or pains in this world could compare to the eternal bliss or misery of the next one. "Nothing of pleasure and pain in this life," he wrote, "can bear any proportion to endless happiness or exquisite misery of an immortal soul hereafter." Thus, the wise person will put little weight upon "the transient pleasure or pain" he finds in this world as against promise of "that perfect durable happiness hereafter."[23]

He asks, then, why men fail in this calculation and risk eternal damnation. He takes it as an analytical truth that all men seek their own happiness. Yet, he argues, we are prone to value lesser degrees of happiness to greater ones. Since this cannot be explained as a failure to desire our own good, it must be that our judgment is frequently wrong in ascertaining where our long-term interests lie. We tend, in particular, to discount the future so thoroughly that present pleasures lead us to ignore far greater absent goods just as "objects near our view, are thought to be greater than those of a larger size that are more remote."[24]

Of course, if there were no "prospect beyond the grave," men would be quite right to satisfy all their earthly desires with no thought of morality.[25] This is why atheism is a crime, and one of such proportions that it should "shut a man out of all sober and civil society."[26] Without the promise of an afterlife, "the inference is certainly right, *let us eat and drink*, let us enjoy what we delight in, *for tomorrow we shall die*."[27]

Human weakness leads us to value present goods more highly than the greater ones beyond the grave and to allow them to determine our conduct. Yet this focus on nearer goods is built into our very capacity to act in the world. Locke rejects in the *Essay* the "conventional view" that the will is determined by the greatest good presented to the understanding. One reason for so doing so is that "moral rectitude," no matter how well understood fails to determine the will without an accompanying desire, or feeling of "uneasiness" in its absence. Beyond this, however, Locke contends that if the conventional view were correct, contemplation of so great a good as the afterlife would "seize the will," fixing the mind upon it and trapping it in continual contemplation.[28] It would, in short, make men unsuited for society and the quite legitimate pleasures they derive from contributing to it and from the company of others.

In this conception, men can only achieve their ultimate aim by pursuing it indirectly. It is axiomatic that we all seek our own happiness, to slake the thirst of "uneasiness" felt in the absence of some good. If this is true, it would seem that good conduct does not emerge from rational reflection on the good but upon feeling the appropriate type of uneasiness. How we come to feel this right uneasiness then becomes a central question in morals and one that increasingly concerns Locke. To be sure, there is a cognitive component to this uneasiness, but Locke's argument for the inertness of reason and his concentration on desire make it clear that he would not agree with Plato, or Thomas Aquinas, in equating knowledge with virtue.

Despite its incapacity to move the will, the free use of reason plays a large role in Locke's moral thought. In fact, an essential feature of the arguments of the religious dissenters surrounding Locke was to defend what one of them, Andrew Marvell, described as a "reason religionated and christianized" against the challenges of blind appeals to authority in ecclesiastical matters.[29] Such a defense had vast political implications, as was evident in the criticism the dissenters offered of such proponents of absolute sovereignty as Hobbes and Samuel Parker because they denied the competence of individuals to judge right and wrong, good and evil for themselves in a personal relation with their God.[30]

What and how much does one have to *know* in order to organize one's life around the Christian virtues? Locke comments extensively on this question, especially in the *Reasonableness of Christianity*. He does so first in the context of a discussion of the historical development of moral philosophy.

Locke credits pre-Christian philosophers with making some progress in ascertaining the nature of man's duties toward others. Yet, this progress only went so far for two main reasons. First, reason is inadequate even when it is practiced by the best philosophers. "It is plain," Locke argued, that "human reason unassisted failed men in its great and proper business of morality."[31] The heathen philosophers were, in Locke's view, akin to the blind men feeling the elephant to ascertain its form. Absent the light of revelation, moral knowledge grew only incrementally, with no promise that it would ever arrive at completeness.

Equally important, the words of the philosophers had no authority with "the greatest part of mankind," which lacks the "leisure or capacity for demonstration," who "cannot know, and therefore . . . must believe."[32] As much as Locke rejected the notion that individuals had to rely on ecclesiastical authority to interpret scripture for them, he rejected the possibility that morality could emerge in any satisfactory form without the authority of scripture itself. This was certainly the case among the many although it would be wrong to suggest that Locke recommends religion as the opiate of the masses. Much like Hobbes, Locke had little faith in the capacity of the learned and the wealthy to bridle their affections.

> Had God intended that none but the learned scribe, the disputer, or wise of this world, should be Christians, or be saved, thus religion should have been prepared for them, filled with speculations and niceties, obscure terms, and abstract notions. But men of that expectation, men furnished with such acquisitions, the apostles tell us . . . are rather shut out from the simplicity of the Gospel; to make way for the poor, ignorant, illiterate who heard and believed promises of a Deliverer, and believed Jesus to be him.[33]

For Locke, the poor were in a privileged position because of their superior receptiveness to revelation. His compliment may seem backhanded since their advantage lies in their lack of time or capacity for serious reflection. But theirs is a privileged position nonetheless and Locke is far from claiming that the poor are being led astray by anyone in nurturing their faith.[34]

Clearly, Locke did not reject the enterprise of serious reflection on morals. He was known to engage in this practice himself. However, absent the recognition that "Jesus is the Christ," it is equally plain that he did not see reflection on morals as advancing very far in either the minds or the hearts of men. Without it, all the weighty tomes on casuistry do no good, while, if one has this basic belief in Jesus, such works are merely superfluous. The belief in the rewards and punishments after the grave should concentrate the mind quite well on righteousness. Of course, it often does not do this well enough and we turn now to this problem.

Locke on Moral and Civic Education

For Locke, moral and civic motives emerge from an education that is a training as much of the will as of the intellect—if not more so. Locke's notion of education in the moral and civic virtues relies strongly on inducements in the form of rewards and punishments that work upon the will, as it were, surreptitiously. Moral practice in personal or civic associations emerges from what Locke describes as a concordance of "Conscience, Reason and pleasure."[35]

Locke wrote his main work on education, *Some Thoughts Concerning Education*, with an explicitly civic concern in mind. His is an education in the bourgeois virtues of civility, liberality, and justice. These virtues are not conceived in perfectionist terms, that is, as expressions of a fully developed human nature. Rather, they are conceived as internal restraints of character on primary, predominantly selfish instincts, restraints that are required if men are to live together in peace. Education in the liberal virtues Locke has in mind is as essential to maintaining the security and prosperity of the liberal nation-state as are effective political institutions. "[It is] impossible to find an instance of any Nation, however renowned for their Valour, who ever kept their Credit in Arms, or made themselves redoubtable amongst their Neighbours, after Corruption had once broken through, and dissolv'd the restraint of Discipline."[36] Locke shows a concern with the harmful effects of "corruption" on the polity (a point worth noting by republican revisionists who would reserve this term and the concern it represents to nonLockean republicans). Further, he explicitly rejects the notion that institutions can prevent injustice if men do not feel a desire to abide by the guidelines these institutions establish.

The civic virtues Locke discusses essentially consist in the "Power of denying our selves the Satisfaction of our own Desires, where reason does not authorize them."[37] This formulation should not be read as suggesting that Locke was an ascetic. Reason authorizes a great many satisfactions. Rather, the interest of this remark derives from its conception of virtue as a *power* over the self and from the question it raises: How do the dictates of reason become effective guides to actions? Locke's answer to this question is somewhat confusing. He wants to suggest that just actions will result if only reason is consulted fairly. Yet his periodic equations of reason with self-interest, along with his belief in the propensity for us to discount the future in a pronounced way, give grounds for thinking that just the opposite may result.

This is indicated when, for example, he describes the "natural reason" all men possess as a "touchstone" by which they can distinguish "truth from appearances."[38] This faculty, given us by God to discern truth, does not always guide our actions for two main reasons. Either it is atrophied through disuse, as is inevitably the case with manual laborers given the drudgery of their tasks.[39] Or, the faculty is "spoiled and lost" as a result of the "assuming prejudices, overweening presumption and narrowing [of the] minds" of men.[40] The latter explanation is similar to Hobbes's analysis of the sources of resistance to his political doctrine. In any case, Locke has little doubt that, however true his political principles may be, however much in accord with God's will as expressed through natural reason, the path between truth and action is a circuitous one. "If a true estimate were made of the Morality and Religions of the World, we should find that, the far greater part of Mankind received even those Opinions and Ceremonies they would die for, rather from the Fashions of their Countries, and the constant Practice of those about them, than from any conviction of their Reasons."[41] He expresses a similar point, with an added complication, when discussing the virtue of honesty and the best means of inculcating it in children. Shame and habituation, he writes, "will be better Guard against *Dishonesty* than any Consideration drawn from interest; Habits work more constantly, and with greater Facility than Reason: Which, when we have the most need of it, is seldom fairly consulted, and more rarely obey'd."[42]

This passage is as interesting in its equation of reason and interest as in its assertion that rational dictates are rarely followed. Locke implies that reasoning from interest *could* supply incentives for honest conduct if it were more fairly consulted. Yet the rational prudence Locke points to could provide only a probable motive for acting justly. The calculation made concerns the probability of one's dishonest conduct being discovered; rational individuals would differ in their assessments of risk. It is largely this consideration, I suspect, that encourages Locke to discount purely rational motives for honest conduct.

It could be argued that habituation to this duty is necessary in the education of children because of the undeveloped state of their rational faculties and need not apply to adults. Indeed, Locke offers support for this reading in his general discussion of the importance of habituation in moral education. He suggests that "kind words and gentle admonitions" are more effective moral guides for children than the learning of rules which requires the assistance of memory.[43] Success in habituation is achieved "when constant Custom has made any one thing easy and natural to them, and they practice it without Reflection."[44]

Yet the superior reliability of habit over reason with regard to moral actions is as much in evidence among adults as among children—hence Locke's stress on the centrality of customary opinion in providing even the beliefs we are willing to die for. Moreover, grown men, even the gentlemen he is addressing, are not much more reliable than children when interest and duty conflict. "The Foundations on which several Duties are built, and the Foundations of Right and Wrong, from which they spring, are not perhaps, easily to be let into the Minds of grown Men, not used to abstract their Thoughts from common received Opinions."[45]

Moreover, the advanced reasoning powers of adults do not necessarily make them more honest, since reason is a tool that can be applied equally well to narrowly self-regarding as to other-regarding uses. In fact, the distinction between child and adult is less significant with respect to motives for virtue than is an innate quality adult and children share, the "love of dominion." This love, Locke argues, is "the first Original of most vicious Habits that are ordinary or natural."[46] And it is a trait as distinctly human as is reason itself. No other creature is "half so willful and proud, or half so desirous to be Masters of themselves and others, as Man."[47]

Given an instrumental conception of practical reason, and given that the ends it is likely to serve if unattended are those determined by man's innate love of dominion, it is fortuitous that moral reasoning has an ally in malleable passions, which can serve as a basis for a sense of justice. It was left to the Scottish Enlightenment thinkers to develop the moral psychology on which Locke relies but which he does not fully elaborate. It is sufficient for him to note that the sources of that morality required to sustain a constituted polity can be inculcated by what amounts to a desire to conform to the expectations of others. Only this desire makes shame and habituation the effective tools in moral education that they are.

This reading finds support in the central role played by reputation in Locke's thoughts on moral education. Locke's writings on education are generally, and justly, considered humane and progressive. They minimize the use of corporal punishment, compared to the standards of his time, and show respect for the reasonableness of the child.[48] Locke accepts the notion that good actions should be rewarded and bad ones punished but he seeks to substitute psychic rewards and punishments for physical ones. He writes, in fact, that "Good and Evil, *Reward and Punishment*, are the only Motives to a rational Creature: these are the Spurs and the Reins, whereby all Mankind are set on work and guided."[49]

Locke's advance, in humanistic terms, is in expanding the range of goods and evils that can be used as sources of motivation. The rewards and punishments "whereby we should keep Children in order," Locke writes, are primarily "esteem and disgrace." These can act as "powerful incentives" to the mind, once it is brought to contemplate them and can act as "the true Principle, which will constantly work, and incline them to the right."[50] The child's "love of credit" and "apprehension of shame and disgrace" is passed on to the adult as a concern for maintaining a good reputation.

A sound regard for reputation among one's gentlemen peers, once implanted, is a most effective guide to conduct throughout one's life. Reputation, Locke writes, is *not* "the true Principle and Measure of Virtue."[51] The latter comes only from God and is apprehended by natural reason. Reputation is, rather, a psychic reward external to the true principle and provides motives to adhere to it. A psychic reward is required to make virtues such as honesty and justice practical, given the omnipresence of narrowly self-regarding motives for action. Thus, although reputation is not the measure of virtue, it is, in the real world of people with competing private ends to pursue, people whose natural reason easily becomes clouded, "that which comes nearest to it."[52] It makes of virtue a non-self-abnegatory practice requiring neither saints nor heroes to act in light of it.

One puzzle in relating Locke's writings on education to his more philosophical works is the virtual invisibility of God in the former. Reading Locke's thoughts on education, one is led to wonder, for example, why atheists cannot be tolerated in a political community if they are correctly habituated to good moral and civic practices. To be sure, there is reference in *Some Thoughts Concerning Education,* to specifically religious education, but it is neither central to the work structurally or substantively. Locke recommends that children read a sanitized history of the Bible or carefully chosen selections from it. He further suggests, in advice as applicable to adults as to children, that constant acts of devotion are more suitable to religious education than are "curious Enquiries into [God's] inscrutable Essence and Being."[53]

The injunction against atheists is perfectly understandable on one level. They lack the fear of divine punishment and hence have no disincentive to satisfy immediate earthly desires even when doing so conflicts with moral duties. Moreover, they lack the fundamental understanding of themselves as products of God's workmanship and hence the obligations such as not to harm others and to respect property that are grounded in this understanding. Yet Locke's remarks on discounting the future and his discussion of the customary wellsprings of belief set strict limits on the extent to which such religious understandings provide guides for action even for professed believers. He expresses a most thoroughgoing sense of these limits in the *Essay*, in which he argues that the "law of fashion" plays a more central role as a basis for conduct than even the law of God.

> He who imagines commendation and disgrace not to be strong motives to men to accommodate themselves to the opinions and rules of those with whom they converse, seem little skilled in the nature of history of mankind: the greatest part whereof we shall find to govern themselves chiefly, if not solely, by this *law of fashion*; and so they do that which keeps them in reputation with their company, little regard the laws of God or the magistrate. The penalties that attend the breach of God's laws some, nay perhaps most men, seldom seriously reflect on: and amongst those that do, many, while they break the law, entertain thoughts of future reconciliation, and making their peace for such breaches. And as for the punishments of the commonwealth, they frequently flatter themselves with the hopes of their impunity. But no man escapes punishment of their censure and dislike, who offends against the fashion and opinion of the company he keeps, he recommends himself to.[54]

One illegitimate solution to this puzzle is to suggest that Locke's discussion of natural law duties are no more than rhetorical devices deployed to protect himself from prosecution or to offer "opiates" to the masses.[55] There is no reason to use Locke's rather unphilosophical educational writings as a code to interpret everything else he wrote and one would be hard-pressed to find advice even in them that is contrary to religious belief.

The mature Locke does tend to focus attention on what he called the "original and nature" of ideas rather than on establishing their ultimate truth.[56] Locke was quite aware of the consequences of this turn in his thought, as expressed in a letter to Tyrrell regarding a discussion of the grounds of ethics Locke had promised but failed to include in the *Essay*. Locke writes that he should not be criticized for failing to provide something that formed no part of his intention (although this is a somewhat disingenuous claim). The purpose of the *Essay* is not moral demonstration of natural law, for "some men's supposition of such a law, whether true or false" is, in fact, quite sufficient to show the "original and nature" of moral ideas. In other words, he sees it as less important to demonstrate moral truths than to show how they come to hold the practical force in human affairs that we know them to possess. This was very much the way in which Scottish Enlightenment figures from Hutcheson through Hume would pose the central concerns of moral philosophy. For Locke, this focus does not show a rejection of natural law but merely a shift in emphasis and Locke's reasonable belief that the agenda of the *Essay* was ambitious enough even excluding Tyrrell's requests.

Locke holds closely to his intentions in describing the origins and nature of moral beliefs and moral conduct as well. In so doing, he offers not a demonstration of ethics but a phenomenological description of moral practice and an explanation of how morality comes to have the weight it does in everyday life. In following this strategy and in grounding his ethics in a hedonistic psychology and theory of motivation, Locke is less at odds with the later, more thoroughly secular, Scottish thinkers considered in the next chapter than may be supposed. To be sure, Locke would have been uncomfortable positing a separate moral sense, as did Hutcheson, or with the radically skeptical turn in Scottish thought found in the works of Hume. Yet, there is an affinity in the "historical, plain method" of moral inquiry employed by Locke and these thinkers.[57]

The conception of virtue offered by Locke is far different from classical visions of virtue.[58] The civic virtues function less as an expression of a well-rounded character in the Aristotelian manner than as restraints on what Hume would later call "primary," or selfish dispositions. Locke treats exercise of virtue, public or private, largely in instrumental terms. It is valued for the good it produces, whether political stability or affable social relationships, not for the well-being it brings to its practitioner. Indeed, the essential motivating factor, the desire to be esteemed by others, points away from arguments, central in ancient thought, that focus on the benefits to the self of having a virtuous character. Locke is not concerned with showing that only the virtuous life is truly happy (absent fears of eternal punishment) or debating whether the virtues are one or many as Plato, or Aristotle, or Aquinas had before him.[59]

That Locke's understanding of civic virtue rejects these central pillars of classical thought should not surprise us. It is not the role of a liberal state as he understands it to enable citizens to realize their *telos*. Nor is it the role of the state to define this *telos* in terms of an authoritative conception of the good life. Locke rejects these functions but continues to recognize the need for citizens to be disposed to perform the public duties required to sustain a just state. Given these constraints, Locke offers a psychology of citizenship and conception of public virtue that is suitable for liberal regimes. The subsequent development of this psychology in Scottish thought is the concern of chapter 4.

4

The Psychology of Citizenship:
The Scottish Connection

Antiquity always begets the opinion of right; and whatever disadvantageous
sentiments we may entertain of mankind, they are always found to be
prodigal both of blood and treasure in the maintenance of public justice.
DAVID HUME, "Of the First Principles of Government"

Perhaps no phrase of David Hume's better displays his remarkable capacity to
mix wit with a dose of cynicism to yield a rather profound insight.[1] However
much we may think ill of our fellows we at least have to credit them with a
prodigal willingness to spill each other's blood (for, of course, a good cause).
Contained in this gibe is the observation that stable government rests on its
ability to engage both the interests and the affections of its subjects. How it
comes about that government does this is Hume's question. How it can be made
to come about, given strict limits on appeals to antiquity, is a question addressed
by the authors of *The Federalist* and their Anti-Federalist rivals.

The originality of the Americans' reflection on this subject derived largely
from the fact that, unlike Hume, so new a nation had no "antiquity" to which
to appeal. Also unlike Hume, the constitutional founders had to address the
pressing issue of whether, or how, loyalties to one sovereign could be passed
to another. This problem was compounded by the fact that the original
sovereigns—the states—had a stronger claim to whatever psychological bounty antiquity could provide than did the new national government. If the Anti-
Federalists were generally creative in dealing with the issue of civic
allegiance, it should be no surprise that, given this additional strain, the
Federalists were more creative still.

However much the constitutional founders fashioned their own answers to
this perpetual political concern, they drew upon their political heritage and contemporary European political thought to do so. Particularly apposite were the
ideas of David Hume and other major figures of the Scottish Enlightenment who
grappled with problems in moral and political philosophy, including Francis
Hutcheson, Adam Smith, and Thomas Reid. Hume was particularly useful to
Madison and Hamilton in that he provided the best available discussion of civic

motivations from a secular perspective. Hume, Smith, and Hutcheson offer understandings of how allegiance and even virtue emerge without active inculcation by a political regime. Constitutional debates over capacity of the proposed government to foster the allegiance of its citizens were much less ideological and much more empirical than is commonly supposed. The Federalists drew quite freely on Humean notions of the bases of political allegiance and the psychological theories which undergird them. And, while doubts about authorship make the tracing of direct lines of influence to the Anti-Federalists impossible, the cast of their arguments shares the empirical and psychological tone associated with Scottish thought on the subject. The Anti-Federalist writings examined in this book also display some instructive parallels with Hutcheson's ideas on the importance of benevolence as a political bond.

Scottish Enlightenment thought on civic virtue and allegiance is intrinsically interesting and merits our attention on its own terms and in terms of its place in the development of liberal understandings of citizenship. Moreover, using it as a key to unlock American political ideas cannot succeed without first asking whether these ideas make sense to any rational audience, including the constitutional founders and ourselves. However, treating the American case involves three further dimensions. The first is the more purely historical. Were the works of the Scottish thinkers in question available and read in late eighteenth century America? The second, is whether there are compelling reasons to believe that Scottish thought *influenced* Madison, Hamilton, and other readers as witnessed in arguments the latter make on allegiance and civic virtue. Finally, even if there is such evidence, what value is there in returning to Scottish thought rather than exploring early American civic concerns solely on their own terms?

I want to suggest that a recourse to the Scottish Enlightenment illuminates the manners in which Americans thought about the relation between the citizen and the state, a direct item of contention between Federalists and Anti-Federalists in the constitutional ratification debates. Scottish thought was less important when it came to stating and defending political first principles. The language in which basic institutions and fundamental rights were justified was strongly Lockean in character for both Federalists and Anti-Federalists, though Hume and Smith, in particular, can fairly be described as liberal in their basic political orientation.

The empirical and psychological character of Scottish Enlightenment consideration of the issue of civic virtue (and other issues) mirrors the Federalist and Anti-Federalist approaches, which, as against most republican revisionist views, did not implicate fundamental ideological commitments to any great degree. Their differences were more about means than about ends. Two key issues were called into question. First, could an extended republic provide the protections of natural and civil rights which is the raison d'être of the liberal state? Second, and related, could an extended republic gain the support of it citizens without the benefit of the personal ties and affections that can bind representatives to the people in small republics with small electoral districts?

An answer to the latter question depends on certain fundamental presumptions about the ties that bind citizens to the state, which in turn rest on a deeper theory of motivation for action per se. Hamilton and Madison adopt an especially Humean stance in arguing that a sound administration over time will gain the allegiance of citizens and in pointing to the limitations of the ties of benevolence the Anti-Federalists see as crucial to political as well as familial loyalties. The Anti-Federalists, in their reliance on this natural sentiment, present a theory closer in structure to that of Hutcheson. In turn, some of the criticisms of Hutcheson's moral psychology carry weight here as well. A recourse to the Scots thus helps us not only to clarify but also to criticize a political psychology that is largely implicit in the writings of the constitutional founders.

Though I am careful to differentiate the relevant Scottish thinkers—Francis Hutcheson, David Hume, Adam Smith, and Thomas Reid—a general word on the Scottish style of political and moral thought is in order. David Hume's promise at the beginning of his *Treatise of Human Nature* to apply the "experimental method" of Francis Bacon to morals is indicative of this style and was seconded by such diverse figures as Adam Ferguson in social history and Adam Smith in political economy. In the field of morals, this scientific, empirical turn took the form in Hutcheson, Hume, and Smith of virtually converting moral discussion into a branch of psychology. In their writings there is an affinity to Locke's later views of his own goals in pursuing moral philosophy. The task is not to demonstrate moral truths but to show how they come to acquire their undeniable practical force.

In politics and economics, there was a stress on what one historian has described as the emergence of "spontaneous order."[2] Such writers as Adam Smith, Adam Ferguson, and Hume stress the extent to which social and political institutions evolve out of an array of forces over which individuals have little control rather than out of conscious design. Smith's analysis of the market is the classic example of a system that is seen to advance public good though no one participates in the system with public good as the intended result. In the political sphere such reasoning could easily result in a sort of conservatism in the quite literal sense of the term. In Hume's work especially, precedent and custom place a heavy weight on the scales of political change, tipping them against reforms that may eke out more social utility or a more rational design of government.[3] This too is a trait the authors of *The Federalist* share, despite the enormous political and cultural differences between Great Britain and the United States. Of the Scots one might examine, the four mentioned are especially noteworthy both because they offer the best reflection on the subject at hand and hence help most in clarifying the founders' views and because trails of influence can and have been traced for each. Before taking up Scottish thought in further detail, let us turn briefly to the questions of availability and influence.

The Scottish Connection: What Did the Americans Know and When Did They Know It?

There can be little question that major works of the Scottish Enlightenment were widely available in America by the constitutional period.[4] This was not so evident even twenty years ago despite the pioneering work of Douglass Adair in pointing out the parallels to the point of paraphrase in Madison's borrowing from David Hume. Adair's work was a beacon guiding others such as Garry Wills, in popularizing the notion of a Scottish influence particularly on Jefferson (for example, Hutcheson) and the authors of *The Federalist*.

The writings of Francis Hutcheson had wide cachet in colonial America, as they had in eighteenth century Europe. His influence in Great Britain was so pronounced that Jeremy Bentham could complain near the end of the eighteenth century, some seventy-five years after Hutcheson's first published work, that his "moral sense" theory, a theory that posited the existence of a separate sense to perceive moral duties and innate desires to act on them grounded in benevolence, reigned throughout Europe.[5] In America, moral sense theory influenced a diverse range of thinkers from Jonathan Edwards to Charles Chauncy. Hutcheson is cited by an equally varied group of writers of the revolutionary period and beyond including Jefferson, Madison, Franklin, James Wilson, and Benjamin Rush.[6]

The response to moral sense thought was not, however, altogether favorable, especially among American divines of the colonial period. This is seen in a most relevant way for our purposes in the response of John Witherspoon (1723–1794), the Princeton teacher who taught political and social philosophy to James Madison. Witherspoon was a Scottish Presbyterian minister of deep Calvinist piety. He came from Scotland to teach at the fledgling College of New Jersey at Princeton in 1768. James Madison was his most famous pupil but no fewer than nine members of the Constitutional Convention of 1787, nine governors, and ten senators in the early republic passed through his program.[7] Witherspoon's philosophical training took place at the University of Edinburgh, where Thomas Reid's "common sense" response, which relied on "self-evident moral truths" as a bastion both against Hutcheson's moral sense thinking and the radical skepticism of Hume, were being formed.[8]

Hume was more to be feared than Hutcheson because of his apparent atheism and a skeptical philosophy that was seen by many to undermine widely accepted notions of moral responsibility along with religious faith. But the Calvinist Witherspoon would not abide Hutcheson's moral-sense thinking, largely for what he saw as its facile harmonization of morality with instinct, as indicated in this satirical observation: "It illustrates the truth of Mr. Hutcheson's doctrine: that virtue is founded upon instinct and affection, and not upon reason; that benevolence is its source, support, and perfection; and that all the particular rules of conduct are to be suspended when they seem to interfere with the general good."[9] However much "virtue and happiness are connected by the divine law and in the event of things, we are made so as to feel towards them as distinct."[10] Virtue, and attendant notions of duty, do not derive their moral value from advancing human happiness but are independently recommended to our minds. Witherspoon contends that humans are equipped with the capacity to form a clear and distinct conception of virtue that does not rest in its genesis or meaning on prior emotions however benevolent or altruistic they may be. To claim any less is to reduce divine law to a species of human desire.

Witherspoon was an orthodox Presbyterian and part of the attraction in appointing him as president of the College of New Jersey was that, unlike clergymen native to or with a longer tenure in the colonies, he had not been involved in the divisive battles between Old Light and New Light Presbyterians that emerged out of the Great Awakening. He was, moreover, unusually eclectic for a clergyman of his time in the range of readings he would recommend to his students. This was in part because he was as confident in the truths of common sense philosophy as he was in his Calvinist faith, so that he was not threatened by the dispersion of false doctrines. He was, in fact, a forceful advocate of religious tolerance and urged in the course of his lectures on moral philosophy that "we ought to guard against persecution on religious account . . . because such as hold absurd tenets are seldom dangerous. Perhaps they are never so dangerous, but when they are oppressed."[11] It is probably more than coincidence that Madison was later to express an equally strong endorsement of religious tolerance, given what is known of their close relationship and mutual admiration.[12]

Witherspoon's tolerance extended so far as to include in his curricula works of David Hume, works far more destructive in his view than any by Hutcheson. Despite his noxious doctrines, Hume was nonetheless ranked by Witherspoon among "the most laudable Authors (mostly British)" to have emerged since the Protestant Reformation.[13] Although he included Hume's *Essay Concerning Human Understanding* on a short list of major philosophical works, he also warned that Hume "seems to have industriously endeavored to shake the certainty of our belief upon cause and effect, upon personal identity and the idea of power [meant here in the philosophical sense of the time as a capacity for agency]; it is easy to raise metaphysical subtleties and confound the understanding on such subjects."[14]

Witherspoon was far from being the only divine in America to be troubled by Hume's metaphysics, which could indeed be deeply corrosive of religious faith and moral agency. This less than enthusiastic reception of Hume's metaphysics is captured in the satiric verse written by a young Yale student in 1773.

> Then least religion he should need,
> Of pious *Hume* he'll learn his creed
> By strongest demonstration shown,
> Evince that nothing can be known . . .
>
> Alike his [Voltaire's] poignant wit displays
> The darkness of the former days,
> When men the paths of duty sought,
> And own'd what revelation taught;
> E'er human reason grew so bright,
> Men could see all things by its light,
> And summon'd Scripture to appear,
> And stand before its bar severe,

> To clear its page from charge of fiction,
> And answer pleas of contradiction;
> E'er myst'ries first were held in scorn,
> Or *Bolingbroke*, or *Hume* were born.[15]

By and large, America's practicing politicians of the founding period, unlike its divines and philosophers, tended to focus on Hume's political insights and be less concerned with the more abstract problems raised by his epistemology. This ordering reflects in large measure the works of Hume that were available to Americans in this period. His *History of England* and political essays were far more widely available than his *Enquiries*, which were in turn more accessible than the *Treatise*.[16] It also reflects the philosophical and religious temperament of the new nation. Americans were not by and large predisposed to follow Hume down the skeptic's trail he had blazed even as their best and brightest drew on the deep reserves of Hume's political wisdom. In fact, the decidedly unskeptical "common sense" philosophy of Thomas Reid was to become a dominant strain in American intellectual life from the 1790s through the middle of the nineteenth century.

It would be unfair to say that educated Americans of the constitutional era exhibited the kind of scorn for philosophy *tout court* that Tocqueville was to describe some fifty years later, or Allan Bloom bemoan one hundred and fifty years after that. The most cursory readings of the founding debates shows that ideas mattered to the founders, though not necessarily ideas about metaphysics or epistemology.[17] Yet there is little indication that political leaders of the constitutional period worried themselves about the deeply unsettling implications of Hume's skepticism.[18] Even Jefferson's criticisms of Hume, among the sharpest found in America, critiqued most strongly his Tory leanings as displayed in the *History* rather than his philosophical hubris. Americans active in politics could, in short, accept much of Hume's political wisdom without following his pyrrhic path toward skepticism and agnosticism.[19]

There were, of course, those like Madison who were conversant with the full range of philosophical discourse of the period and could discourse learnedly on such topics as the relation of "liberty and necessity" and personal identity. Madison engaged in private correspondence with former college classmate and future Princeton president, Dr. Samuel Stanhope Smith, among others, on such purely metaphysical themes and apparently displayed a wide range of knowledge of the works of Locke, Hume, Henry Home (Lord Kames), and other major sources.[20] James Wilson too must count among the more philosophical framers. He was to become an avowed advocate of common sense philosophy and to draw heavily on the works of Reid in his law lectures, and seemed to be more troubled by Hume's "abstract philosophy . . . commonly called metaphysics" than with his political sympathies.[21]

Political reactions to Hume varied from Jefferson's revulsion at Hume's alleged "Toryism" to the unmitigated admiration found in Hamilton's writings. It is nonetheless instructive that as diverse political figures as Jefferson, Hamilton, and Benjamin Franklin expressed admiration for Hume's political insight.[22] This is most surprising perhaps in Jefferson's case, since he is among the most vehement of Hume's American critics on political grounds. Hume's *History of England* was to Jefferson a "book which has undermined the free principles of the English government . . . and has spread universal toryism over the land."[23] Yet Jefferson is disappointed as only a one-time admirer can be. He had read Hume's *History* as a young man and had copied out sections of it in his commonplace book. In a letter written in 1810, Jefferson recounts, "the enthusiasm with which I devoured it when young, and the length of time . . . which were necessary to eradicate the poison it had instilled in my mind."[24] It should be added that Hume, for his part, was by no means "Tory" by the American definition. In 1775 he described himself as "an American in my principles" and had written as early as 1771—four years before Burke's more famous remonstrance to the same effect—that "our Union with the America . . . in the Nature of things cannot long subsist."[25]

Despite this, Jefferson was to recommend reading Hume to several young men seeking his advice on political education. He advises Peter Carr to read Hume's *History* and he recommends "several of Hume's political essays" to Thomas Mann Randolph, Jr., as also being worthwhile.[26] Randolph was to inform Jefferson on the progress of his studies and did so in a letter dated April 14, 1787: "Being certain that Politics was a science which would lead to the highest honours in a free state, and the study of which by many members would be of the greatest utility to the community in an infant one, I resolved to apply chiefly to it. From this time Montesquieu and Hume have been my principal study."[27] Jefferson, one suspects, greeted this news with the ambivalence brought out by the combination of admiration and contempt which characterized his attitude toward Hume.

Alexander Hamilton, not surprisingly, was decidedly unambivalent in his admiration of Hume. Hamilton offers the only direct quotation of that "equally solid and ingenious writer" in *The Federalist*. Appropriately, Hume is cited in the context of arguing against those who would delay ratification of the Constitution until amendments were made to better secure rights. Hamilton asks its readers to be cognizant of the limitations of reason in designing institutions and to allow time for working out the Constitution's defects. As Hume observes,

> To balance a large state or society . . . , whether monarchical or republican, on general laws, is a work of so great difficulty that no human genius, however comprehensive, is able, by the mere dint of reason and reflection, to effect it. The judgments of many must unite in the work; experience must guide their labor; TIME must bring it to perfection, and the feeling of inconveniences must correct the mistakes which they *inevitably* fall into in their first trials and experiments."[28]

The political thought of Hamilton and Hume are perhaps no more consonant than in this belief that the best should not become the enemy of the good and that political institutions are perfected with experience rather than by conscious design ex nihilo.

Hamilton learned from Hume about designing political institutions as well as on the perils of maintaining them. Indeed, his tutor at King's College was a graduate of Glasgow University, the university of Hutcheson, Smith, and Reid, and there is clear evidence that Hamilton was not only aware of but favorably cited Hume and Smith well before the constitutional period.[29] Writing in 1775, he quotes that "celebrated author [Hume]," extensively on the subject of checks on political authority. Hume's essay "Of the Independence of Parliament" was particularly useful to Hamilton. Hamilton shared Hume's assumption that all men must be assumed to be knaves in designing institutions even if they are not all knaves in fact. Hume had added "every court or senate is determined by the greater number of voices, so that, if self-interest influences only the majority (as it will always do), the whole senate follows the allurements of this separate interest and acts as if it contained not one member who had any regard to public interest or liberty."[30] Hamilton responds by applying Hume's observation to the American problem of justifying a revolution: "What additional force do these observations acquire when applied to the dominion of one community over another!" He concludes: "From what has been said, it is plain that we are without those checks upon the representatives of Great Britain which alone can make them answer the end of their appointment with respect to us—which is the preservation of the rights of the governed. The direct and inevitable consequence is, *they have no right to govern us.*"[31]

This is, to be sure, a rather strained reading of Hume's essay and not altogether logical in its own right. The need for independence only follows from the lack of sufficient checks on Parliament if it is impossible to improve upon those checks within the context of a dependent relationship, and Hamilton does not make this claim. The passage is more interesting to us in prefiguring the design of government developed in *The Federalist* in its fear of majoritarianism and the stress placed on checks and balances.

This brief survey can do no more than suggest that works of the Scottish Enlightenment were available and read by leading figures in late-eighteenth-century America. Scottish thought was no monolith, however, and early Americans picked and chose among its principles in a manner that largely reflected ideological and religious prejudices. Though it is difficult to generalize, Americans were more at home with the intuitionism of "common sense" thought on the philosophical level than with Hume's radical skepticism. Hume was nonetheless a source of political insight—and controversy. The constitutional founders' conceptions of citizenship—and the relevance of Scottish political and moral thought to them—is our next topic.

Can Virtue Be Reduced to a Feeling and Morality to a Science? The Hutchesonian Origins

If John Locke stumbled into a psychologization of virtue to fill the space between natural law and selfish men, Francis Hutcheson (1694–1746) leapt into the breach feet first. He did not quarrel with the notion of man as God's

workmanship but neither did he try to ground moral obligations in our crea-
turely status. It is perhaps a cause for surprise, moreover, that Hutcheson, who
offered the first pure statement of the utilitarian principle, relied on a considerably more complex theory of motivation than Locke (or later, Bentham).
Like Locke and like his Scottish successors, however, Hutcheson was especially concerned with locating "exciting causes" of action.

Hutcheson preceded Hume in the claim that reason could not be such a
cause. He claims, in a manner Locke or any of his predecessors in the natural
law tradition would reject, that ultimate ends are not discovered by reason
and, as importantly, not in need of rational defense. Thus, Hutcheson argues
that to ask for a justification for love of country or love of mankind and for
actions taken in the name of either displays a profound misunderstanding of
what morality is all about.

> What reason can a benevolent being give as exciting him to hazard his life in
> a just war? This perhaps, "such conduct tends to the happiness of his country."
> Ask him, why he serves his country? he will say "his country is a very valuable
> part of mankind." If his affections be really *disinterested*, he can give no *ex-
> citing* reason for it: The happiness of mankind in general, or any valuable part
> of it, is an *ultimate end* to the series of desires.[32]

Presumably, once we reach the end of the series of desires we have discovered
the ultimate grounds of morality and our motive for action. This is a curious
if comfortable view of morality in its facile harmonization of morality and
desire—too comfortable for such critics as Thomas Reid and James Madison's
teacher at Princeton, John Witherspoon.

This harmonization is witnessed in Hutcheson's definition of reasonable
action. "He acts *reasonably*," Hutcheson wrote, "who considers the various
actions in his power, and forms *true opinions* of their *tendencies*; and then
chuses to do that which obtain to the highest degree *that*, to which the *instincts*
of his nature incline him, with the smallest degree of those things from which
the *affections*, in his nature make him averse."[33] It is fortunate, given this
maximizing notion of rational action, that a dominant instinct is one for public
good. Moreover, it is for the most broadly conceived public good, the happiness of mankind in general.

Hutcheson is not always careful in his language and the choice of the word
instinct for the inclination he describes here is not altogether felicitous.[34] He
uses it to refer to the humans capacity for feeling a particular sort of pleasure,
the receptor of which is our moral sense. Hutcheson does not ordinarily reduce
this moral sensitivity to an instinct, although it is an innate aspect of human
nature. It is more akin to our capacity to experience aesthetic pleasure, although we may not be schooled in art history or art appreciation.

The notion of a distinct moral sense is wrought with confusions. It is not
clear, for example, whether Hutcheson held that moral approval is simply the
fact of having appropriate kinds of feelings or whether those feelings are occasioned by the presence of a moral goodness that exists independently and
is apprehended intuitively.[35] This confusion is exemplified in Hutcheson's

claim that "Moral Goodness . . . denotes our Idea of some Quality apprehended in Actions, which procures Approbation, and Love toward the Actor, from those who receive no Advantage by the Actions."[36] Is it the case, then, that the sense and expression of approbation is what makes the action morally good or that the apprehension of moral goodness gives rise to this sense and its expression? Put another way, does the goodness of the action depend upon that feeling's being present?

Hutcheson is, at best, confusing on this score largely because his notion of what a moral justification entails is rather poor. Moral approval, in contrast to other sorts of approval (for example, that for being nattily dressed), only makes sense in reference to moral principles. The principles must be logically prior in just the same way as one must have a conception of what it is to be well dressed before approving of a particular fashion statement. It is hard to see, therefore, how the pleasurable excitation of the moral sense is the ultimate (and ultimately groundless in any other than an empirical psychological sense) source of all justifications in morals.

As there is no moral sense organ comparable to other sense organs, a good bit of thinking must be done before we can even identify our feeling as a moral one. While no one in her right mind can confuse, for example, the sensation of taste with that of sight (though as any good chef knows, food that looks good is more satisfying to the eater), it will not be at all clear in many actions whether our approval springs from universal or more particularized forms of love, including self-love. Deciding which it is requires an act of judgment in which we ask whether our feelings are appropriate to the situation. More precisely, we must ask whether the conduct in question was guided by the moral principles that should apply given the circumstances.[37]

The plausibility of Hutcheson's notion of morality rests on his altruistic psychology and its generous if not exalted notion of human instinct. To be sure, Hutcheson does not see saintliness as a moral requirement. That is to say, he does not contend that the individual is obligated to "sacrific[e] all positive interests and bear . . . all private evils for the public good."[38] He thus distinguishes "innocence" (what we might call the natural obligation of minimal altruism) from heroic or saintly virtue. He does not offer a precise point at which obligatory actions turn into supererogatory ones but suggests that the key to locating this point is what was to become the utilitarian standard—that each count for one and none for more than one. In Hutcheson's words, "every man may look upon himself as part of the system, and consequently not sacrifice an important private interest to a *less* important interest of others."[39]

Nonetheless, it is apparently natural according to Hutcheson that persons view their actions from this disinterested perspective, giving no more weight to their preferences and desires, or to those of their loved ones, than they do to those of strangers. They are motivated to do so by a sentiment of universal benevolence. Such a view enabled him to avoid the complexities found in Hume's and Smith's accounts of the relation between the "artificial" virtue of justice and the "natural" one of benevolence and the conflicting demands these virtues could make on our actions.

I will later suggest that in the American context the Anti-Federalists come close to paralleling what we might call the "naive Hutchesonian" view of moral sense thinking at least in relation to the ties that bind the polity together. These ties, in this view, are formed by unmediated feelings of benevolence. The political consequence of this view is to contend that the size of the polity should not extend beyond the range of benevolent sentiments people can feel. The Federalists' treatment, I will suggest, corresponds *and* draws directly upon the Humean innovations in moral sense theory as well as on his application of it to political matters. The innovations of Hume and, to a lesser degree, of Smith concern us next.

Hume and Smith: Custom, Imagination, and the Philosophy of Virtue

When Adam Smith published his classic work in moral philosophy, *The Theory of Moral Sentiments*, he soon received a letter of praise from David Hume. Hume relayed from London that "the public seem disposed to applaud it extremely" and that the "mob of literati are beginning to be very loud in its praise."[40] Hume fully shared in these public judgments of Smith's work, and, in fact, joined in the praise of Smith once again in the last year of his life when he read *The Wealth of Nations*.[41]

The respect Smith and Hume had for each other was based on warm personal ties and a remarkable similarity—though not identity—in their philosophical projects. Both sought to provide a scientific understanding of morality by grounding it in psychology and prevailing material and political conditions. Both explored and sought to reconcile the competing psychic and moral demands imposed by self-love and the natural virtue of benevolence on the one hand and the artificial virtues needed to preserve a polity—justice and allegiance—on the other. Each can be described fairly as a liberal in political outlook although neither was politically doctrinaire.[42] Both noted the centrality of custom and habit in preserving norms of conduct—personal and political—which would not fare so well if subject to frequent rational scrutiny.[43] Finally, both were what we might call secular conservatives reluctant to upset the customs that legitimated political power. Yet, unlike nineteenth century conservatives such as Joseph de Maistre and Louis de Bonald (and even unlike Edmund Burke, with whom they shared so much), they feared as much the irrationalism that could be introduced into the polity by religious enthusiasms and, by implication, other forms of superstition and zeal.[44]

In *The Theory of Moral Sentiments* Smith differentiates the empirical approach to morals common to Hume and himself from the rationalist approach that was prominent in Great Britain in the early years of the eighteenth century. Samuel Clarke and William Wollaston were especially prominent philosophers who sought to locate morality in the "fitness of things," which was to be discovered by reason. They sought an objective grounding for morality that could not be reduced to psychological states or even to intersubjective conventions. Smith objects to such an approach on analytical and empirical grounds. It is, he argues, "altogether absurd and unintelligible to suppose that the first perceptions of right and wrong can be derived from reason .... It is by finding, in a vast variety of instances, that one tenor of conduct constantly pleases in a certain manner, and that another constantly displeases the mind, that we form the general rules of morality."[45] Moral maxims, Smith argues, are not different from maxims of other sorts in being arrived at through "experience and induction."[46]

Hume too praises the application of a modern experimental approach to morals in the introduction to his philosophical masterpiece, *A Treatise on Human Nature*. This early work was sadly neglected in Hume's day, a fate Hume largely attributed to what he saw as its ponderous style.[47] In any case, he observes that the "science of man is the only solid foundation for the other sciences, so the only solid foundation we can give to this science itself must be laid on experience and observation."[48] He points to the works of Locke, Hutcheson, and Mandeville, among others, as beginning to apply Lord Bacon's experimental method to morals with great effect.[49]

This empirical strain leads Smith and Hume to apply Locke's "historical, plain method" to moral and political enquiry. Each was less concerned with arriving at true principles of justice, for example, than with exploring the interests of men that induced them initially to adopt such rules and later to abide by them. It is nonetheless worthwhile to tease out from their writings the political principles to which they might subscribe, although any attempt to box these thinkers into categories of moral and political philosophy in common usage today (are they utilitarians or contractarian liberals?) will be frustrated.[50]

Hume's frequent appeals to the "public good" in defending property arrangements and political institutions have led many critics to read him as a proto-utilitarian. Yet the term *public good* is used in too loose and general a sense to push this too far. Hume nowhere states that the last iota of utility should be eked out of the social or political system, as Bentham might later maintain. In fact, there is no moral imperative in his work, as there is for Hutcheson, to promote the greatest good of the greatest number.[51]

Indeed, a better case can be made for ascribing an implicit liberal contractarian political philosophy to Hume. And, while we are more interested in his notion of the ties that bind citizens to their polity by fostering a sense of allegiance, it is worth noting that Hume is not so far from the generally liberal contractarian principles of the American founders even in terms of political principles. David Gauthier has made this case, suggesting that Hume accepts a species of "hypothetical contractarianism" in that he legitimates "systems of property and government ... in terms of the consent they would receive from *rational* persons in a suitably characterized position of free choice."[52] The original-choice situation Hume describes in his essay "Of the Original Contract" exemplifies Gauthier's point:

> The people, if we trace government to its first origin ..., are the sources of
> all power and jurisdiction, and voluntarily, for the sake of peace and order,

abandoned their native liberty, and received laws from their equal and com-
panion . . . . If this, then, be meant by the *original contract*, it cannot be
denied, that all government is, at first, founded on a contract. . . .[53]

This is, formally at least, a reasonably clear enunciation of a social-contract
theory. The people come to a mutually beneficial agreement in the form of a
contract as they are by nature equals and are capable of impeding each others'
pursuit of the good.

Whether Hume is a contractarian in spirit could more reasonably be
debated. He offers no moral justification for the original contract of the sort
we find in overt exponents of social contract theory from Locke through Kant
and on to Rawls or Nozick. Hume does not, in other words, suggest that this
initial agreement is anything more than a modus vivendi among potentially
antagonistic individuals. There is no sense that it is morally required for
respecting the inviolability of persons.

Ironically, Smith may be more a contractarian liberal "in spirit," although
he nowhere follows Hume in defending a notion of an original contract. Smith
accepts, for analytical purposes at least, the notion of equal individuals who
possess, "antecedent to the institution of civil government," the rights of self-
defense and of punishing offenders.[54] Upon establishing government, "the
most sacred laws of justice . . . are the laws which guard the life and person
of our neighbour; the next are those which guard his property and possessions;
and last of all come those which guard what are called his personal rights, or
what is due to him from the promises of others [emphasis added]."[55]

Smith's adoption of nonutilitarian reasoning is witnessed in part in the
reluctance with which he concedes to the sovereign activities that not only
prevent harm to individuals, but promote the public good. The sovereign, he
suggests, has a duty to "promote prosperity" of the commonwealth by dis-
couraging vice and impropriety. This authorizes him to "command mutual
good offices to a certain degree." Yet, this is a power the sovereign must
exercise with the greatest reluctance. "To push it too far," Smith writes, "is
destructive of all liberty, security, and justice."[56]

That Smith describes the rules of justice as sacred rather than as merely
useful implies a respect for persons that requires that such rules cannot be
overridden lightly. His ordering of these rules so that rights of persons are
prior to those of property or contracts points in the same direction. His reluctance to condone the use of state power to promote the good when conflicts
with liberty, security and justice are at stake, and the low weight he assigns
to consequences in assessing moral value are clearly anathema to utilitarians.
Though we may wish that Smith was clearer in stating the conditions for overriding rights for the public good, his priorities are clearly liberal ones and
perhaps more in accord with contractarian formulations than those of Hume.

The difficulty in identifying a clear-cut underlying political philosophy in
even as self-conscious a pair of thinkers as Smith and Hume derives in part
from their pluralistic understanding of the sources of moral and political conduct, and, indeed, of the vagaries of human conduct in general. It is a

predominant theme in *The Theory of Moral Sentiments* in particular that judgments of moral approval or disapproval involve a wide range of faculties and
emotions. Thus, Smith offers a phenomenology of moral approval that serves
to refute attempts to reduce the sources of morality to interest, reason, utility,
and even to a separate and distinct "moral sense." Approval consists first in
the sympathy we feel with the motives of the moral agent. Second, we sym-
pathize with the gratitude felt by the recipient of the action. Third, we observe
that the conduct of each is "agreeable to the general rules by which those two
sympathies act." Finally, we consider such actions as part of a larger system
of actions that "tends to promote the happiness either of the individual or of
the society, [thus] they appear to derive a beauty from this utility. . . . "[57]

Smith's account of moral approval is admirably cognizant of the diversity
of moral ends and qualities of conduct we consider praiseworthy. Yet neither
Smith nor Hume fully escapes the flaws found in Hutcheson's account of
moral approval. There is a failure in each case to clarify the relationship between feeling and moral judgment. Hence it is hard to know whether qualities
are moral *because* they give rise to a sentiment of a certain type or whether
these sentiments arise only when we are confronted with moral goodness, that
is, because they are really estimable. As a consequence of this uncertainty,
the relation these authors seek to posit between the content of morality and
the motivation to act on it is also nebulous.

Both Smith and Hume recognize that the capacity of a given action to
produce pleasure is not a sufficient test of its morality. Rather, in Smith's
words, the action must please "in a certain manner." In almost identical language, Hume contends that "we do not infer a character to be virtuous, because
it pleases: But in feeling that it pleases after such a particular manner, we in
effect feel it is virtuous."[58] Hume's language is odd because he describes a
feeling about a feeling as what ultimately confers the appellation of virtue or
vice on an action. Hume's second-order feeling, by which we come to see an
action as virtuous, is better conceived of as a judgment, and as one made from
a disinterested position. As Hume puts it, "'Tis only when a character is considered in general, without reference to our own particular interest, that it
causes such a feeling or sentiment, as denominates it morally good or evil."[59]
Yet, here the motivational confusion is introduced. It is a sine qua non of
Hume's thought that actions are motivated by the passions since they are ex-
perienced by concrete individuals. What remains unclear in his theory is how
a judgment that an "impartial spectator" would come to about the worth of
an action moves *me* to that action.[60]

The best response Hume offers to this problem is a linguistic one. A disinterested viewpoint, he argues, is built into the language of morals itself. And
insofar as individuals use this language, and seek the concurrence of others
in their judgments, they cannot help making universal claims.

When a man denominates another as his *enemy*, his *rival*, his *antagonist*, his
adversary, he is understood to speak the language of self-love, and to express
sentiments, peculiar to himself and arising from his particular circumstances
and situation. But when he bestows on any man the epithets of *vicious* or

odious or *depraved*, he then speaks another language, and expresses sentiments, in which, he expects, all his audience are to concur with him. He must here, therefore, depart from his private and particular situation, and must chuse a point of view, common to him with others: He must move some universal principle of the human frame, and touch a string, to which all mankind have an accord and symphony.... And though this affection of humanity may not generally be esteemed so strong as vanity and ambition, yet, being common to all men, it can alone be the foundation of morals, or of any general system of praise or blame.[61]

Hume suggests that by entering this moral-language game we are implicitly recognizing its rules and those rules require the adoption of a moral point of view. The passion that determines that these rules *matter* to us is the universal (though universally undervalued) "affection for humanity."

According one critic virtue and vice are for Hume "publicly available aspects of man's world which serve as the occasion of specific feelings."[62] Thus, to describe an action as virtuous is not merely to say that it produces a pleasurable sensation in me but that it *should* produce such a sensation and generally does so. Moral language is therefore not simply a means of expressing emotions but a recognition of an *occasion* for the expression of a suitable moral sentiment. Further, there is no such thing as a private moral language, so that sentiments of approval or disapproval necessarily appeal to a universal standard.

Yet to say that describing an action as virtuous means that it should produce a feeling of a certain sort begs a question. If it *is* virtuous, the presence or absence of a feeling should count for very little in its appraisal. The center of moral debate then shifts to the *reasons* one might give for considering the action virtuous in the first place. At this point, feelings are simply doing too little work, certainly less than Hume's position can tolerate. As he would put it, morality ceases to be a "practical study, nor has any tendency to regulate our lives and actions."[63]

Further, we are left with the problem of motivation. As we have seen, Hume holds that moral approval or disapproval are the considered feelings of the moral evaluator once she abstracts herself from her selfish passions and preferences. Yet, the "feelings I do not have, but would have, if certain allowances were made for the fact that my actual feelings may be biased or rest on mistake, obviously cannot move me to action."[64]

Finally, Hume does not have much of a response to those who might refuse to play the moral language game (or play it only disingenuously) or to those who simply concede the "affection for humanity" a very low place on their list of goods. They can be judged wrong only from a point of view they refuse to accept and the only compelling reason for accepting this point of view is an affection they do not possess or possess to too limited a degree.

Thomas Reid: A Response to Humean Morals

It is reasonable to suppose—though we certainly have not proven—that no satisfactory account of the sources and principles of morals can be as empirical as Hutcheson, Smith and Hume sought. Nor can feeling play as central a role in deriving moral principles. Indeed, the criticisms we have developed of Hume and Smith, as well as of Hutcheson's moral sense theory are not wholly original ones. Many American colonists conversant with law and philosophy, including signers of the Declaration of Independence such as Witherspoon, Jefferson, James Wilson, and Benjamin Rush, were conversant with the debate between rationalists such as Samuel Clarke and Wollaston and moral-sense thinkers broadly defined from Hutcheson through Hume.[65] They were aware particularly of the common sense criticisms offered of moral sense school by their sharpest Scottish critic, Thomas Reid (1710–1796).

Reid himself had been influenced profoundly by Hume's *Treatise on Human Nature*. Indeed, responding to it, in particular seeking to refute Humean skepticism, formed the basis of his life's work. Ironically, Reid's work also served as a vehicle for transmitting Hume's philosophy to America. The distinguished American intellectual historian, Henry May, sums up Hume's influence on late eighteenth century American thought as follows. Hume was "popular as a historian, selectively admired as a political and social theorist, feared as a critic of religion, and known as a philosopher or psychologist mainly through those who answered him."[66] Reid figures prominently among the last group.

Reid replaced Adam Smith in the University of Glasgow chair in moral philosophy in 1763 and wrote several major and influential works while holding it. The one work written early enough to be familiar to Americans by 1787 was *An Inquiry into the Human Mind, on the Principles of Common Sense*, which was published in 1764. Reid's greatest works—*Essays on the Intellectual Powers of Man* and *Essays on the Active Powers of Man*—were written after his retirement from Glasgow University in 1780 and were first published in 1785 and 1788, respectively. Reid's commonsense philosophy, began to gain adherents during the Revolution, but gained wide popularity on booksellers' lists and in college curricula from the 1790s through the middle of the nineteenth century.[67]

The gist of Reid's attacks on Hume were metaphysical and, more important, moral. Reid attacks the "ideal system of understanding," whose origin is found in Descartes and Locke and culminates in the thought of George Berkeley and Hume. He attributes pernicious effects to idealism and attempts to replace it with a philosophy closer to the common sense of mankind. The idealist tradition Reid attacks was one that questioned so fundamental a fact as the existence of the external world. Descartes had placed doubt about the source of sense experience at the origins of his philosophy and Berkeley and Hume followed him in claiming that we do not experience external bodies directly but only, if at all, through sensations. Sensations of what are often described as secondary qualities of objects—heat, cold, color—cannot be held to establish the existence of that object. None of these thinkers doubted the existence of a world outside their minds, but all were concerned over the certainty of any claims we could make for its existence.

The moral implications of this epistemological skepticism were profound.

If we cannot know for certain that there exists an external world, how can we evaluate the consequences of our actions in it? And if we cannot do this, what is left of long-accepted notions of moral responsibility and personal accountability? These moral concerns were never far from Reid's mind in his attack on idealism, nor of those who accepted Reid's commonsense alternative in both Scotland and the United States.[68]

Reid's epistemological defense of "realism," that is, the belief in the existence of nonideal things, relies heavily on the notions, first, that there are innate ideas, and, second, that God is not a deceiver so that the data of our senses as processed through our perceptive faculties of sight, hearing, and so forth are trustworthy. His short answer to idealism is simply that humans are so constructed as to develop true beliefs about the existence of external objects. In his terminology, this is built into our nature as "percipient" and not merely sentient beings.[69] We can trust in these beliefs as our Creator does not intend our deception. This is a dogmatic resolution relying on two critical notions the post-Cartesian idealists had good reasons to reject. Nonetheless, it does enable Reid to set limits to the corrosive effects of Humean skepticism. There is at least considerably less to be skeptical about. And it is a validation of the commonsense beliefs of mankind, thereby narrowing the gap between philosophers and the common man's understanding of the bases of knowledge and belief.

Reid's application of commonsense philosophy to morals is, if anything, even more dogmatic. The intent behind it is to call into question what he calls the sentimentalist view of morality advocated in different forms by Hutcheson as well as Hume and Smith. Thus, Reid criticizes moral theories based on "sympathy" in a letter to Lord Kames. "I have always thought," Reid writes, "that Dr. [Adam] Smith's system of sympathy is wrong. It is indeed only a refinement of the selfish system; and I think your arguments against it are solid."[70] Reid contends, and not without merit, that moral evaluations do not reside solely in the feelings of the moral actor or the feelings of approval or disapproval they generate in the spectator. When we say that someone has a moral duty to undertake some action, we are saying that action *ought* to be undertaken whether or not that person has a desire to do so and whether or not that action will be favorably received. To hold that moral actions are defined by their capacity to produce good feelings or because they are useful is to lose a sense of the independent force of morality as it is understood in common language. "It is true that every virtue is both agreeable and useful in the highest degree; and that every quality that is agreeable and useful, has a merit upon that account. But *virtue has a merit peculiar to itself*, a merit which does not arise from its being useful or agreeable, but from its being virtue [emphasis added]."[71]

Reid's moral philosophy can best be described as a form of rational intuitionism. In the moral sphere, he challenges Hume's skepticism by simply asserting that people are given to make correct moral judgments intuitively, that is, through a clear insight into moral truth that relies neither on feeling nor subtle reasoning.

A clear and intuitive judgment, resulting from the constitution of human nature, is sufficient to overbalance a train of subtile reasoning on the other side.
Thus the testimony of our senses is sufficient to overbalance all the subtile
arguments brought against their testimony. And, if there be a like testimony
of conscience in favour of honesty, all the subtile reasoning of the knave
against it ought to be rejected without examination, as fallacious and sophis-
tical, because it concludes against a self-evident principle; just as we reject
the subtile reasoning of the metaphysician against the evidence of sense."[72]

Those thinkers who center their positions on moral sentiment cannot deny
this proposition without losing the reason-giving force even they want to claim
moral statements have.

Scottish Rationalism and Empiricism Among the Founders

The Scottish thinkers we have examined up to this point were engaged in a
rich philosophical discourse concerning the nature and origins of moral beliefs
and practice. We shall pursue shortly the course of discussion I take to be
most relevant to the constitutional debates: that on the sources and nature of
allegiance and civic virtue. I have preceded this discussion with a rather
detailed look at Scottish moral philosophy for two reasons. First, several
scholars who have done so much to document Scottish influence on the founding, especially Adair and Wills, have been less careful in their interpretation
or said little about Scottish thought.[73] I will argue below that Wills in fact is
quite wrong in his reading of Hume's account of the ties that bind a polity
together. Second, the writings of these philosophers on diverse subjects from
epistemology to politics form a single argument. This is certainly the case
with Hume and Smith. We shall see some clear parallels, for example, between
Hume's account of the belief in causality as the habitual association of events
and his account of why and how people come to accept political rulers and a
distribution of property as legitimate. There is a logic to his ideas that is
missed by interpreters who focus exclusively on his political writings. Indeed,
we cannot evaluate the influence of ideas or how they may have been (mis)un-
derstood if we do not first seek to understand them in their own terms.

There is one implication of this plan of study I wish to avoid, however.
While Hume and others clearly recognized the linkages among metaphysics,
epistemology, and political philosophy in their own work, I do not want to
suggest that intelligent readers, whether in the eighteenth century or in the
present, must accept Humean philosophy, for example, in toto. Indeed, I do
not think this was the case with Madison and Hamilton, who clearly admired
Hume's writings on politics though Madison was conversant with a broader
range of his thought. When it came to political "first principles," a great many
Americans, including the constitutional founders, relied on Lockean notions
of natural rights and Reidian notions of "self evident" truths. Thus, in
Federalist 31 Hamilton notes that in any disquisition "there are certain
primary truths, or first principles, upon which all subsequent reasonings must

depend." This is true in the "science of morals and politics," although the principles of these do not have the same certainty as those of mathematics.[74] For Hamilton, as for Hobbes and Locke, passion and self-interest obscure moral judgment more often than the difficulty of the subject.

Whether we look to Madison, who appeals to a "fundamental and undeniable truth" in his justly famous "Memorial and Remonstrance," or to Jefferson's self-evident truths in the Declaration of Independence, or to Thomas Paine, who appeals to the common sense of mankind in urging the American revolutionaries to defend their "natural rights," we see a similar epistemic presumption.[75] When it comes to first principles Americans, and certainly the constitutional founders, shared more with Locke and Reid than they did with Hume or Smith, who had little use for self-evident truths that exist independently of experience and convention. As Morton White so persuasively argues, the authors of *The Federalist* appeal both to "Lockean" reason and "Humean" experience.[76] Moreover, there is nothing illogical in this philosophical division of labor. The constitutional founders were, as we shall see, decidedly Lockean when they defined political first principles. Locke's rationalism was of less use, as Locke himself recognized, in explaining how people came to *act* in accordance with those principles. This is in large measure a matter of feeling, not just of reason. On this score, it should not surprise us that Scottish moral philosophy was of more use to the founders.

Hume and Smith: Justice, Allegiance, and the Philosophical Politics of Virtue

While the efforts of moral sense thinkers to ground morality in desire is not ultimately convincing, it *is* persuasive to argue that, given a range of morally acceptable *political* arrangements, the one that shows itself best able to elicit sentiments of support from potential members has at least a prima facie advantage over alternatives. It is so, moreover, whatever one thinks of the moral ontology undergirding this view. And this case must rest on some theory of the wellsprings of conduct that are drawn upon to form a sentiment of allegiance. It is equally necessary to consider motives for action and the circumstances that engender them which *inhibit* the formation of ties of allegiance.

Hume clearly believes that, in all but the most exceptional circumstances, the weight of custom shifted the balance of sentiment toward the existing government, whatever its particular merits or demerits. Moreover, there is a normative imperative not to pursue sudden changes in government despite its flaws.

> Some innovations must necessarily have place in every human institution; and it is happy where the enlightened genius of the age give these a direction to the side of reason, liberty, and justice. But violent innovations no individual is entitled to make. They are even dangerous to be attempted by the legislature.

More ill than good is ever to be expected from them. And if history affords examples to the contrary, they are not to be drawn into precedent and are only proofs that the science of politics affords few rules which will not admit of some exception. . . . [77]

No doubt some of Hume's insistence on this point derives from a temperament that tended to value order and stability over other ends. Hume's reactions to political events perhaps indicate this better than his philosophical works. For example, his reaction to the imprisonment of John Wilkes for slandering George III and the resulting violent protests is expressed in the following letter to Turgot: "Here is a People thrown into Disorders . . . merely from the Abuse of Liberty, chiefly the Liberty of the Press; without any Grievance, I do not only say, real, but even imaginary; and without any of them being able to tell one Circumstance of Government which they wish to have corrected."[78]

Hume's preference for order (even leading here to a cavalier dismissal of restrictions on liberty of the press as a legitimate grievance against government) has, however, a theoretical foundation as well. It derives from the philosophically grounded consideration that the nature of passionate attachments to an entity, as indirectly implicated in the daily personal concerns of our lives as the government of a large state, is always threatened with being overwhelmed by more particular attachments. In addition, both a regard for property rights, virtually synonymous with justice in Hume's view, and allegiance to the political regime are fictitious, imaginative ties that gain their strength through habitual association. Some prior consideration of the contrast between justice and other moral rules is required to bring these themes to light.

If feelings of benevolence were less confined to immediate acquaintances than we know them to be, or if nature were more bountiful than we know it to be, neither the rules nor the sense of justice would be necessary. Sadly, neither of these conditions hold. Thus, material scarcity and limited benevolence see to it that rules of justice are necessary. Such rules, Hume argues, are required to protect individuals in their possessions and, by so doing, they promote the public good. "Few enjoyments," Hume writes, "are given us from the open and liberal hand of nature; but by art, labour and industry, we can extract from them in great abundance. Hence the ideas of property becomes necessary in all civil society: Hence justice derives its usefulness to the public: And hence alone arises its merits and moral obligation."[79] Hume is as adamant as Locke in asserting that "whatever is produced or improved by a man's industry ought, for ever, be secured to him."[80] To be sure, Hume, and Smith as well, differ from Locke in defending this position by appeals to public utility rather than natural rights. Yet neither saw any fundamental opposition between public good and private property rights of the sort just described. And they follow Locke as well in recognizing that these rights impose the corresponding duties on others to "respect the life and person of our neighbors" as well as their "property and possessions."[81]

A sense of justice is required to assure the stability of property rights and holdings. Yet, this sense must compete both with what Hume describes as the "primary" or selfish instincts and with limited benevolence as a motive for action. The primary instincts impel us, in Smith's phrase (on this matter there is a full harmony of views between Hume and Smith), to "indulge ... at the expense of other people, the natural preference which every man has for his own happiness above that of other people. . . . "[82] It is this inclination that a sense of justice must curb.

> The case is precisely the same with the political or civic duty of *allegiance* as with the natural duties of justice and fidelity. Our primary instincts lead us either to indulge ourselves in unlimited freedom or to seek dominion over others; and it is reflection only which engages us to sacrifice such strong passions to the interests of peace and public order.[83]

The reflective element in the sense of justice makes it an artificial virtue in Hume's parlance. Unlike benevolence, justice does not spring naturally from the heart. As suggested above, this distinction is not an altogether helpful one: feelings of benevolence may be natural in Hume's sense, but actions tending to the well-being of loved ones equally demand reflection. Think of a parent refusing a child a drink of water before surgery upon doctor's orders. Nonetheless, it is a distinction Hume makes and holds to with some consistency, and it points to a conceptual difference between justice and other virtues that is far more defensible.

A central aspect of this difference is that just persons must be guided in their conduct by a system of rules rather than by the expected consequences of individual actions.

> For if it be allowed (what is, indeed, evident) that the ... consequences of a particular act of justice may be hurtful to the public as well as to individuals; it follows, that every man, in embracing that virtue, must have an eye to the whole plan or system, and must expect the concurrence of his fellows in the same conduct and behaviour. Did all his views terminate in the consequences of each act of his own, his benevolence and his humanity as well as his self-love, might often prescribe to him measures of conduct very different from those, which are agreeable to the strict rules of right and justice.[84]

Justice as a virtue requires that citizens distance themselves from natural affections as regulators of conduct. It also requires distancing oneself from generally accepted criteria of moral worth. The "laws of nature which regulate property, as well as all civil laws ... deprive, without scruple, a beneficent man of all his possessions, if acquired by mistake, ... in order to bestow them on a selfish miser, who has already heaped up immense stores of superfluous riches."[85] Presumably, if the beneficent one is known through personal ties, the moral sense will be that much more confounded.[86]

A sense of justice also requires a proper conception of self-interest. This conception is not a self-abnegatory one. Hume is perhaps nowhere more "Madisonian" in his emphasis on the futility of denying the force of self-interest as a guide for one's conduct and on the need for interest to be redirected into socially beneficial channels.

No affection of the human mind has both a sufficient force, and a proper direction to counter-balance the love of gain, and render men fit to society, by making them abstain from the possessions of others. Benevolence to strangers is too weak for this purpose; and as for other passions, they rather inflame this avidity, when we observe that the larger our possessions are, the more ability we have of gratifying all our appetites. There is no passion, therefore, capable of controlling the interested affection, but the very affection itself, by an alteration of its direction.[87]

Hume contends that, if every man were wise enough to perceive the confluence of his personal interests with those of society, he would show a steady adherence to the rules of justice that make stable society possible. Unfortunately, men tend to give undue weight to "a lesser and more present interest," a condition that makes government both necessary and potentially unstable. Thus, both self-interest too narrowly conceived and "our natural uncultivated ideas of morality . . . conform themselves to the partiality of our affections. . . . "[88]

If reflection on self-interest properly understood forms the core of a sense of justice, it is aided by a general feeling of benevolence or humanity that, although weaker than immediate ties to loved ones, undeniably exists and gives an attachment to general rules some force. "The interests of society," Hume argues, "are not, even on their own account [apart from considerations of personal advantage] entirely indifferent to us."[89] We see in this argument that Hume does not ground moral sentiment in utility alone. Hume argues that we must ask the further question—utility for what? If we had no interest in the well-being of our fellows, the utility of rules of justice would not stir our passions and thus become a motive for action. Usefulness moves us *only because* "the happiness of society, recommends itself directly to our approbation and good-will."[90]

Smith's view of the sense of justice is much like that of Hume. Justice is the "main pillar" of society, so that its observance is essential in a way in which natural virtues such as friendship and gratitude are not.[91] A developed sense of justice is required to counteract more selfish instincts and the rather weak links among men provided by universal sympathy.

Men, though naturally sympathetic, feel so little for another, *with whom they have no particular connection*, in comparison to what they feel for themselves; the misery of one, who is merely their fellow-creature, is of so little importance to them in comparison even of a small conveniency of their own; they have it so much in their power to hurt him, and may have so many temptations to do so, that if this principle did not stand up within them in his defence, and overawe them into a respect for his innocence, they would, like wild beasts, be at all times ready to fly upon him; and a man would enter an assembly of men as he enters a den of lions [emphasis added]."[92]

Enlightened, that is, long-term, interest and this sentiment of universal sympathy are the sources for a sense of justice. Smith differs from Hume in giving a fuller description of how sympathy works. It is not utility alone, or even love of humanity, that explains, for example, the deep resentment we feel for the harms done an innocent victim. It is, rather, a direct identification with that person and a consciousness of ill desert that nature has implanted in the human breast. The intensity of the feeling of resentment cannot be explained on utilitarian grounds since the harm done one innocent person is not likely to undo the whole system of justice. Moreover, if utility were the sole grounds of moral approbation, "we should have no other reason for praising a man than that for which we commend a set of drawers."[93]

Similarly, Smith argues that property relations are reinforced by the sympathetic and imaginative bond the poor come to feel for the rich. It is a bond that supports justice, assuming that the wealth of the rich has been justly acquired, and it counteracts the illegitimate resentment the poor might feel if their sentiments grew out of a comparison of their well-being with that of the rich.

> When we consider the condition of the great, in those delusive colors in which the imagination is apt to paint it, it seems to be almost the abstract idea of a perfect and happy state. It is the very state which, in all our waking dreams and idle reveries, we had sketched out to ourselves as the object of all our desires. We feel, therefore, a peculiar sympathy with the satisfaction of those who are in it. . . . What pity, we think, that any thing should spoil and corrupt so agreeable a situation! We could even wish them immortal; and it seems hard to us, that death should at last put an end to such perfect enjoyment.[94]

Smith, it should be added, is offering no mere apologia for the wealthy. This sympathetic identification does harm our moral sense, as we frequently see the "respectful attentions of the world" drawn more strongly toward "the rich and the great" and not toward the deserving "wise and virtuous."[95] It is discomfiting to Smith as a moral theorist, and a particularly empirical one at that, to note this disjuncture between the characters we should and those we do esteem.

Hume and Smith both contend, though with somewhat different arguments, that our moral sense can be confounded by a range of sentiments and imaginative connections. Thus, self-interest and limited benevolence can either promote or undermine our sense of justice. Much the same can be said for sympathetic identification with the rich (or, though Smith does not say so, revulsion at the sight of the poor). Their epistemic and moral philosophic insights, I suggest, give rise quite naturally to conservatism in the political sphere. Motivations to maintain a political order emerge from a balance of considerations of long-term interest, benevolence, and imaginative association with the upper classes and, as we shall see, the governing elite.

Imagination plays a vital role in stabilizing the virtue of justice and political allegiance. In the *Treatise*, Hume had argued that our belief in the *constancy* and *coherence* of sense objects derives from experiencing these objects over time. Thus, "these mountains, and houses, and trees, which lie at present under my eye, have always appear'd to me in the same order; and when I lose sight of them by shutting my eyes or turning my head, I soon find them return upon me without the least alteration."[96] Imagination is an active power of mind that, once set in motion, is "apt to continue even when the object fails it." Thus, when we see the same mountains, houses, and trees in the same order day after day, we become convinced of their continued existence even when we are not perceiving them. The imaginative power makes it possible for us to maintain a belief in their existence that the broken string of sense perceptions over time could not provide. Thus, Hume can assert that "all reasoning concerning matters of fact arises only from custom, and custom can only be the effect of repeated perceptions."[97]

Hume also sees the virtue of justice and political allegiance as dependent on acts of imagination accompanied by appropriate feelings. In the case of justice, that is, of property relations, Hume contends that the recognition of rights of ownership rests, in a sense, on a fiction. We associate an observable relation between an object and a person with a moral one. A presumption of ownership arises from, first, *occupation*, that is, original possession of an object; then *accession*, an intimate connection between things we own and things they produce (for example, the fruit on a fruit tree); next *prescription*, the duration of ownership; and, finally *succession*, the passing on of property from fathers to children.[98]

These associations make ownership of property appear natural to most observers and, hence, contribute to the stability of property relations. They are distinguished from other imaginative leaps, such as those that give rise to religious superstition, by their social utility.[99] The apparent naturalness of property rights, say those acquired through succession, militates against altering laws governing inheritance even if a case could be made that such rules would enhance economic efficiency or satisfy more members of society. The simple fact that people are inclined to accept these rights as legitimate, based simply on the tendency of the mind to link facts with right, counts for maintaining that schedule of rights that has evolved "naturally" against competing, yet nonexistent, ones.

The duty of allegiance, like that of justice, is explained in the first instance by the human interests government serves and is reinforced by acts of imagination regarding the right to rule. Government is required to compel us to follow rules that are in our long-term self-interest. Much of Hume's criticism of social-contract theory derives, in fact, from what he sees as its needless lack of parsimony for not taking this into account. There is no need to found an obligation to obey government on a promise. Hume is willing to grant that "the duty of allegiance be at first grafted on the obligation of promises," but it "quickly takes root of itself, and has an original obligation and authority, independent of all contracts" grounded in the interests it serves.[100]

Hume does not contend that citizens or subjects actually reflect upon the utility of government and thereby decide to give their allegiance to it. It hardly seems that this is a matter for decision. Antiquity, after all, *always* begets the opinion of right. Interest can explain why people should recognize some sort of authority. It does not explain why we accede to the concrete person(s) or institutions we allow to govern us. And allegiance, like Blake's God, is in the details.

As in the discussion on property, imaginative associations cause subjects to view possessors of power in fact as possessors in right. The first principle of imagination Hume notes is that of *long possession*. This gives authority to almost all established governments in the world even the majority of them who came to power through illegitimate means. For these, "time alone gives solidity to their right; and operating gradually on the minds of men, reconciles them to any authority, and makes it seem just and reasonable."[101]

Where no one has long held the reins of power, the second principle, *present possession* "is sufficient to supply its place."[102] Hume argues that present possession carries greater weight in assuring the stability of government than it does in assuring the stability of property. Violence against present holders of property is more likely, first, because of the stronger countervailing short-term interest—presumably, we can imagine more easily wresting possessions from a fellow than wresting power from a ruler. Second, changes that advance one's interests, which are easily produced in private affairs, "are unavoidably attended with bloodshed and confusion, where the public is interested."[103]

The liberality in Hume's notion of the sort of rulers the people will legitimize is indicated by his inclusion of *conquest* as the third principle governing allegiance. It is, in fact, stronger than present possession as an imaginative bond between people and ruler because it is "seconded" by the notions of glory and honor we ascribe to conquerors and take some pleasure in ourselves. *Succession*, the fourth principle, has its supports as well in the presumed consent of the father monarch and the imitation of succession in private families.

Finally, *positive law* establishing or altering a form of government or line of succession can have a psychological force—albeit a weaker one—that is irreducible to the other four principles under special circumstances. When changes are made in a constitution, the people will "think themselves still at liberty to return to the antient government" unless the new one exhibits "an evident tendency to the public good."[104] The pull toward antiquity is indicated, Hume argues, in the common notion of fundamental laws, which are supposed to be unalterable even by the sovereign. How much these fundamental laws can be altered without jeopardizing popular support is a matter for prudential determination as there is "an insensible gradation from the most material laws to the most trivial, and from the most antient to the most modern."[105] How far a legislature can innovate in the principles of government is, thus, "a work more of imagination and passion than of reason."[106]

The diversity of Hume's principles of allegiance should not obscure a general theme uniting them. In Hume's words, " 'Tis interest which gives the general instinct; but 'tis custom which gives the particular direction."[107] Obedience to the magistrate is a duty that supplements justice by obliging men to act in their long-term interest. But as a sense of allegiance takes hold it is soon consolidated into habit and even reflections on interest cease to be a motivation for obedience. Hume devotes a good bit of space in his political essays to describing this process of habituation.

Hume's problem is to discover why men, if they are not inclined to conform themselves to the duties of justice, will be so inclined toward the "factitious duty of obedience." The core of his answer is simply stated: "Order in society . . . is much better maintained by means of government, and our duty to the magistrate is more strictly guarded by the principles of human nature than [is] our duty to our fellow citizens."[108] The psychological insight offered here is profound. Dispositions to obey and feelings of allegiance toward the magistrate are more deeply grounded psychologically than are duties to our fellows. The former do not require the cognitive skills nor the (unnatural) impartiality toward loved ones required by a sense of justice in order to be practical.

This is so, first, as the initial leaders of polities, who attain their positions "by consent, tacit or express," do so by demonstrating "superior personal qualities"—virtues such as valor, integrity, or prudence—which recommend themselves directly to followers. Second, the leader's power to reward services to him gives his officers a motive to support him. Finally, as the polity develops, "habit soon consolidates what other principles of human nature had imperfectly founded, and men, once accustomed to obedience, never think of departing from that path in which they and their ancestors have constantly trod and to which they are confined by so many *urgent and visible motives* [emphasis added]."[109]

In this indirect way, the duty of allegiance feeds into regulative dispositions. Obedience toward the magistrate, as Hume writes elsewhere, becomes so familiar that men cease to inquire into its "origin or cause," any more than they inquire into the "principle of gravity . . . or the most universal laws of nature."[110] Duties to one's fellows, which only weakly motivate us in their own terms, are reinforced—in a sense, are personalized—by the magistrate. At the same time, allegiance, upon becoming habitual, has received the tacit endorsement of ancestors and is brought into the sphere of intergenerational familial affections as well. Each of these bring stability enhancing practices more firmly under the guard of the principles of human nature as Hume's empirical psychology understands them.

Hume returns to this theme in one of his seminal political essays, "Of the First Principles of Government," which begins with an empirical observation and a note of surprise. Given the force of their numbers, we cannot help being surprised at the "easiness with which the many are governed by the few and the implicit submission with which men resign their own sentiments and passions to those of their rulers."[111] The surprise is occasioned by an understanding of the sentiments and passions themselves. Recognizing political authority requires the resignation of both natural, selfish passions and social ones, insofar as the latter are channeled in directions harmful to the state. Social sympathy *is* a psychological foundation of the sense of allegiance states require. Yet it *cannot*, in itself, confer any legitimacy on a political objective. It can, in fact, be a political vice. "Popular sedition, party zeal, a devoted obedience to factious leaders; these are some of the most visible, though less laudatory effects of this social sympathy in human nature."[112]

If a liberal government is to be stable, it must engage men's affections as well as their interests. In Hume's terms, it must be supported by "opinions of *right*" as well as by "opinions of *interest*."[113] The latter are required because our understanding of moral psychology would impel us to reject as unviable any form of government that consistently required self-abnegatory acts by its citizens. It is unlikely that we would support for any extended time a form of government that was not perceived to be generally advantageous.

The opinion of right is required because there are many particular instances in which the sense of general advantage of having a government is too weak to override the particular disadvantages individuals experience when supporting the state imposes costs on them. This opinion is, therefore, less clearly justified on prudential grounds than is the opinion of interest. The latter, Hume suggests, will tend to develop if subjects sense that the state is soundly administered. The former results less from the *function* of government than from its *durability*. Antiquity, after all, always, begets the opinion of right.

Hume suggests that the virtue of allegiance only fully takes hold of citizens once it ceases to be based on reflection. Given sound administration over time, this virtue will naturally, that is, unconsciously, develop. It will, in short, become habitual. At the juncture at which this habit emerges, it becomes pointless to speak of "civic virtue" in cognitive terms, however much its origins may be found in interest. Civic virtue consists in the bond of sentiment the citizen feels for community, government, and political leaders. And this is in itself an argument for conserving existing institutions, statues, and customs. Frequent, even if well-planned, innovations undermine the sentiment that inspires habitual obedience. And without this habit, the essential rules of justice of the society would be threatened.

A Humean Politics of Virtue: Some Preliminary Links to the Founding

Hume's *Enquiry Concerning the Principle of Morals* contains one of the stock figures of liberal political thought, a character described as a "sensible knave."

> Though . . . without a regard to property, no society could subsist; yet, according to the imperfect way in which human affairs are conducted, a sensible knave, in particular instances, may think, that an act of iniquity or infidelity will make a considerable addition to his fortune, without causing any considerable breach in the social union and confederacy. That HONESTY IS THE BEST POLICY, may be a good general rule; but it is liable to many exceptions: And he, it may, perhaps, be thought, conducts himself with most wisdom, who observes the general rule, and takes advantage of all the exceptions.[114]

The knave is not likely to find *any reasons* convincing for abiding by rules of justice. No prudentially grounded argument is going to influence him, because he has already quite reasonably calculated that defection from the rules is more advantageous to him than compliance with them.

A this point in his argument Hume reintroduces the issue of moral sentiments. If members of a political community are to be disposed, by and large, to undertake civic duties, this disposition must come from a moral sentiment, not from reflection on interests. The knave's long-term interests are, to be sure, bound up with the preservation of law and order both of which are violated by his actions. But he would be irrational to assume that his acts of knavery threaten the continued existence of society. If his "heart rebel not against such pernicious maxims . . . he has indeed lost a considerable motive to virtue; and we may expect, that his practice will be answerable to his speculation."[115] From Hume's perspective, it is fortunate that there are reasons to believe that most hearts do rebel against such maxims most of the time.

Hume does not hold to the implausible view that a polity can be stable without an inclination on the part of its members to make it so. The presence of something like civic virtue is a prerequisite for stable government. Nor, however, is Hume a Pollyanna about basic human motives or conduct, although a recent work dedicated to showing a Humean influence on the American founders casts him in just this role.

Perhaps the best-known recent effort to call attention to a Humean influence on the authors of the *The Federalist*, especially James Madison, is that of Garry Wills. Wills's analysis is insightful on a great many concrete points and he traces lines of influence plausibly and effectively. He nonetheless misleads us because his fundamental understanding of Humean moral and political philosophy is deficient. It places excessive stress on the role of universal benevolence.

Madison's world, Wills writes, was "the world of the American Enlightenment—a world of the classical virtues reborn. . . . "[116] Hume pointed the way to this world not only by his commonsense approaches to meddlesome problems of political philosophy and practice, but also by his optimistic good faith in the benevolence of the human species and the capacity of men for virtue. His theory and observation of the moral sentiments had taught him that virtue provides its own rewards. Madison, Wills tells us, was a Humean in all these ways. He held a conception of public virtue with a meaning and importance that today we can hardly fathom. He believed that there were men of extraordinary virtue who would be selected by their peers as public servants and that their peers had the virtue and wisdom to choose them and reward them accordingly.

If we do not recognize Madison in this light, this merely shows how much we as a society have changed. Madison was a product of his times, and given "all those cultural changes that have taken place between his time and ours," he is barely recognizable to us.[117] His ideals are likely to seem maudlin, so much so that even political candidates not noted for their modesty refuse to claim for themselves the elevated virtue that Madison took as a sine qua non for sound political leadership. Madison was a brilliant political thinker as well as designer and advocate of political institutions but, alas, a poor prognosticator. His world, and Hume's, has disappeared. The virtue is gone, left for the historian to recapture.

Wills is intent to show that while Publius, like Hume, was aware of the "darker side" of human nature, deep down he believed that man was good. How do we reconcile those "few dark passages" on human nature in *The Federalist* with "the reliance on virtue as preserving the American republic?" We rank them. Although Publius designs a system of government, in part, to check selfishness, and although Hume is similarly aware of man's moral flaws, both believed that the "actual motive that [generally] prevails in human action" was "the moral sense, or social virtue."[118]

Wills's analysis has the effect not only of consigning Madisonian thought, Humean roots and all, to a distant past; it trivializes it as well. Wills's reading would be plausible perhaps if he were analyzing Hutcheson, but considerations of the goodness or badness of human nature are anathema to Hume's moral and political thought and focusing on them cannot begin to do it justice. In Hume's own words, the "question . . . concerning the wickedness or goodness of human nature, enters not in the least into that other question concerning the origin of society."[119] Nor do they enter into its maintenance.

One simply does not find in Hume, or in Smith, a description of human passions or interests as inherently and universally good or evil. If men are benevolent—and they are—benevolence itself is too limited in scope to be the social bond for a large, complex polity. Men act unjustly out of benevolence as easily as they do out of selfishness. Moreover, the very social sympathy that forms the basis of the moral approbation attached to justice and allegiance can cause great harm to the public interest. Hence, Hume notes that the social sympathy inherent in our nature can be damaging if it attaches itself to the wrong sorts, e.g., party zealots or factious leaders.

If men are honorable—and they are—honor is a "check" upon conduct only under certain circumstances. It is eroded by party politics. "Honor is a great check upon mankind; but where a considerable body of men act together, this check is in a great measure removed, since a man is sure to be approved of by his own party for what promotes the common interest, and he soon learns to despise the clamor of his adversaries."[120]

If, on the other hand, men are self-interested—and they are—then they must be governed by self-interest. Ambition, that is, must be made to counteract ambition. If men are rational beings—and they are—it is not always recommended that magistrates appeal to the reason of their subjects in justifying their political authority. Some such notion is behind Hume's animus toward social-contract theory and its voluntaristic implications. Even when it is plainly true that magistrates derive their authority from an "original contract," it is best that they do not advertise this. "Magistrates are so far from deriving their authority, and the obligation to obedience in their subjects, from the foundation of a promise or original contract, that they conceal, as far as possible, from their people, especially from the vulgar, that they have their origin from thence."[121] Magistrates who do not so conceal the origins of their authority risk fostering the presumption that obedience is a matter of choice. Reasoned consideration of the necessity of justice and allegiance are anchors for these virtues but subjection of the magistrates' right to rule to the sorts of rationalistic critiques of power natural-rights theorists are fond of can corrode "opinion of right" and, hence, political stability.

Instead of a simple consideration of the goodness or badness of human nature, Hume and Smith offer subtle, anti-reductionist theories about the social virtues and the mental and psychological characteristics that actuate them in political affairs. Their theories are ideally suited for statesmen aimed at convincing each other and citizens that the form of government they propose is not only just but able to engender popular support. Though Hume and Smith offer enough argumentation to piece together the theories of justice on which they rely, their concerns are predominantly empirical. Indeed, for Hume, as the sense of allegiance increasingly becomes habitual, it detaches itself from the moorings of conceptions of justice altogether. We grow to like whatever government we are under merely because it grows old.

Much of the debate over the ratification of the American Constitution revolved around the very sorts of questions Hume explored with such insight. Deep-seated theoretical disputes about the worth of a liberal and republican, forms of government are rare. Debates, on the other hand, on the viability of the proposed constitutional government that refer specifically to its capacity to engender the allegiance of citizens and upright conduct in its office holders are rife. Let us turn our attention to the constitutional founders by exploring the "first principles" of the authors of *The Federalist*. Showing how these Americans and their opponents thought about fostering civic virtue given by and large liberal principles will be our next concern.

II

The Constitutional Founders' Theories of Citizenship

5

The Federalist: Liberal Commitments

In defending the newly drafted Constitution of 1787 in the New York State ratifying convention, Alexander Hamilton comes close to stating a general theory of constitutional design as pursued by a wise legislator. "Men," he argues, "will pursue their interests. It is as easy to change human nature as to oppose the strong current of selfish passions. A wise legislator will gently divert the channel, and direct it, if possible, to the public good."[1] Elsewhere Hamilton paraphrases Hume in making much the same point.

> Political writers, says a celebrated author, have established it as a maxim that, in contriving any system of government, and fixing the several checks and controls of the constitution, *every man* ought to be supposed a knave; and to have no other end, in all his actions, but *private interest.* By this interest we must govern him; and, by means of it, *make him co-operate to public good,* notwithstanding his insatiable avarice and ambition. Without this, we shall in vain boast of the advantages of *any Constitution.*[2]

One might wonder whether Hamilton's strongly stated pessimism regarding human nature does him more harm than good in his defense of the proposed Constitution. If the tendencies of man are as rapacious as Hamilton suggests, is it wise to consolidate and expand the powers of a government that is at some distance removed from popular control? Indeed, this was a common Anti-Federalist refrain. The Federalists, they contended, relied *too much* on the virtue of officeholders and too little on such institutional checks on power as could be provided by small electoral districts, rotation in office, and short terms of office.[3]

Given these criticisms, it is not surprising that Hamilton seems to sacrifice consistency to assuage these fears. One point made with some frequency by the Constitution's opponents is that the relatively small size of the House of Representatives would make that body subject to intrigue and corruption. Hamilton asks us to suppose, as is reasonable, that the House reaches a size of two hundred members in time: "is not this number sufficient to secure it against corruption?" To those who suggest otherwise, "human nature must be a much more weak and despicable thing than I apprehend it to be."[4] To be sure, the prudential argument for the stability of the proposed system is not long withheld. These two hundred, Hamilton adds, could not cause all that much harm within their two-year term in office even if they were corrupted.

Despite this apparent inconsistency, there is no reason to doubt Hamilton's sincerity in believing that representatives will be more dutiful than the Anti-Federalists fear. Indeed, Madison had relied upon a similar contention in chiding his opponents in the Virginia ratifying convention for their singular lack of faith in the people's virtue. His confidence in their virtue forms the basis for his defense of the small, sixty-five member House of Representatives as proposed in the Constitution. He refuses to believe that there are even sixty-five men in the nation who can recommend themselves to the voting public and yet be narrowly self-seeking. Those who could believe this, Madison suggests, have so little faith in man that they call into question his capacity for self-government. "Were the pictures which have been drawn by the political jealousy of some among us faithful likenesses of the human character, the inference would be that there is not sufficient virtue among men for self-government; and that nothing less than the chains of despotism can restrain them from destroying and devouring one another."[5]

This reliance on virtue in arguing for the proposed Constitution should lead us to doubt a pure "possessive individualist" interpretation of these thinkers, which seems to allow no role for the more elevated sentiments in determining human conduct. Neither Hamilton nor Madison could consistently assume man to be a knave without calling into question the very form of government they proposed. Does this challenge to a pure possessive-individualist reading of these authors lead us to take a further step and question their commitment to core liberal political principles? Here I must urge caution.

A commitment to liberalism must be demonstrated in terms of the political institutions and practices one recommends and the *reasons* one gives for them. Skepticism about the capacity of people to act consistently on moral principles is compatible with a wide range of political theories and beliefs about man's nature. It should not be taken to serve as an instance of any particular ideology. It is important to assess the reasons used to justify certain practices, since some practices, say rotation in office, can be supported on liberal or republican grounds. At the risk of some simplification, a liberal might defend this practice as an effective check on the power of the governed. A (weak) republican would point to the salutary effects it has in stimulating political participation and, therefore, public virtue, both of which are intrinsically good for developing a well-rounded character. And there is no *necessary* inconsistency in defending a practice on both these grounds.[6]

Given apparent commitments to a liberal political philosophy and a reliance on "civic virtue," might we conclude that Madison and Hamilton alternate between two available modes of political discourse? Their liberal skepticism regarding human nature is mitigated, it might be argued, by a republican faith in public virtue. This sort of synthesis is appealing if only because it promises to make peace between two current canonical interpretations of the founders' thought. Yet, it too depends on a premise that has not been established.

References to virtue can be seen as external to liberal commitments only if it is assumed to be somehow inconsistent for liberals to rely on and discuss virtue among citizens of liberal states. If, however, there is no reason to make this assumption (and, as I have argued, there is good reason to reject it), then caution must be urged here as well. To ascertain whether evocations of virtue are inconsistent with liberal principles, it is first necessary to elucidate those principles as expressed by Publius (the pen name of the authors of *The Federalist*). Doing so is the task of this chapter. Once this is accomplished, we can proceed with an analysis of the particular conceptions of civic virtue—and their Humean roots—offered by the authors of *The Federalist*.[7]

Liberal Justice and Self-Interest: Problems of Coordination

Madison and Hamilton, despite variations in emphasis, rely quite consistently on liberal contractarian reasons in supporting the Constitution of 1787. Hamilton generally takes a more instrumental tack in employing liberal conceptions in a defense of the Constitution, while Madison is more likely to draw upon the moral core of the liberal tradition. Yet these are differences in degree, not kind.

Hamilton sees the decision to adopt the Constitution as, at least in part, a problem in persuading self-interested actors to form a government best-suited to their long-term interests. Hamilton seeks to persuade his readers that a government "equally energetic" if not identical in all details to the proposed Constitution accomplishes this goal. The arguments he uses in doing so are classically contractarian and appeal to the interests of free, rational beings deciding upon a state that will provide the stability to enable them to pursue their conceptions of the good life.

In *Federalist* 15, Hamilton most directly likens the Constitution to a social contract. In doing so, he constructs an argument on classical liberal lines. The state governments under the Confederation play a role identical to that of the individuals in Hobbes's state of nature. That is, they are entities pursuing their own ends unconstrained by laws backed by sufficient force. The law-making and law-enforcement powers of the national government are not supported by adequate sanctions. Thus, they amount to "nothing more than advice or recommendation" and are not the "resolutions or commands" they appear to be.[8] This distinction directly parallels Hobbes's definition of positive law in *Leviathan* as "not counsel, but command" and his distinction between the laws of nature, which are no more than "qualities that dispose men to peace and obedience," and laws proper, which are backed by the sword.[9]

Further, the inconveniences of the state of nature are essentially the same for each. Hamilton writes that, in an association such as the Confederation, "where the general authority is confined to the collective bodies of the communities that compose it, every breach of the laws must involve a state of war and military execution must become the only instrument of civil obedience."[10] Thus, if one state fails to contribute to the collective security of the confederation, it is as much a threat to another state's security as the external enemy they are jointly sworn to resist. In such a situation, they are in a state of war with each other and the risks of actual war are correspondingly high.

For Hamilton, a rational plan of escape from these inconveniences is for the states to contract with each other to establish a sovereign with sufficient power to ensure the independence of each state from the use of force by the others and the contribution of each to the collective goods required by the union as a whole. This contract requires the states to surrender some liberty to direct their own affairs by yielding to the national government a share of sovereignty over their citizens. In return, they gain the security and independence (if not as broad in scope, at least more assured) that they could not adequately provide for themselves individually or jointly under the Confederation. Such a contract must form a government "equally energetic," if not identical in all details, to that of the proposed Constitution of 1787.

This plan is the only solution to the problem of a weak form of cooperation which has become untenable. After a brief description of the inadequacies of the Confederation, Hamilton writes that such an arrangement does "not deserve the name of government nor would any prudent man choose to commit his happiness to it."[11] Not consenting to the proposed Constitution indicates an inability to recognize where one's long-term interests lie. In classic liberal fashion, Hamilton does not define the nature of the happiness the prudent man ought to pursue. He does suggest, though, that wherever this happiness may lie, prospects of gaining and maintaining it over time are incompatible with the state of war that currently exists.

Madison, in *Federalist* 10, also expresses the logic of classical liberalism, although not as explicitly as Hamilton. The thread of his argument is worth tracing, since it shows much about the moral foundations and the practical functions of the liberal state. Madison describes government's purpose as protecting the "faculties of man" from which rights of property—as well as economic inequalities—originate.

> The protection of these faculties is the first object of government. From the protection of different and unequal faculties of acquiring property, the possession of different degrees and kind of property immediately results; and from the influence of these on the sentiments and views of respective proprietors ensues a division of the society into different interests and parties.[12]

This passage is more assertion than argument and contains several unjustified conclusions. It is not self-evident, for example, that diversity in faculties gives rise to property rights, much less to the broad right of acquisition Madison seems to have in mind. Nor is it clear that faculties, insofar as they are equated with "natural endowments," can establish entitlements of any sort. They are, in the mind of Rawls (among others), arbitrary from the moral point of view. It is less important, however, to criticize Madison on these grounds than to see why he presented his position in these somewhat obscure terms.

When Madison speaks of government's protecting faculties, he is offering an argument for citizens' political obligation to the liberal state he is proposing. At the same time, he is using a yardstick provided by the liberal contractarian tradition to measure the defects of the confederated governments. The moral core of that tradition is that only through voluntary agreement to rules of justice, on condition of like agreement by others, can one exercise one's will with minimal external constraints. More pointedly, the strongest case the liberal state can make for the obedience of its subjects is that without it they are unable to exercise faculties freely, and thus, to act as autonomous agents.

Madison makes much the same point in *Federalist* 51, where he uses the language of the social contract and expresses clearly a liberal egalitarian ethic. "In a society," he writes, in which "the stronger faction can readily unite and oppress the weaker, anarchy may be as truly said to reign as in a state of nature, where the weaker individual is not secured against the violence of the stronger." Under these conditions, even the stronger are "prompted, by the uncertainty of their condition, to submit to a government which may protect the weak as well as themselves."[13] As Hobbes had argued, not even the strongest is so strong as to be able to fend off all aggressors. The social contract provides a political equality of weak and strong in place of a natural inequality. Though Madison, like Hobbes, points to the interested motive even the strong have for coming to such an arrangement, it is clear that the moral worth of the government is derived from its capacity to protect the weak, that is, those minorities who would not withstand the onslaughts of a majority faction. Any other reading would be inconsistent with the stress on preserving civil and political liberties from the threats of factions that Madison expresses throughout *The Federalist*. Unlike Hobbes, Madison counts more than political stability in his criteria of good government.

This contractarian argument can readily be applied to the choice presented in the ratification process. Madison does so in *Federalist* 45 by contending that the purpose of the Revolution was to secure for Americans those goods which could not be secured under the arbitrary rule of the British. These goods are the "peace, liberty and safety" of the American people defined generally as their "happiness." Any government that threatens these goods is not deserving of support for all the reasons noted above. This is as true of state governments under the Confederation as of the British colonial governments. If, he writes, the national union is essential to the American people's happiness, it is "preposterous to urge as an objection to it . . . that such a government may derogate from the importance of the individual States."[14]

The obligation owed state governments exists to the extent that they are able to secure individual liberties and general welfare. If they are not performing this task adequately, or if a diminution of their powers is required for its performance, their legitimacy decreases proportionately. It may be that supporters of the Confederation have praiseworthy reasons for defending state sovereignty. Among these could be a sense of affection for the locality, or, theoretically, a classical republican-inspired idea of the small state as the locus of active citizenship. Nonetheless, the moral weight of these reasons would be slight if states were not adequately "protecting faculties." That they are not doing so is, of course, precisely Madison's contention.

That Madison equates faculties with skills in acquiring property indicates that there is a bourgeois or "possessive individualist" component in his liberalism. This does not suggest that he is unconcerned with the "common good." His whole public life belies this contention. Moreover, he does not ascribe *only* self-interested motives to human nature. Nonetheless, Madison defines the term *common good* and sees it as problematic in a particular, ideologically constrained way. Since there are inevitable scarcities of goods to be possessed in market economies, and since exercising faculties is essentially equated with acquisition, society is necessarily ridden with conflicts over scarce resources. Further, men naturally feel a passionate attachment to their own property, as well as to opinions, religious beliefs, and the like. And, by implication, they feel a natural aversion to what they see as impediments to their pursuit of the goods they desire. These passions are easily inflamed and manifest self-love in the narrowest sense. They dispose "men to vex and oppress each other [rather] than to co-operate for the common good."[15] This notion of the passions justifies Madison's remark that factions are sown in the nature of man. And this in turn establishes the necessary function of the liberal state as regulating competing interests, or, more starkly, breaking and controlling the "violence of faction."

Hamilton and Madison use explicitly contractarian arguments to establish central points of the Federalist position: Hamilton to show the necessity of enhanced national power to avoid a "state of war" and Madison to delegitimize, in a sense, state governments by showing the basis of *any* government's claim to legitimacy. That they argue in these terms in what are essentially works of political persuasion indicates that they attributed a wide acceptance of these premises even to their critics.

Moreover, despite the quite legitimate claim that can be made for the originality of *The Federalist* on issues of institutional design, the problems they address are endemic within the liberal tradition. They acknowledge that such problems as the adequacy of contributions to the collective goods required by the union and respect for individual and minority rights have become more acute with the waning of the "transient enthusiasm" of the revolutionary era.[16] Yet this is inevitable; the enthusiasms of revolutionary politics are transient indeed and their continuance would not be desirable even if possible. *The Federalist* represents not so much a loss of faith in republican virtue as a recognition of the intractable instabilities in liberal politics that result from both motivational and structural causes.

The motivational factors have been emphasized in the literature, particularly by writers who reject what they take to be Publius's conception of "human nature."[17] And there is little question that Publius believed that the most frequently observed motives for social action were not the sort that encouraged the recognition of political obligations. Madison's contention that government is the greatest reflection on human nature in its less angelic aspects is a case in point, as is his claim that faction is sown in the nature of man. Hamilton seconds this assessment in *Federalist* 15. He argues that those who oppose strengthening the enforcement function of the national government betray "an ignorance of the true springs by which human conduct is actuated." These are the "original inducements to the establishment of civil power . . . [since] the passions of men will not conform to the dictates of reason and justice without constraint."[18]

Despite the frequency of these considerations on human nature, it would be misleading to place too much weight on them in evaluating Publius's plan of justice or the causes of instability in it. This is so for three reasons, the first of which applies to Madison, and the latter two equally to Hamilton. First, Madison accepts as a truism the notion that society was founded on a contract (even if a hypothetical one) that required the assent of every individual to be established. In a letter to Jefferson, he repeats the Lockean argument that *only* unanimous consent could legitimate the principle of majority rule. This is so because, without presupposing original unanimity, political decisions made by majorities could not be conceived as acts to which the minority has voluntarily acquiesced. They would, therefore, be mere assertions of force and minorities would not be under a moral obligation to abide by them. Yet, if individuals were motivated to an overwhelming degree by a love of power and dominance, as the cited passages of *The Federalist* admittedly imply, it is hard to see how either the original motive to cooperate or subsequent ones to be bound by adverse political decisions could arise.[19]

Second, while Madison and Hamilton use contractarian arguments to defend the Constitution, it is important to note that their problem is to justify a specific government that will affect the distribution of wealth and power among already-situated social actors. This distinguishes their problem from that of pure contract theorists whose contractors are conceived to be in a presocial state. The men they describe, who must decide the fate of the proposed Constitution, are presumed to have personal preferences, interests, and motivations that are a product of their socialization—not of "human nature" per se. Madison goes so far as to suggest that motives to defect from rules of cooperation inevitably will arise in a society constituted in accordance with liberal principles. Some such idea is behind Madison's contention in *Federalist* 10 that "liberty is to faction what air is to fire."[20] As long as individuals are free to exercise a right of choice, it is preordained that they will act factiously, that is, against the rights of other citizens and the "permanent and aggregate interests" of the community.

That they act in this manner results from the relation between reason and the natural passions of self-love. But it is to their personal property, as well as to their opinions concerning the valued ends of life (religious and political opinions, for example), that these passions attach themselves. None of these values exist in a state of nature. The competitive motives Madison sees as a source of faction are politically relevant only because a political-economic system is in place that allows for liberal capitalist competition.

Thus, Madison's claim that factiousness is sown in human nature, however much it may express a Calvinist pessimism, should also be read politically as a statement that reflects his commitment to a liberal capitalist political economy. It rests on a fundamental understanding of individuals as choosers of self-selected ends who, given unequal natural endowments and the condition of free economic exchange, acquire different degrees and kinds of property to which they form passionate attachments. Madison's problem is to establish that liberal democracy is empirically viable *even though* its very structure is one that encourages destabilizing, privatistic dispositions.

That both Madison and Hamilton remain optimistic about man's capacity for self-government despite these tendencies suggests a third reason for de-emphasizing their evaluation of "human nature" in explaining their politics. Each argues that, although the structural problems of liberal democratic co-operation are constant, the passions that serve as wellsprings of human conduct are *malleable*.

The specifics of this line of argument must be delayed until the next chapter. It is enough to note here Madison's belief that enough virtue could be generated among citizens to observe liberal democratic norms. This belief is evident in his Virginia ratification convention remarks and in *The Federalist*. He states in *Federalist* 55 that, in addition to the undeniable "degree of depravity in mankind," there are other qualities that justify "a certain portion of esteem and confidence." Republican government, he adds, "presupposes the existence of these qualities in a higher degree than any other form."[21] It is, in fact, untenable in their absence.

Throughout *The Federalist*, as well as in other writings, Hamilton and Madison show a keen awareness of the reasons the liberal state can offer citizens for undertaking civic duties. Yet they also are aware of the limited degree to which reasons can be relied on to promote desired modes of conduct. Madison argues explicitly in "The Vices of the Political System of the United States," a piece that foreshadows *Federalist* 10 in its analysis of the dangers of majority faction, that establishing a practice of political obligation will not follow from making a theoretical case for its necessity. Madison considers what should be sufficient motive for majorities to restrain themselves from abusing "the rights and interests of the minority, or of individuals."[22] He then explains why they would not show this restraint. Neither prudence, respect for character, nor religion are sufficient to restrain narrowly acquisitive motivations.

Respect for character, Madison argues, is indeed a salutary motive for moral conduct in individuals, although even here it "is considered as very insufficient to restrain them from injustice." The problem is more pronounced when collective actions are considered. The "efficacy" of this motive "is diminished in proportion to the number which is to share the praise or the blame."[23]

Religion as a motive to restrain unjust acts is also found wanting. Religious belief is at times "kindled into enthusiasm" and when it is so, "its force like that of other passions is increased by the sympathy of the multitude."[24] Yet, religion even in its "coolest state" is not infallible and "may become a motive to oppression as well as a restraint from injustice."[25]

Perhaps we are on safer grounds, then, in considering a "prudent regard to their own good as involved in the general and permanent good of the community" as a motive restraining injustice.[26] This motive is derived from reasoning based on what is best for one's long-term interests. A prudent regard for my own good is motivation to respect other's rights because the common good (defined as the stability of government and the generality of its laws) is the condition for each individual's acquiring and maintaining desired objects. If today I can best satisfy my desires by violating other's rights, tomorrow the situation may be reversed. Madison then echoes Hume in suggesting that, although this consideration ought to be "of decisive weight in itself, [it] is found by experience to be too often unheeded. It is often forgotten, by nations as well as by individuals, that honesty is the best policy."[27]

The problem of self-restraint is not, however, precisely the one of forgetting Madison describes. If dishonesty often prevails, it is because honesty is not always the best policy when judged by the dictates of rational prudence. Madison shows an awareness of this when considering several of the concrete defects of the Confederation. For example, he offers three reasons for believing that, although the members of the Confederation require union, their contributions to its maintenance are likely to be insufficient without adequate sanctions.

The first reason concerns the distribution of costs and benefits across member states. "Every general act of the Union," he notes, "must necessarily bear unequally hard on some particular member or members of it." For example, tariffs that protect manufacturers may adversely affect agricultural interests and states. Second, in a situation of competition over scarce resources, the "partiality" of members to their own interests will lead them to "exaggerate the inequality" of costs where it exists, and "even suspect it where it has no existence." Finally, even virtuously intentioned members are likely to come up short as they will reason that "the voluntary compliance of each other may prevent the compliance of any, although it should be the latent disposition of all."[28]

Madison's reference to the "latent" disposition of all to cooperate points to the need to establish the conditions under which this disposition is most likely to be acted upon. The Confederation's failure to do so is one of its main vices. Its design exhibits a "mistaken confidence that the justice, the good faith, the honor, the sound policy of the several legislative assemblies would render superfluous any appeal to the ordinary motives by which the laws secure the obedience of individuals." The defects Madison refers to are "want of sanction to the laws, and of coercion in the government of the Confederacy."[29] In the absence of adequate coercive powers, the idea of a just state is a contradiction in terms. Hobbes had made the point first that without laws backed by force, it is not appropriate to discuss the self-interested motives of individuals in terms of justice or injustice. In a condition in which each is a threat to every other, each has legitimate grounds in seeking all means necessary to preserve his own life regardless of the consequences to others' well-being. Only when an enforcement mechanism is in place that can assure each within reason that his life and assets will be protected, can invasion of others' rights (which are themselves the results of enforced cooperation) be considered unjust. Seen in this light, the full force of Madison's claim of the Confederation's incapacity to provide motives for just conduct comes into view.

Hamilton shares the essentials of this Hobbesian analysis. In *Federalist* 7 he notes that "without any umpire or common judge to interpose between contending parties . . . the sword would sometimes be appealed to as the arbiter of [the states'] differences."[30] Further, however harmful the resort to force may be, it cannot be considered unjust under the present, confederal arrangements. Stating that a future source of discontent among the states is likely to be increased commercial competition, given unequal advantages of states and regions, Hamilton writes: "The habits of intercourse, on the basis of equal privileges . . . would give a keener edge to those causes of discontent than they would naturally have independent of this circumstance. *We should be ready to denominate injuries those things which were in reality the justifiable acts of independent sovereignties consulting a distinct interest.*"[31] It is not unjust for states to act on their distinct interests if an effective enforcement mechanism to regulate commerce is lacking. This is true even when doing so is injurious to the union as a whole. No state can be reasonably assured that the others will do any differently. In fact, Hamilton had argued in a different context that there are good reasons to doubt other states' forbearance if voluntary compliance is the only means of providing for it.

> Though the states will have a common interest; yet they will also have a particular interest. . . . [A]s a part of the union it will be in the interest of every state, that the general government should be supplied with the revenues necessary for the national purposes; but it will be the particular interest of every state to pay as little itself and let its neighbors pay as much as possible.[32]

He adds that since "particular interests have always been more influential upon men than general," the states will always act as "so many eccentric powers" supporting the national government only when it is prudent for them to do so.[33] Without an adequately coercive national government, any other norm of conduct could not be considered consistent with rational behavior. Moreover, the more virtuous state leaders would lack even the satisfaction of claiming that the less forbearing ones were unjust or wrong.

In sum, Madison and Hamilton are well aware of the self-interested motives for conduct that are likely to be encountered in (though not exclusively in) liberal polities. Their consideration of these motives is cogent and "realistic." It leads quite directly to Madison's well-known analysis of the requisite means for "breaking and controlling the violence of faction" developed in *Federalist* 10. It leads as well to Hamilton's sophisticated discussion of deciding to adopt the Constitution as analogous to deciding upon a government from a state of nature—and to his call for a more "energetic" government than that provided under the Articles of Confederation.

Yet, there are two distinct ways in which this attention to the problems of coordinating the actions of self-interested individuals, so often stressed in readings of "Madisonian" liberal democracy, is not a complete description of Publius's liberal commitments or view of human nature. First, neither Madison nor Hamilton take self-interest to be the whole story of human motivation, as necessary as the assumption that people pursue self-interest much or most of the time is to designing sound institutions. Second, both defend liberal institutions not merely as modi vivendi enabling warring factions to live together in peace (though this is no small thing), but also on decidedly moral, noninstrumental grounds. This second point deserves expansion.

Liberal Justice: Entitlements and Moral Worth

The authors of *The Federalist* are clearly aware of free-rider problems and the sorts of instabilities that plague polities that grant wide charters of liberty. Yet, this would not be enough to define them as liberals at least in the quasi-Kantian manner in which we have been using that term. In fact, the constitutional design they defend is not valued merely as a modus vivendi, that is, as a device to keep self-interested actors in check. Rather, it has, especially in Madison's essays, an independent moral justification that requires, but is not reducible to, the provision of law and order. If this were not the case, we might be more inclined to see an antithesis between moral virtue and liberalism. If true, however, the notion of a language of virtue internal to liberal discourse seems more plausible. Dispositions that promote good things are, after all, themselves good and can fairly be described as virtues.

What then is the goodness, the moral worth, of the political order Madison and Hamilton work so hard to secure? Here a familiar difference between the views of the two thinkers takes on some importance. Hamilton is more prone to emphasize the harms dissolute government has done to America's "national dignity and credit" while Madison emphasizes the harms it has done in light of its duty to protect the fundamental rights of its citizens.[34] Differences between the two over the scope and powers of the national government and over the future course of the nation as a commercial or agrarian republic were to become more pronounced and, as most schoolchildren know, lead to the political split between the two in the Federal era. Up to the time of *The Federalist* these differences are, however, matters of degree, not kind.

Even for Hamilton, whose liberal credentials are more prone to challenge than Madison's, the social contract is more than a modus vivendi, more than a device required to secure internal order and facilitate the achievement of national greatness. This is seen in part in Hamilton's early vindication of the convening of the Continental Congress and its drafting of the "Declaration of Rights and Grievances" to George III. Much in the style of the Declaration of Independence, Hamilton deems to present "first principles" before presenting a list of specific grievances against king and parliament. Among these are the assertion that the "only distinction between freedom and slavery consists in this: In the former state, a man is governed by the laws to which he has given consent . . . : In the latter, he is governed by the will of another." In the one case, his "life and property" are his own, in the other, they are his only at the pleasure of his master.

Americans, Hamilton continues, are

> "intitled to freedom . . . upon every rational principle." All men have one common original [i.e., God]: they participate in one common nature, and consequently have one common right. No reason can be assigned why one man should exercise any power, or pre-eminence over his fellow creatures more than another; unless they have voluntarily vested him with it.[35]

Only after stating these Lockean principles of natural right does Hamilton proceed to appeals to the British constitution and to specific compacts between Great Britain and the colonies to make his case.

One must read into Hamilton's remarks the usual (if not more than the usual) caveats one attaches to assertions of the rights of "all men" in classical liberal texts. The class of those who count as "men" for Hamilton is highly restricted and I make no effort here to convert him into more of a social egalitarian or less of a skeptic regarding the good will and wisdom of "the people" than he actually was.[36] It is nonetheless significant that his grievances against the British government are thoroughly liberal and contractarian.

Americans do not merely crave freedom; they are entitled to it because they are human beings, that is, as a matter of natural right. All are fundamentally equal with regard to this right's having one "common original" in their Creator, so that no one's claim of preeminence over others can by justified without consent. Claims of preeminence are the very core of injustice and violate the equal concern and respect Americans, like all people, merit.

It is even more apparent that Madison's liberalism is far more than the bargaining solution to the problem of competing interests that is often described by readers of *Federalist* 10. The argument in this document is more profoundly moral than is often recognized. By characterizing the role of the state as the "protection of faculties," Madison emphasizes the importance he places on the state's assuring the autonomous functioning of each individual in the commonwealth. Factions, whether based on different religious commitments, on commitments to competing demagogues, or on different amounts and types of property are to be controlled not only because they lead to instability but also because they often promote injustice. The unconstrained religious zealot is no advocate of religious tolerance any more than the demagogue is of free and fair debate. Indeed, when either political or religious factions are unconstrained by representative institutions in an extended republic the likelihood is increased that an "unjust and interested majority" can "outnumber and oppress the rest."[37]

Madison does not discuss his conception of justice in any detail in *Federalist* 10, so one is forced to look elsewhere to find it. There is perhaps no better place to look than to his classic defense of religious freedom presented to the Virginia legislature to develop Madison's conception of "first principles." What is wrong with a bill requiring citizens to pay a relatively small sum to support an established religion? Such a requirement, Madison contends, is profoundly obnoxious to the dignity and respect that are the birthrights of all rational creatures. Madison reminds his fellows that Virginia recognizes in its own Declaration of Rights that "all men are by nature equally free and independent" even if it sometimes forgets what this entails. The bill in question violates this presumption of equality by requiring that citizens favor one conception of religious worship not because they are persuaded by it but because they are compelled to do so by the state.

Moreover, the *right* to worship as one sees fit is the correlate of a *duty* each person has toward his Creator. Madison is never more Lockean than when he deals with on this point. Each person is duty-bound "to render to the Creator such homage, and such only, as he believes to be acceptable to [the Creator]."[38] This duty is prior to any the person undertakes as a member of a political community and, therefore, cannot be overridden by communal preferences as defined by a majority. It is the nature of just social agreements that they require no more from one party than they demand from another when fundamental rights are at stake. Thus,

> whilst we assert for ourselves a freedom to embrace, to profess and to observe the Religion which we believe to be of divine origin, we cannot deny an equal freedom to those whose minds have not yet yielded to the evidence which has convinced us. . . . It degrades from the equal rank of Citizens all those whose opinions in Religion do not bend to those of the Legislative authority.[39]

This language was to be echoed by Madison and his fellow delegates in the declaration issued by the Virginia ratifying convention urging the ratification of the Constitution. During that convention, Madison had argued that "there is no shadow of right in the general government to intermeddle with religion. Its least interference with it would be a most flagrant usurpation."[40] After asserting that there are "certain natural rights of which men, when they form a social compact cannot deprive or divest their posterity," the delegation urged a bill of rights to reassert this and better assure their protection.[41] Among these natural rights was one of religious worship. "That religion or the duty we owe our Creator and the manner of discharging it can be directed only by reason and conviction, not by force or violence, and therefore all men have an equal, natural right and unalienable right to the free exercise of religion according to the dictates of conscience."[42] Parenthetically, Madison adds in a later piece that it is no defense of established religion to claim that religious faith is the social cement of the civic order. There is a sharp aversion to a Rousseauian civil religion in his remarks. It is crude, even cynical, he argues, to use religion "as an engine of Civil policy." To do so is "an unhallowed perversion of the means of salvation."[43] That the Madisonian state is obligated to remain neutral with respect to religious worship can be derived from the duty each person has to worship God in a manner deemed most pleasing to Him.[44] The nature of this manner remains fundamentally contestable and its determination devolves to the individual.

This defense of religious worship cannot be extended to all the rights Madison defends, however central it is to Lockean liberalism. Nonetheless, it is clear that Madison extends his neutrality principle beyond the case of religious worship. Moreover, the proposed Constitution will assure the state's neutrality among conceptions of the good, a task at which state governments under the Articles were failing. In Madison's short catalogue of the "vices" of the political system under the Articles, Madison contends that

> the great desideratum in Government is such a modification of the sovereignty as will render it *sufficiently neutral* between the different interests and factions, to controul one part of the society from invading the rights of another, and at the same time sufficiently controulled itself, from setting up an interest adverse to that of the whole Society [emphasis added]."[45]

Monarchies fail this test. Though the monarch is "sufficiently neutral towards his subjects," he frequently sacrifices their interests to his own aggrandizement. In small republics, there is rarely a strong central government to be feared by the whole society but the "sovereign will" is "not sufficiently neutral toward the parts composing it."[46]

Madison's argument for the best way to secure neutrality presented in this piece prefigures his argument in *Federalist* 10. An "enlargement of the sphere" will "lessen the insecurity of private rights."[47] This is not because people in large republics are less susceptible to the narrowly partial or self-regarding prejudices of those in small ones but because there are more obstacles to their success in achieving them.[48]

Among those fundamental rights an "enlarged sphere" will help protect are freedoms of speech and of the press. Madison had little cause to offer a philosophical defense of free speech during the debates over the Constitution. It was, after all, not a contested principle. In fact, the Anti-Federalist opposition argued, if anything, for a specific and forceful assertion of it in a bill of rights.[49] Madison considered the nature of this right most directly while working on the Virginia and Kentucky Resolutions in response to the passage of the Alien and Sedition Acts in 1798. And even here he is more intent on arguing against a narrow interpretation of the meaning of the free speech clause of the First Amendment to the Constitution—that it was meant only to bar prior restraint on publications and not *all* regulation of the press by the national government.[50]

Madison does provide, however, a brief defense of free speech qua free speech in the following form. The power to regulate the press is an especially fearful power to vest with government as "it is levelled against the right of freely examining public characters and measures, and of free communication thereon, which has ever been justly deemed the only effectual guardian of every other right."[51]

Madison's claim will be familiar to readers of John Stuart Mill's *On Liberty*. To be sure, freedom of the press results in "some degree of abuse" that may occur from the improper use of any good thing. Yet, as Madison eloquently states, "it is better to leave a few of its noxious branches to their luxuriant growth, than, by pruning them away, to injure the vigour of those yielding the proper fruits."[52] As a case in point, Madison contends that free dialogue was a necessary condition leading to the adoption of the 1787 Constitution by bringing to light both its strengths and the defects of the Articles of Confederation.[53] When public characters and measures cannot be examined freely their defects cannot be brought to light. The truth emerges, Madison suggests, from a debate that explicitly allows for the statement of even patently false or excessive ideas.

In sum, the liberal commitments of Hamilton and Madison are seen in their understanding of the problem of social cooperation among citizens with competing goals, a problem that classical liberal thinkers from Hobbes on had formulated and sought to resolve. Yet this is only part of the story. Madison's defense of the Constitution, more than Hamilton's, is moral as well as instrumental. Whether we look at his derivation of property rights or his defenses of freedom of worship and speech, rights-based contractarian arguments play vital roles. Essential to each is the notion that the liberal state *must* offer justifications of political power that are defensible from the standpoint of *each* individual, and not merely for the aggregate good they produce. Moreover, a liberal polity rests on a public dialogue in which this exercise of power can be justified to free, equal, and rational persons.

We may quarrel with particulars of Madison's arguments (as I have with his discussion of property rights) but this general outline seems clear. Free speech is vital and is a "guardian" of other rights as it is *essential* to a public dialogue within which power can be justified. Free discussion may point to the defects in whole forms of government (for example, in the debate over the Articles of Confederation) or in the conduct of particular wielders of power in a settled polity. Freedom of worship is an absolute principle since individuals have prior duties to their Creator which cannot be overridden by political majorities. Also, given inevitable uncertainties about the "proper" manner for worshiping God, *any* public law regulating forms of worship is fundamentally unjustifiable to other citizens. It can only be, therefore, an exercise in force, not in reason or persuasion and is objectionable on that ground as well.

There is much that can be questioned in Madison's conception of justice if taken as a whole. What cannot be questioned is that Madisonian justice rests squarely in the liberal social contract tradition and on a fundamental premise of liberal equality. When the state "protects faculties" or respects religious diversity, it is doing not only what is expedient but what is right.

Now citizens left to their own devices will fail quite often to act as justice demands. There is no denying Madison's, or Hamilton's, "realism" on this score. They do not believe, however, that the people are incapable of the sorts of virtues required to sustain a liberal state. More important, the likelihood that people will act to maintain a just order is quite a different sort of question than that of offering criteria of justice itself. Madison's and Hamilton's pessimism on the propensity of citizens to do as justice requires does not negate the moral nature of the derivation of principles of justice. The following chapter will take up the question of the sources and types of civic virtue the authors of *The Federalist* see as necessary and possible in the American context.

6

Publius's Liberalism and Civic Virtue

This sir, is my great objection to the Constitution, that there is no true responsibility—and that the preservation of liberty depends on the single chance of men being virtuous enough to make laws to punish themselves.
—PATRICK HENRY, THE VIRGINIA RATIFYING CONVENTION

Ambition must be made to counteract ambition. . . . It may be a reflection on human nature that such devices should be necessary to control the abuses of government. But what is government itself but the greatest of all reflections on human nature?

—JAMES MADISON, *Federalist* 51

Patrick Henry's "great objection to the Constitution"[1] is fascinating on a number of counts. Supporters of the Constitution[2] are derided for their facile faith that the virtue of those in power is a sufficient safeguard of liberty. It is an objection he turns to time and again. Thus, he informs his fellow convention delegates that "notwithstanding what gentlemen say of our representatives, I dread the depravity of human nature," wishing to protect against it "by proper checks." He "will never depend on so slender a protection as the possibility of being represented by virtuous men."[3] Moreover, "all checks founded on anything but self-love will not avail" to protect liberties.[4]

Henry's view that the best defenders of the Constitution rely excessively on "virtue" in their proposed new order is a startling claim to readers of *Federalist* 10 and 51, where the decidedly nonangelic aspects of human nature are given prominence. Indeed, it is a valid though partial response to Henry to say that he simply misunderstands and underestimates the "auxiliary precautions" built into the Constitution and thus overstates the extent to which the mere good will of officeholders is required to assure their fidelity to duty. Much of the ingenuity of the system, in particular its claim to attach the interests of the officeholder to his constitutional place, is simply lost on Henry.[5]

Yet this response is not the only one that can be made to Henry's objection.[6] As much as the authors of *The Federalist* share his goal of preserving liberties, they do not intend to denigrate the virtue of those in government charged with their preservation nor that of the people who are to put them into power. Rhetorically, this is a clever strategy. The Federalists, charged with elitism by their opponents, deride the opposition for its lack of confidence in the wisdom and virtue of "the people." But it is a point of principle as well. Neither Madison nor Hamilton believe that the proposed constitutional order will remain stable if rulers and citizens are not disposed to see to its maintenance, although, as we shall see, the motives each has to do so differ.

That citizens would not be disposed to support the government of a large republic is another claim the Anti-Federalists make with some frequency. Publius spends considerable space in refuting this, as he does in supporting his confidence in the fidelity of rulers. In both cases he relies on a complex and, in some regards, original conception of political psychology. His arguments tend to be empirical ones hypothesizing on the causal connections between political and social structures and motivations of individuals to sustain them. In both their empirical form and their substantive content, they echo the most fully articulated political psychology Madison and Hamilton had available to them: that of David Hume.

The political first principles Publius relies on are liberal contractarian ones. This is seen both in his conception of the Constitution as a solution for problems of cooperation peculiar to that tradition of political discourse and in his defense of individual rights and the corresponding obligation to respect the rights to life, liberty, and property of others. Publius shows an acute awareness of the potential instabilities of liberal polities. Publius considers the actual ends individuals are likely to pursue (primarily those of independence, wealth, and power). He then assesses the difficulties the motivations to pursue these ends pose to a rationale for cooperative behavior. This concern impels Publius to develop an argument aimed at establishing the viability of liberal democracy in the United States. To paraphrase Madison, the intent is to find a republican cure for the diseases incident to republics. The solution involves both institutional restraints on governmental powers and an understanding of the bases of allegiance, grounded in a complex moral psychology.

Madison and Hamilton contend that the requisite civic dispositions, the sentiments and habits needed to sustain a liberal polity, are reasonably likely to develop under the proposed constitutional government. Publius presumes as much as in arguing that such traits as *habitual obedience* of law by citizens, *fidelity* by rulers in performing public duties, and *deference* by small-propertied or, in the future, propertyless masses, to ruling elites were needed for stable government. He argues that the main political factors that would foster these traits are the soundness and durability of administration. This argument aids Publius in contending specifically, against the Anti-Federalists that *time* and not the *size* of the polity was the source of the sentiment of allegiance. Therefore, he could hold that, in time, the sentiments of allegiance, which at present principally accrued to state governments, would be transferred, in some degree, to the national one.

Liberal democratic governments require that considerable numbers of ordinary citizens and public officials take seriously the regime's rules of justice and act on the virtues appropriate to them. Any set of political principles and the institutions they inspire that do not engender a citizenry's willingness to sustain them will not endure. A critical exploration of the arguments used by the authors of *The Federalist* to address this issue follows. It includes an evaluation of their effectiveness against the opposition of their time. But it is also concerned with their contribution to political theory, in particular, an American theory of liberal citizenship. With regard to the latter, I will suggest that the Humean stress on habit and custom as bases for allegiance has some troubling implications for both committed liberals and republicans interested in fostering a full-throated political dialogue.

The Obligations of Citizenship: From Theory to Practice

The problems Madison and Hamilton faced in attempting to demonstrate that the proposed constitutional system of government would engender support and remain stable can be summarized as follows:

1. *The obligation argument.* One ought to undertake actions aimed at sustaining the liberal state, which provides the security and benefits one requires as a free agent pursuing self-selected ends.

2. *The empirical-conduct problem.* Human actions are frequently not in accord with the first proposition for a variety of reasons, but mainly because honesty is often *not* the best policy from the standpoint of rational prudence, or from that of the commonly observed selfish or narrowly benevolent passions.

3. *The coercion requirement.* Adequate state sanctions are required for a criterion of justice, for without confidence that others are likely to comply with laws, no one can reasonably be asked to forgo the acquisition of all means they deem necessary for self-protection.

4. *The limits-of-coercion problem.* Though power is required to preserve liberties, there is a point at which power becomes a threat to those liberties. It does so when it reduces, beyond some minimally acceptable point, the sphere of personal freedoms the liberal state is designed to protect.

5. *The virtue requirement.* Liberal democratic states therefore need citizens and rulers with the capacity for moral forbearance in order to be sustained and not to degenerate into tyranny or anarchy.

The onus of Publius's viability argument is to show that the requirement of virtue can be satisfied without violating fundamental freedoms. In none of these five propositions does Publius employ concepts or see problems not also evident to most of his audience. Publius breaks new ground only in arguing that the requirement of virtue can be met under a federated, national republic. Reconstructing this argument requires, first, an examination of Publius's moral psychology. It also requires drawing up a civic personality profile to which he would subscribe. I will suggest that Publius's concept of "human nature" and his notion of civic virtue are linked by way of his understanding of the natural and prudential motives for conduct that incline people, as he imagines them, to exhibit the civic virtue he thinks necessary.

The first of two problems of allegiance and civic virtue pertains to those traits as displayed by ordinary citizens. The second and equally pressing concern is that of the fidelity of public officials to their duties. Though Madison and Hamilton have confidence in the capacity of the proposed constitutional system to engender both while protecting against weakness in either, somewhat different psychological explanations are offered for each.

The allegiance problem pertaining to ordinary citizens is addressed by Hamilton in *Federalist* 27, in which he begins with a general psychological observation. Hamilton states that there are two general rules, that help explain the sources of a sense of allegiance and the concomitant disposition to act on it. First, he suggests that the people's "confidence in and obedience to a government will commonly be proportioned to the goodness or badness of its administration." Exceptions to this rule depend "so entirely on accidental causes" that they are not worth considering in any depth.[7] His second generalization is more strictly psychological, although with political implications: "Man is very much a creature of habit," so that

> the more the operations of the national authority are intermingled in the ordinary exercise of government, . . . [and] the further it enters into those objects which touch the most sensible chords and put in motion the most active springs of the human heart, the greater will be the probability that it will conciliate the respect and attachment of the community. . . . A government continually at a distance . . . can hardly expect to interest the sensations of the people.[8]

Hamilton's suggestion that sound administration and habit are sources of a sense of allegiance directly parallels Hume's notion of this sense in his discussion of *opinions of interest* and *opinions of right*. The former are required so that citizens sense that the existing government is generally advantageous to their interests, which it is if it has sufficient power to perform, and adequately does perform, the essential tasks of the liberal state. These tasks, amounting to the provision of peace, internal order and justice, and promotion of prosperity through the regulation of commerce, are described throughout *The Federalist* and are listed in Article I, Section 8, of the Constitution. Opinions of right are required to promote regime-supporting behavior, since the sense of general advantage is frequently overridden by the sense of the particular disadvantages that maintaining the plan of cooperation imposes.

Yet even as Hume and Publius share theoretical affinities on this point, they employ their arguments with different intentions. While Hume's allegiance argument is one step removed from current political debate (although his attempt to cut the ground out from under explicit natural-rights thinkers has a clearly conservative political intent), Publius makes his case as a statebuilder with an active political opposition. He therefore must demonstrate that the government he proposes can not only meet the virtue requirement within liberal norms, but that it is better equipped to do so than the alternative(s) suggested by his Anti-Federalist opponents. Moreover, he must do so despite his recognizing that the state governments, whose powers he seeks to diminish, have marked advantages over a national one in appealing to the interests and affections of their citizens.

In *Federalist* 45, Hamilton argues that the states will retain several of these advantages even upon accepting the proposed Constitution. This is explained in part by the states' retention of powers extending "to all objects which, in the ordinary course of affairs, concerns the lives, liberties, and properties of the people, and internal order . . . , and prosperity of the State."[9] And "being the immediate and visible guardian of life and property, . . . regulating all those personal interests and familiar concerns to which the sensibility is most immediately awake," states have an advantage over the national government in "impressing upon the minds of the people affection, esteem, and reverence toward government."[10]

The utility of state government is more evident to citizens than are the benefits they will receive from a strong national one, because states are the main protectors of rights through their justice systems and the main providers of collective goods. Thus, they are the main beneficiaries of that sense of approbation which derives from prudential sources. Since the objects of national government relate to "more general interests," it will be "less apt to come home to the feelings of the people; and . . . less likely to inspire an *habitual sense of obligation* and an active sentiment of attachment [emphasis added]."[11] The only noted exception to this tendency was the period of "transient enthusiasm" felt for the national congress during and immediately after the Revolution. Before long, however, the "attention and attachment" of the people turned back to state affairs.[12]

State governments benefit from a sense of approbation derived from the social and selfish passions as well. With regard to the latter, states control the dispersal of those "regular honors and emoluments which produce an attachment to government." Thus, "all the passions . . . , of avarice, ambition, interest, which govern most individuals, and all public bodies, fall into the current of the States, and do not flow into the stream of the General Government."[13] In Hamilton's view, the fact of this source of state loyalty is liable to render any confederacy unstable, since acts of national sovereignty are likely to be resisted by those whose official power and prestige are weakened by them.

With regard to the social passions, Publius takes note of the nonprudential or natural attachments which accrue more to the states. Madison mentions in *Federalist* 46, for example, the ties of "personal acquaintance and friendship, and of family and party attachments" between office holders and voters that reinforce state loyalties.[14] Such ties are evidently grounded in feelings of benevolence and trust toward those with whom we have intimate contact, though he sees no need to elaborate on this point.

It is important to note, however, that natural loyalties to the locality, however praiseworthy their source, cannot be used in themselves as arguments against the legitimacy of the proposed federal government. Hamilton makes this point in *Federalist* 15, where he notes that the natural "predilection" felt for "local objects . . . can hardly fail to mislead the decision" to sufficiently empower a national sovereign.[15] If local affections, in fact, if passions of any sort, blind one to recognition of principles of justice which must be instituted on a national scale to be effective, there is no virtue in them. This point reinforces Madison's argument that the importance of individual states is a secondary consideration when compared to that of any government's capacity to provide for the happiness of its people.[16]

Publius's enumeration of motives ranging from avarice to benevolence gives an indication of the type of legitimacy problems his proposed government is likely to face. The requirement of virtue can only be met if the interests and passions of men, taken as they are, can be channeled to support the state. Hamilton states the problem in his June 18 speech to the Constitutional Convention, which he concludes by arguing that "government must be so constituted as to offer strong motives [of support] . . . [i]n short, to interest all the *passions* of individuals . . . [a]nd turn them into that channel."[17]

Hume had explored with great acuity the ways in which the passions and interests become converted into supports for the political regime. Publius's particular argument is that the constitutional government is able to engender support even without the bounty of custom (initially) which was so essential to Hume's account of allegiance. To establish this point, he must persuade his audience that the primary attachments and prudentially based sentiments that currently accrue to the states can be reduced in force, while others can be redirected sufficiently to provide support for the national government.

Fundamental to Hamilton's argument on civic allegiance is the notion that the government must be deemed generally advantageous by the bulk of citizens to gain their support. This is the sense behind Hamilton's first general rule cited above. Without some grounding in this prudentially based motive, it is unlikely that the national government could ever sufficiently command the loyalty of citizens so as to override their natural attachments to the states. Hamilton observes this by noting as a "fact of human nature" that

> affections are commonly weak in proportion to the distance or diffusiveness of the object. Upon the same principle that a man is more attached to his family than to his neighborhood, to his neighborhood than to the community at large, the people of each State would be apt to feel a strong bias toward their local governments than toward the government of the Union; *unless the force of that principle should be destroyed by a much better administration of the latter* [emphasis added]."[18]

Hamilton does not explain why this sense of general advantage is of sufficient force to override natural, benevolent sentiments that primarily benefit the states. But it is less surprising that he could make this argument regarding state loyalties than if it had been made pertaining to family or neighborhood affections. In those instances, it would seem patently absurd to suggest that such attachments could be overridden by more general interests. That this case can be made regarding the states reflects Publius's opinion, as expressed by

Madison but consented to by Hamilton, that the individual states are already too large in population and area, and too diverse in interests, to bear much resemblance to small, local units. The states do not even have much in common with the ancient republics, which could claim with some validity to be bound in a single purpose by ties of benevolence. The ancient republics' "dimensions [were] far short of the limits of almost every one of these [American] states."[19]

Hamilton's thesis seems to be that a certain affection for the central government will steal into the hearts of its citizens if it performs its functions reasonably well. He claims that the national government can gain its citizens' allegiance as it becomes "more intwined" with the ordinary lives of citizens. Yet, it poses no threat to the states even as loyalty to it grows. Though Hamilton does not say so directly, one can surmise that *if* it comes to pass that the citizens of New York, Virginia, and other states come to feel a stronger attachment to the nation, this indicates a failure on the part of the individual states in their basic tasks of protecting rights and providing public goods. Attachments to the national government emerge in a manner that is non-threatening to the states and is noncoercive. It relies largely on the consolidation of general advantage into habit.

One can draw from Hamilton's discussion of this process a positive as well as a negative connotation. From a liberal point of view, it is surely desirable that citizens fulfill civic duties voluntarily and do so because the state is seen as an important instrument in the preservation and, indeed, encouragement of their private pursuits. There is no derision intended by describing the state's function as "instrumental" here. One can feel a great deal of affection for instruments that are vital to one's own good, as the carpenter might toward a lathe or plane, for example. The carpenter will likely feel a desire to look after those tools, to clean and polish them to keep them in good working order and perhaps even pleasing to the eye and hand. That one has some such feeling toward the state is an indication, according to Hamilton's diagnosis, that things are going properly.

From a republican perspective, Hamilton's line of argument is disconcerting, especially in its view of the ends of the state. For civic republicans, political institutions are justified primarily in terms of their capacity to provide opportunities for the development of the moral and rational faculties of citizens through civic participation. It should be clear that Hamilton shows no such understanding of the role of the state in the place where one might most expect it: that is, in a discussion of the basis of the affection the individual feels for the political regime. Hamilton displays no great interest either in offering a definitive conception of the "good life" or in arguing for the national government (or the state governments, for that matter) as a means to its realization.

There is, however, a second, more subtle, concern that either a committed liberal *or* a republican critic of Hamilton might make. This has to do with the psychological nature of the attachment he—and Madison—describe. Although attachment to the state has its origins in an opinion of interest, as it takes hold as an opinion of right it is stripped of virtually all cognitive content and becomes little more than a habit not subject to rational criticism. Now there is nothing inherently antirepublican about stressing the importance of habit or, indeed, a stress on the emotional bases of attachment toward the political order. We do not think less of the patriot if he cannot explain his love of country. Moreover, if Aristotle is the fountainhead of classical republican thought, it is worth remembering that moral education was principally for him the inculcation of good habits. Morals, he contended, can only be taught to the person who already possesses a good character.[20]

Nonetheless, it *is* consistent with contemporary understandings of republicanism that political first principles should not be taken as givens, but should be subject to public deliberation and alteration if the moral understanding of the political community so requires.[21] Liberals too, if liberalism is taken to be a dialogue requiring justification of political power to a community of free and equal rational beings, should seek a similar sort of justificatory dialogue. And it was just such a dialogue that Hamilton and Madison hope to avoid, at least once the messy business of constitution making was settled.

Madison expresses a desire to avoid this justificatory dialogue perhaps more sharply than Hamilton. Madison's aversion is grounded in an understanding of the need for government to attain the habitual support of its citizens and the ways in which debates about first principles and constitutional reform can inhibit the habituation process. It is also based in part on his beliefs about the socioeconomic development of the polity, which would make resolutions of constitutional controversies more difficult in the not too distant future. These views are expressed in responses to Jefferson, both in *The Federalist* and elsewhere, on the desirability of frequent constitutional conventions, and in what I will call his propitious-moment argument.

Madison rejects Jefferson's radical contractarian idea that living generations can bind only themselves, since an explicit consent to the terms of the social contract by the governed is a condition of legitimate rule. Madison recognizes that Jefferson's idea embodies the "spirit of Philosophical legislation," that is, that the principle is correct in theory.[22] Nonetheless, Jefferson's call for periodic constitutional conventions must be rejected on empirical grounds. In a world of disinterested philosophers, it is conceivable that periodic renegotiation of the terms of social cooperation would usher in mutually beneficial reforms that reflect the acquired wisdom of new generations under new circumstances. Taking human beings as we know them, however, we can expect that each party will try to renegotiate the contract in terms most favorable to himself regardless of the just claims of present property holders to the current distribution of social product. Under temporary laws whose expiration could be readily anticipated, "all the rights depending on positive laws, that is, most of the rights of property, would become absolutely defunct, and the most violent struggles [would] ensue between the parties interested in reviving, and those interested in reforming the antecedent state of property."[23] Frequent supersession of the "obligations dependent on antecedent laws" weakens the "sense of them" and thus "cooperate[s] with motives to licentiousness already too powerful." Under these conditions, no one can count on the rewards of his own industry, so that industry is discouraged and society as a whole suffers because of it. Thus, the notion of tacit consent, despite Madison's recognition of its questionable philosophical standing, is necessary for stability and industry.[24] Further, it ought to be presumed essentially except where explicit discontent with the current state of affairs is too loud to ignore.

Madison addresses with some regularity this theme of fostering the presumption of consent of the governed while opposing the establishment of political mechanisms, such as periodic constitutional conventions, that explicitly renew this consent. A central component of his argument is the idea that habit, or prejudice, is among the most powerful motives to curb licentiousness. To the extent that a habitual sense of obligation is widespread, natural urges toward selfish gain at the expense of the public good will be at least partly neutralized. The weakening of habits of obedience is the consequence most to be feared in proposals like Jefferson's. "Would not," Madison asks, "a Government so often revised become too mutable and novel to retain that share of prejudice in its favor which is salutary aid to the most rational Government?"[25]

He resumes discussion of this theme in *Federalist*, 49 where he again responds to Jefferson's call for frequent conventions. Each convention would "carry an implication of some defect in the government" and frequent ones would "deprive the government of the veneration which time bestows on everything, and without which perhaps the wisest and freest government would not possess the requisite stability."[26] This veneration, a necessary restraint on selfish inclinations, seems to be an offshoot of the general psychological law that time breeds familiarity which, in turn, breeds affection. In the case of government, time does its work as long as certain provisos are met. These provisos are that government be well-administered and perceived to be generally advantageous. Beyond this, love of the republic is not attributed, except very indirectly, to any moral qualities of the state, but simply to the fact that it will grow old.

The habitual obedience to law that Madison describes is a virtue for him only if the laws themselves are just. This means that they respect the rights of minorities, whether of religious sects or of property owners. It is less clear to him, however, that small property owners and the propertyless masses of the future would recognize property rights and respect them in the future. Madison especially fears that impending economic changes would heighten class antagonisms and make this assumption particularly problematic. Here again preserving fundamental rights will depend in part on the success of appeals to sentiments in inculcating a habitual sense of allegiance. It will also depend on settling fundamental constitutional disputes as soon as possible.

Madison's subscription to this propitious moment argument is indicated in the following set of considerations. In the Virginia ratifying convention, he describes as the "great republican principle" the proposition that "the people will have sufficient virtue and intelligence to select men of virtue and wisdom."[27] Yet he suggests in the Philadelphia convention and elsewhere that, as time goes on, it will become increasingly uncertain that the people will act as this principle requires.

> In framing a system which we wish to last for ages, we should not lose sight of the changes which the ages will produce. An increase in population will of necessity increase the proportion of those who will labour under all the hardships of life, and secretly sigh for a more equal distribution of its blessings. These may in time outnumber those who are placed above the feelings of indigence.[28]

Madison further notes that "symptoms of a levelling spirit" are already present and that they "give notice to future danger."[29] At some future time, the near-indigent majority is unlikely to consider existing property distributions or the government that legally enforces them to be either just or generally advantageous. They will then, to paraphrase Hume, have lost a considerable motive to virtue.

It is reasonable to surmise that Madison has this situation of increased class divisions and likely class antagonism in mind when he tried to convince Jefferson that periodic constitutional conventions, by legitimizing renegotiation of existing property relations, are likely to lead to injustice. It is better, he suggests, to resolve constitutional issues now and not to raise them again, since raising them again might invite a reconsideration of rights and be detrimental to justice. The discontent, even the suffering, of the masses does not constitute evidence of injustice or legitimate grounds for renegotiation as long as the current property distribution has not resulted from the violation of rules of just acquisition. These rules embody the "principle of natural law" that each has "an exclusive right to the portions of the ground with which he has incorporated his labor and improvements."[30]

Madison faces a two-pronged problem. First, in the future, the people will be increasingly unlikely to show the moral forbearance required to sustain a liberal democratic polity. Second, any redistribution to remedy their dissatisfactions would be unjust by liberal norms at least as Madison understands them.[31] His response to this problem includes both institutional arrangements and appeals to the affections. And it was an issue he would return to later in life when he reflects on discussions in the Constitutional Convention over property qualifications for suffrage. In the convention, he had suggested, but did not vigorously fight for, a freeholder qualification for congressional elections. "In future times," he had argued, "a great majority of the people will not only be without land, but any other sort of, property." These people will "combine under the influence of their common situation; in which case, the rights of property & public liberty" will not be secure.[32] It is still evident to him some thirty-four years later that propertyless citizens are less likely to respect these rights than secure, propertied citizens. But by 1821 he suggests that this problem must be addressed by other means.[33] The democratization of the American electorate in the intervening years made the prospect of introducing new property qualifications for the vote unpalatable. Under present circumstances, Madison wrote that the security for the holders of property when the minority, can only be derived from the ordinary influence possessed by property, & the superior information incident to its holders; from the *popular sense of injustice* enlightened and enlarged by a diffusive education; and from the difficulty of combining & effectuating unjust purposes throughout an extensive country [emphasis added]."[34]

There is an instructive tension in this later writing between Madison's liberal egalitarianism in the political sphere and the ways in which it can conflict in practice with legitimate claims of property rights. If property qualifications for voting are ruled out by "public opinion," it is no less true that Madison has come to find them objectionable on moral grounds. It is, he notes, "the enterprize inspired by free Institutions, that great wealth in the hands of individuals and associations, may not be unfrequent."[35] And, while Madison fears that such property holders may be unjustly expropriated by propertyless majorities, he also expresses the dangers to public liberty brought about by "a dependence of an increasing number on the wealth of a few."

Moreover, the protection of property cannot justify restrictions on suffrage if "it violates the vital principle of free Government that those who are to be bound by laws, ought to have a voice in making them."[36] The goal of consensual government makes it "indispensable" that the mass of citizens have an electoral voice and, if a choice must be made between "an equal & universal suffrage for each branch of the Government and a confinement of the *entire* right to a part of Citizens," then the former should be selected. It is better for property owners to lose the right to be represented, both as persons qua persons and as a protected class, than for the propertyless to lose their political voice altogether.

The Madison of 1787 seems less troubled by the inegalitarian consequences of liberal capitalist development. His concern is that potentially divisive issues be put behind the nation so that an era of normal politics played according to settled rules could emerge. Yet, even if one senses some regret about these consequences in the Madison of 1821, it is not a regret on which he will act. Liberal principles of justice in acquisition—as he understands them—rule out redistributions that may be justified on other grounds (even, for Madison, grounds of liberal equality). In any case, the Madison of 1787 was primarily concerned that political debates with potentially redistributive consequences be foreclosed for the foreseeable future. Doing so had two advantages. First, it would avoid the inevitable inference that periodic constitutional conventions would give rise to—that there is some defect in the government. Second, it would create a period of stability, which is required for time to do its work on the affections. It would do so, however, at the price of restricting public deliberation on political first principles which republican ideology, and, in my view, a consistent liberal ideology as well, demand.

Communitarian and neorepublican critics of *The Federalist* have stressed the alleged tendency of that work to advocate an essentially privatistic, even apathetic body of citizens. These critics focus their attention on largely on *Federalist* 10 and 51, where Madison expresses perhaps his most cynical view of human nature, pronouncing on the narrowly self-interested motives for political action and the instrumental role played by the state in managing conflict over scarce goods. According to this characterization, within the framework of "Madisonian democracy," political participation is undertaken to promote group or individual interests. These critics stress essential social divisions between those interests with sufficient financial, organizational, and constituency resources to gain access to the political process and the masses lacking these resources. The political activity of the masses, including their electoral participation, is seen to be more expressive than instrumental, the essential function of which is to periodically relegitimize the regime.[37]

There is some support for such a reading of Madison in his remarks quoted in this chapter and it derives in part from an understanding of political psychology he shared with David Hume. The republican critique, however, tends at times to present Madisonian democracy as an amoral bargaining arrangement. Yet the liberties Madison seeks to protect are valuable from the moral point of view and the government that protects them is more than a modus vivendi among equally legitimate claimants to political power and social resources. In examining the arrangements Madison defends to "break or control the violence of faction," we ought not lose sight of his raison d'être for such arrangements. They are essential for persons to be able to develop and act on rational life plans even if these are contrary to popular sentiments or considerations of public good. We may not endorse the full catalogue of rights Madison defends, but this need not concern us here. There is ample room in the liberal tradition today to debate whether, for example, principles of justice require minimally restricted libertarian property rights, or whether they demand a more egalitarian distribution of resources or welfare. What especially impresses Madison is the fragility of basic liberties and the importance of devising institutional means and encouraging habits and beliefs that will protect them. He is particularly sensitive to the need government has for citizens' noncognitive support and he seeks to promote such support with a wide array of psychological appeals.

Madison's defense of a bill of rights during the First Congress is an interesting case in point, since he displays both the sense of fragility already referred to and the subtleties of his political psychology. In the following remark, he considers the ways in which even "paper barriers" can be useful in generating psychological support for the regime.

> It may be thought that all paper barriers against the power of the community are too weak to be worthy of attention. I am sensible they are not so strong as to satisfy gentlemen of every description who have seen and examined thoroughly the texture of such a defense; yet, as they have a tendency to impress some degree of respect for them, to establish the public opinion in their favor, and rouse attention of the whole community, it may be one means to control the majority from those acts which they might be otherwise inclined.[38]

This endorsement of a bill of rights is something of a change of heart for Madison and a concession to political realities.[39] The thrust of Madison's argument here is that paper barriers are not a stone wall; although they cannot protect against hurled sticks and stones, they can at least keep out a mild chill. Curiously, Madison admits that such barriers will be ineffective against the more knavish members of the community who "have seen and examined . . . the texture of such a defense." These ingenious few will devise arguments calling into question the defense of rights the bill of rights presents. Nonetheless, a written document, Madison argues presciently, tends to "impress some degree" of favor among the public at large and "may be one means" to control majority faction.

It is hard to think of another passage of Madison's with more hedges than this one. He is keenly aware that paper barriers are best backed with stone or iron reinforcements. What is more peculiar in this passage, however, is the claim that the *mere existence* of such a document will generate some respect for it and, surreptitiously perhaps, for the principles it embodies. Moreover, they will do so best among citizens who reflect least on these principles, those who do not "examine thoroughly" the texture of such a defense.

Ironically, several recent scholars have traced Madison's initial opposition to the inclusion of a bill of rights in the Constitution to similar sorts of reasoning that we see in his somewhat faint-hearted endorsement of the bill in the First Congress. In *The Federalist*, Madison asks rhetorically whether a bill of rights is "essential to liberty" and reminds his readers that the Confederation had none.[40] Hamilton had made the more extreme claim that "the Constitution is itself, in every rational sense, and to every useful purpose, A BILL OF RIGHTS." The Constitution, he argues, does all such a bill is supposed to do. It "declare[s] and specif[ies] the political privileges of the citizens in the structure and administration of the government"; it defines certain "immunities and modes of proceeding, which are relative to public and private concerns." The "substantial meaning" of a bill of rights is, therefore, found in the proceedings of the Constitutional Convention and, of course, in the document itself.[41] Moreover, protections of liberties are ultimately provided by Humean means, that is, by public opinion.

The question remains why Madison and Hamilton wished to exclude a bill of rights initially despite its popularity and an agreement, especially on Madison's part, with the sorts of rights it would protect. Here one must surmise from the context of the debate over this issue and from writings on other subjects, since there is little textual explanation to be found. The Anti-Federalists tended to conceive of a bill of rights as a statement of unalterable natural rights that should *precede* the text of the Constitution to exhort and to educate readers politically. The problem with this view, argues Herbert Storing, is that it can "undermine stable and effective government."

> The Virginia Declaration of Rights asserted that free government depends on a "frequent recurrence to first principles." The Federalists doubted that. Recurrence to first principles does not substitute for well-constituted and effective government. In some cases, it may interfere. Does a constant emphasis on unalienable natural rights foster good citizenship or a sense of community? Does a constant emphasis on popular sovereignty foster responsible govern-

ment? . . . The Federalists did not doubt that these principles were true, . . . that they provide the ultimate source and justification of government. The problem is that these principles, while true, can also endanger government. Even rational and well-constituted governments need and deserve a presumption of legitimacy and permanence. A bill of rights *that presses the first principles to the fore* tends to deprive government of that presumption.[42]

Walter Berns seconds this analysis of the harmful consequences of a statement of natural rights in the Constitution. "However true," he writes, "such a statement might serve to undermine or destabilize government, even government established on those principles."[43] Both view Madison's skillful managing of the adoption of the first ten Amendments to the Constitution, which eliminated references to "first principles," as the culmination of his work as "Father of the Constitution."

Now it is not clear from Storing or Berns why expounding a theory of fundamental rights cannot foster a sense of community or common good. Contemporary liberals certainly tend to reject such a suggestion. Rawls, for example, argues tellingly that a political community which guarantees to each person that her vital interest will not be traded off for the good of society as a whole or for the "perfection" of some set of its members is likely to engender a stronger sense of community among autonomous citizens than a society based on nonliberal (for Rawls, utilitarian or perfectionist) ideologies.[44]

Nonetheless, Storing and Berns are persuasive in claiming that Madison at least had these fears. And perhaps we understand why he hedges when discussing the potential beneficial effects of a bill of rights as a paper barrier against oppression. We have already seen his reluctance to provide for debate of first principles in the future and to foster a sense of consent of the governed while minimizing the opportunities for actualizing this consent.

To the sophisticated contemporary reader, Madison's concern that these first principles be deemphasized, at least as a popular language for justifying political power is, perhaps, an unsurprising attestation to his much-vaunted realism. Yet, on closer examination, his position becomes clearer and, I suspect for many of us, somewhat disturbing. it contains a paradox deeply embedded in liberal political theory. The conception of the state of nature as a domain in which natural rights to self-determination in the fullest imaginable sense are exercised, though with some inconveniences, forms a base of comparison with life in civil society. And, in some ways, the latter does not measure up all that well. The state of nature is the freer condition, or so it may seem at first glance. In fact, the political state is required to assure that others do not interfere with each person's pursuit of his own ends. Yet, this added security can easily be conceived as a trade-off against liberty. And the pride of men being what it is, it can be expected that many persons will believe that they could have fended successfully for themselves in the state of nature. Thus, social cooperation imposes greater costs on them than on those with fewer or worse natural endowments. And, as Hobbes had recognized, motives toward justice decline in the same relation.

Nonetheless, natural rights are the true principles on which government was founded and preservation of them is the sole basis of its legitimacy. It seems odd, therefore, to claim that these truths should be, in a sense, suppressed and that "constant expression" of them is incompatible with stable and effective free government. To say that this seems odd is not, however, to claim that it is historically unfamiliar. Madison's concerns mirror those of Hume in his essay, "Of the Original Contract." Hume, too, had balanced a "hypothetical contractarianism" against the considerations of political stability. Though he assented to the former, he believed that the latter could not be sustained if one encouraged persistent appeals to arguments grounding political legitimacy in an initial act of consent by free and equal persons.[45]

Yet, is it not more natural to suppose that recitation of a creed enhances rather than diminishes the propensity to act in light of it and to support the institutions that realize it? I am tempted to ask two further questions. First, if it is better from the standpoint of stability that we do not proudly assert our founding principles, then what should our actual beliefs and attitudes toward government consist in? Second, if first principles derived from natural rights express fundamental truths grounded somehow in Reason, Nature, or God, what is the epistemological status of these actual beliefs and attitudes? It is clearly functional for political stability that government has an ample store of prejudice and veneration in its support, just as it was functional for Plato's ideal republic that his "noble lie" be accepted. One wonders how far this metaphorical likeness ought to be extended.

Stabilizing Government (I): Restricting Participation

The Madison we find in the constitutional period is a considerably more ambivalent character than is sometimes portrayed. A tension exists in his thought between the liberal demands of political equality and the right of (relatively) unrestricted private accumulation of capital. His notion of political equality is internally ambivalent since there is a tension between the formal requirement in a liberal democratic state of consent of the governed and the limits he seeks to place on the exercise of this consent through democratic political institutions. Hence, his ideal citizen is not the informed activist of civics textbooks but a rather more passive figure who generally senses the advantages provided by the national government—and the state governments within a federal system—and pursues peacefully his private pursuits.

Hamilton has a similar understanding of the bases of political allegiance. The average citizen, he suggests, will be virtuous enough if the political system is well administered and durable. His thoughts on allegiance are somewhat less interesting than Madison's only because he rarely expresses Madison's ambivalence whether over the role of a bill of rights, or over the relation between political and economic equality or the scope of political participation. It is unimaginable for Madison to follow Hamilton in describing the people as "a great beast." Hamilton was, according to Woodrow Wilson, a great man though not a great American.[46] The political thought of Madison is perhaps more instructive about the nature of our polity as he was clearly both.

Yet even for Madison, the fears of a participatory citizenship are real and he frequently expresses them. He tends, as his republican and communitarian critics have noted, to associate collective political action with mob rule.[47] Moreover, there is little evidence that he or Hamilton believed that the passive, loyal citizen would be losing anything vital *even* though the constitution admittedly sought to create a political system—and climate—that filtered the best of men from the masses through its electoral process. The protection of liberty and the promotion of prosperity were simply taken by these authors to be higher-order goods for most Americans than was direct and frequent political participation outside of the voting booth. It is difficult for the current observer to say that they were all that wrong in this analysis of the political character of their once and future countrymen, at least where issues of more than a narrow and local scope are concerned.[48]

Madison rejects the views, espoused by republican writers, that political participation is useful, even necessary, in enlarging the horizons of political participants and in broadening their concerns from the merely personal to the broadly political. The most important political contribution of the modern period, he believes, is the notion of political representation. The "total exclusion of the people in their collective capacity" was, in fact, the genius of the American republic.[49] This exclusion is vital to allow for the "distillation" of the most virtuous members of the community from the rest. Moreover, "enlarging the sphere," particularly by having larger congressional districts than the Anti-Federalists favored aided in this filtration process.[50] The larger the district, the less likely elections would be decided based on the potentially corrupting influence of personal acquaintance rather than merit.

These features of Madisonian democracy are familiar enough and they raise two pertinent questions for us. First, what is it precisely about political participation that makes it so frightening and potentially dangerous? Second, why are some people more qualified to rule than others? That is, why are some more likely to be faithful to the obligations of public service and why are the Anti-Federalists wrong in attacking their opponents for relying too heavily on the "virtue" of a few to stabilize the political system?

Responding to the first question again relies on a psychological observation Madison derives in all likelihood from Hume and confirms through experience. Hume had noted that "honor is a great check upon mankind," but, alas, that check weakens among men assembled together. There man seeks the narrow approval of those in his part and "learns to despise the clamor of his adversaries."[51] Madison tells us that "bodies of men are not less swayed by interest than individuals, and are less controlled by the dread of reproach and other motives felt by individuals."[52] Hence, "in all very numerous assemblies, *of whatever characters composed*, passion never fails to wrest the scepter from reason. Had every citizen been a Socrates, every Athenian assembly would still have been a mob [emphasis added]."[53]

A frequent style of argument for Madison is first to state an empirical generalization and then to proceed to the historical experience, preferably in the American context that offers an example of it. He does so in *Federalist* 50, where he makes a case against appeals to the people to prevent and correct infractions of the Constitution. Not surprisingly, Madison finds this to be as bad an idea as the Jeffersonian one of periodical conventions to revise that document. The historical evidence he brings to bear displays quite clearly his notion that passion wrests the scepter from reason in all numerous assemblies. Pennsylvania, he notes, had a Council of Censors in 1783 and 1784 whose mission was to police legislative and executive departments against encroachments on each other. A review of their votes shows to "every unbiased observer" that "*passion*, not *reason*, must have presided over their decisions." The same names, he notes, were on opposite sides on virtually every vote, indicating that the votes were based more upon personal loyalties and/or animosities than on the merits of each case: "When men exercise their reason coolly and freely on a variety of distinct questions, they inevitably fall into different opinions on some of them. When they are governed by a common passion, their opinions, if they are so to be called, will be the same."[54] No doubt few observers today would come to as critical a conclusion about this evidence for "party line" voting, although Madison is well within the limits of the accepted wisdom of his times in decrying the influence of political parties.[55] His particular line of argument indicates nonetheless how deeply he is committed to the Humean assumption that collective activity strips participants not only of their honor but of their reason as well. Madison suggests that their votes cannot even be counted as expressions of opinion. This would suggest that the voters are engaged in at least something of a thought process.

Madison presumes in these statements that participation leads to just the opposite result republicans emphasize. In fact, promoting—or at least not diminishing—the virtue of the people *demands* their exclusion "in their collective capacity" from government. This requirement arises from the diminution of personal responsibility, and hence the restraint of honor one generally finds among people in their private capacities.

Neither Madison nor Hume assert that people are inherently dishonorable, only that they will become so if placed in certain contexts. Madison's clear *political* intent is that they not be so placed. Thus, rights are better secured, people's "happiness" is promoted, and people, in all likelihood, do not miss the participatory opportunities they are effectively denied.

Stabilizing Government (II): Keeping Public Officials Virtuous

The electoral system proposed in the Constitution and defended in *The Federalist*, has been described as a device for "distilling" out "the most virtuous" members of the political community so that *only* the virtuous would be placed in positions of power. One recent scholar has offered the following description, claiming that it refutes the "possessive individualist" reading of Madison dominant among contemporary neorepublican critics: "If Madison took a Hobbesian view, he would have been forced to abandon Montesquieu's view of republics. Unless man can transcend private gain for public good, a republic is impossible. An assertion that such virtue is beyond man dooms the enterprise from the outset, as Madison realized."[56] There is considerable merit to this view. In chapter 2 we took the position that even Hobbes's commonwealth could never emerge if the highest-ordered good for all persons were that they vex and oppress each other. People so motivated would feel comfortable taking their chances in Hobbes's state of nature. Moreover, there would be no basis for a stable agreement among them.

However, even if we accept that Madison subscribes to this process for filtering out the "virtuous," we still have an incomplete description of his project. Virtue is a general concept. Madison's particular conception of it as it pertains to political leaders calls for definition. Conceptions of civic virtue are more likely than conceptions of virtue in general to be related to the value structure of a particular political order. There is a complete coincidence of the two, as Aristotle reminds us, only in the good or just state. As criteria of justice change so do conceptions of the virtues appropriate to them. Hence, tolerance becomes a central virtue in the liberal framework and only a subsidiary one at best in classical thought. For Marxists, it is treated as by and large superfluous, since social antagonism, and therefore intolerance, is removed with the elimination of social classes.

What then is the particular conception of virtue Madison and Hamilton rely upon in discussing officeholders? Clearly they cannot expect the passive allegiance among such men as Publius would like to foster among most citizens. Two general comments about his conception will suffice at the outset. First, Publius may have subscribed to a version of F. Scott Fitzgerald's remark about the wealthy. The wealthy are different from the rest of us only in that they have more money. For Publius, the sorts of men they would like to see in positions of power in the new national government are in no sense members of a different social order. It would not even be proper to describe them as a "natural aristocracy." Rather, they are subject to the same psychological incentives and disincentives, the same complex patterns of motivation, as are all men.

Second, it is well to keep in mind the political context within which Publius's arguments are made. He must respond to Patrick Henry's objection that the constitutional system relies too much on rulers to control themselves. It is, I suspect, this need that leads to such an emphasis in *The Federalist*, especially numbers 10 and 51, on the social and institutional checks and balances which have become the focus in this century of much critical commentary on that work. It is imperative, therefore, that Publius convince his readers that public officials will have incentives to be faithful to the prescribed duties of their offices. In making this case, he again relies on a series of empirical generalizations built on an implicit theory of motivation. It is also essential that he reassure those who might question this theory by accentuating the number of institutional safeguards in place to deter the potential tyrant as well as the petty, self-serving knave.

One of the tacks taken by the authors of *The Federalist* to respond to Anti-Federalist skepticism regarding the probity of public officials in the constitutional system is to question the understanding of human nature out of which this concern arises. Thus, Hamilton observes that the "supposition of universal venality in human nature is little less an error in political reasoning than the supposition of universal rectitude. The institution of delegated power implies that there is a portion of virtue and honor among mankind, which may be a reasonable foundation of confidence. And experience justifies the theory."[57] There is an apparent inconsistency in this observation with Hamilton's endorsement of Hume's view that all men should be assumed knaves when designing political institutions. This is *only* apparently inconsistent, since it is based on the quite realistic expectation that even when all the possible precautions are built into the system, opportunities for malfeasance will remain. "Ethics regulations" can only go so far if the will to act ethically is absent.

Whatever one makes of Hamilton's theoretical consistency, the political importance of making this point is not the least bit obscure. He wants to claim that the Anti-Federalist premise that virtually any opportunity for self-aggrandizement will be taken is simply not justified by experience. We are, to be sure, imperfect beings and should guard against our imperfection. In doing so, however, we should not cut off our noses to spite our faces as we would do if we refused to create an "energetic" government because of irrational fears of abuses of power.

Madison expresses very much the same view in discussing the fidelity of members of the House of Representatives to their duties. "Duty, gratitude, interest, ambition itself," he notes, "are the cords by which they will be bound to fidelity and sympathy with the great mass of people." He recognizes the possibility that such motives may be insufficient "to control the caprice and wickedness of men," but asks, What choice is there?; "are they not all that government will admit, and that human prudence can devise?"[58]

The Anti-Federalists were hard-pressed to disagree with this realistic assessment of the tools with which we must work to assure fidelity. They did question, however, that the proposed Constitution provided for the most effective use of such tools. Small states with small electoral districts were generally considered necessary means to generate the bonds between ruler and subject and the fidelity of rulers. That powers must be checked and that such checks must be in large part social and psychological was a premise Federalists and Anti-Federalists shared. They differed most sharply over their beliefs about the sorts of conditions that would inspire appropriate motivations and, of course, on the structure of institutions that would bring these motives to the fore. And, although one should not attribute causal significance to it, on this point the better argument won.

How the complex motives Madison and Hamilton cite function as supports for fidelity is best seen by discussing their arguments, first, for the basic aims of constitutions in general and, second, for particular institutions in the constitutional design. Madison states what he takes to be the "aim of every political constitution" in *Federalist* 57. This aim "is, or ought to be, first to obtain for rulers men who possess most wisdom to discern, and most virtue to pursue, the common good of the society; and in the next place, to take the most effectual precautions for *keeping them virtuous* whilst they continue to hold their public trust [emphasis added]."[59]

The notion of keeping someone virtuous is puzzling at first glance in that we ordinarily think of virtue as springing from the depths of one's character. From the classical point of view, it is hard to imagine why the truly virtuous person would have to be "kept" that way by some outside force. The Aristotelian virtues, one recalls, are a unity and lead to the happiness of the person who possesses and displays them. The virtuous person has discovered the good life and has no motive to seek such goods as wealth or power—which are only instrumentally valuable—once he has achieved the fullest possible happiness through virtuous actions. Madison clearly does not have this conception in mind. To keep a public official virtuous is to see to it that he does his duty. This does not necessarily entail the claim that doing so is for his own good as well as that of those entrusted to him. Nor does keeping him virtuous necessarily involve appeals to the officeholders' more altruistic sentiments, although these do indeed play some role in Publius's scheme.

What then does keeping someone virtuous entail? There is first and foremost the restraint of free and frequent elections which allow the public to remove the "unvirtuous" from office. Second, there are the familiar "auxiliary precautions," which work to counteract ambition with ambition in government. The separation of powers among the three branches and divided powers within the legislative branch serve to give "those who administer each department the necessary constitutional means and personal motives to resist encroachment of the others."[60] This second constraint relies on the interests of those on whose power I might encroach. But Madison and Hamilton each note that self-interest properly understood leads more often to fidelity to duties than the Anti-Federalists expect. Finally, there are a number of psychological incentives—like gratitude—which steal in on the officeholder and tend to tie him more firmly to his duties to constituents and to the nation.

Duty, gratitude, interest, and ambition itself are the irreplaceable filaments that bind leaders to their public duties. Strengthening these threads and providing institutional safeguards in the event that they fray is the essential task of constitution making. Moreover, their workings, Publius contends, are both more subtle and more reliable than critics of the Constitution note. Interest, for example, provides both an external and an internal restraint on narrowly selfish actions by officials. The external manifestation simply recognizes the likely reactions of those who are encroached upon.[61] Interest as a self-restraint requires a bit more analysis.

It is clear from *The Federalist* that persons often have interested motives to act "factiously" and seek to shift the avoidable costs of cooperation to others. At the same time, interest is connected with the notions of a reasoned conception of duty.[62] The notion of having an interest in something incorporates the idea of an ability to calculate the effects of a number of possible present courses of action on that thing's future viability. This in turn assumes a willingness to sacrifice present satisfactions to future ones where the former, if acted upon, adversely affect the object of interest.[63]

This understanding is evident in the Constitutional Convention when, for example, Madison considers interested motives for the people's agreeing to certain limitations on their political activities as found in the Constitution. Madison asks why the people would approve of a relatively long-termed Senate even though this imposes a constraint on their right to replace unsatisfactory representatives. The people, he suggests, know that they are "liable to temporary errors, through want of information as to their true interest." They might reflect further that they were likely "to err also, from fickleness and passion" and see that a "necessary fence against this danger would be to select a portion of enlightened citizens, whose limited number and firmness might seasonably interpose against such counsels."[64] An interested citizen ought, and on many occasions is even likely, to resist the sirens of potentially harmful passions.

Hamilton argues in a similar vein that self-interest can even at times promote a useful deference on the part of the less educated members of society. There are interested alliances in society as, for example, that between merchants and the lower-class "mechanics and manufacturers." The latter two groups know their limitations and will, therefore, tend to defer to merchants in politics out of largely self-interested motives. Hamilton makes this argument to counter the frequent Anti-Federalist contention that a representative assembly must be, in effect, a statistical sample of the population at large.

> Mechanics and manufacturers will always be inclined, with few exceptions, to give their votes to merchants in preference to persons of their own professions or trades. [They] know that the merchant is their natural patron and friend; and they are aware that however great the confidence they may justly feel in their own good sense, their interests can be more effectually promoted by the merchant than by themselves. They are sensible that their habits in life have not been such as to give them those acquired endowments, without which in a deliberative assembly the greatest natural abilities are for the most part useless.[65]

If Madison's notion of interest entails accepting some constraints now that I might reject in a later heated moment, Hamilton's entails ignoring the vice of pride that might impel me to do for myself what others could better do for me. Interest provides a motive on the one hand for fidelity to the regime and on the other for deference to an elite, both of which are stabilizing forces in Publius's republican scheme of government.

Further, the idea of having an interest suggests a capacity to weigh risks and substitute the pursuit of one satisfaction for another when the first allows for an acceptable level of satisfaction while the second, higher level is less secure. Due to the differing risk assessments of equally rational individuals, this substitution cannot be considered a rule of reason as such. Nevertheless, it is more reasonable to assume that this strategy of minimizing risk will be acted upon than to assume that it would be ignored entirely. Further, this strategy is evident in two controversial positions of the Federalists: first, in the claim that representation in the House of Representatives is large enough to prevent "tyranny" or "aristocracy," and second, in Hamilton's support for an unrestricted right to presidential reelection.

As to the first, Madison counters Anti-Federalist charges that, given the small number of representatives and their distance from the people, congressmen will inevitably form cabals among themselves and disregard constituent interests and constitutional mandates. One of Madison's arguments is that representatives have motives toward fidelity that the Anti-Federalists ignore owing to a simplistic assumption that in any instance where power can be abused, it will be. One of these motives is a recognition by congressmen that the existing system is the source of the authority and esteem they now enjoy. "[I]t must generally happen that a great proportion of the men deriving their advancement from their influence with the people would have more to hope from a preservation of the favor than from innovations in the government subversive of the authority of the people."[66] Whatever the satisfactions tyranny might offer, a significant majority of representatives would probably forgo that pleasure so as not to risk losing the present, not inconsiderable, satisfactions of office.

On this point too Madison seems to have learned from Hume. Hume had noted that in both republics and civilized monarchies, the "supreme authority" has many "honors and advantages" to bestow on magistrates. "The only difference is that, in a republic, the candidates for office must look downward to gain the suffrages of the people. . . . To be successful in the [republican] way it is necessary for a man to make himself *useful* by his industry, capacity or knowledge. . . ."[67] Clearly motives to be industrious emerge from considerations of self-interest. And to fail in these good qualities puts one's office, and the attendant honors and emoluments, at risk. Madison adds only an assessment that most people will be sufficiently averse to risk to stay on the path of virtue.

As to the second position, Hamilton argues that not restricting the reelection of the president promotes his fidelity. Without this provision, his risk-benefit calculus shifts in a harmful direction. "An avaricious man who might happen to fill the office, looking forward to a time when he must at all events yield up the emoluments he enjoyed, would feel a propensity, not easy to be resisted by such a man, to make the best use of the opportunity he enjoyed while it lasted, and might not scruple to have recourse to the most corrupt expedients."[68]

If, on the other hand, he could expect to "prolong his honours by his good conduct, he might hesitate to sacrifice his appetite for them to his appetite for gain."[69] In the case of the President, as well as in the case of Congress a substitution of satisfactions takes place that exemplifies interested motives for fidelity.

Hamilton's discussion of interested motives of and restraints on the presidency is rife with subtle observations. Against those who want the president to possess the sole power to make treaties, Hamilton warns that the "history of human conduct does not warrant that exalted opinion of human virtue which would make it wise in a nation to commit [its] interests. . . . to the sole disposal of a magistrate created and circumstanced as would be a President of the United States."[70] This justifies senatorial advice and consent to treaties, thus restraining the president. This restraint, however, is relaxed a bit by allowing unlimited reelection. Here, Hamilton contends, we are on safer ground. We are not relying on the "superlative virtue" history teaches to be so rare but on the calculation of interests and risk that is engaged in by all rational agents.[71]

If the authors of *The Federalist* follow Hume in seeing to it that it is "by interest we must govern [man]" and "by means of it" make him "cooperate to the public good," they also display the antireductionist tendencies Hume and Adam Smith display in their discussions of moral motives.[72] Interest alone is not adequate to the task of assuring fidelity to public duties. The gratitude of elected officials, especially members of the House of Representatives, to those who put them in office plays a role as well.

Here again, this description of public virtue bears little resemblance to the more exalted classical republican notion. The gratitude Madison describes in *Federalist* 57 as a motive for fidelity on the part of House members feeds quite directly on man's insatiable pride and sensitivity to distinction. Representatives, he argues, "will enter into the public service under circumstances which cannot fail to produce a temporary affection at least to their constituents. There is in every breast a sensibility to marks of honor, of favor, of esteem, and of confidence, which, *apart from considerations of interests*, is some pledge for grateful and benevolent returns [emphasis added]."[73] Madison seems to want to assure potential opponents of the Constitution that their fears of representatives forming cabals of the rich and powerful narrowly pursuing their own aggrandizement are largely unfounded. They are so not only because of the checks and balances built into the constitutional design and not only because of the interested motives of public officials. There is also at work a universal disposition to return benevolence to those who have honored us. Madison can thus claim quite rightly that he is not relying on an unlikely "superlative virtue," to assure fidelity but upon the far more commonly observed—and hence more stable—sensitivity to marks of distinction.

Lest even this view appear too optimistic to some, Madison quickly notes that instances of ingratitude are "but too frequent and flagrant, both in public and private life." But, he adds, "the universal and extreme indignation which it inspires," is proof enough of the "energy and prevalence of the contrary sentiment." And for those who cannot even find it in their own experience to make this concession, Madison adds that it is the representative's "pride and vanity" that will "attach him to a form of government which favors his pretensions and gives him a share in its honors and distinctions."[74] One senses that Madison hopes that if he can convince his readers that even such generally harmful character traits as these can tie the representative to his constituents, the system is indeed more stable and less prone to a cabal of the elite than his opponents contend.

Finally there are more or less pure considerations of duty. Their role emerges most clearly in Madison's discussion of the Senate. The degree of disinterestedness Madison ascribes to the Senate under the Constitution is surprising by contemporary standards and poses a challenge to proto-pluralist interpretations of his thought. In particular, the Senate is not distinguished from the House, as it generally can be today, merely by the different sizes of their constituencies. Madison sees a difference in principle between the two bodies when, for example, he argues in the Philadelphia convention against a proposal that the states pay their senators directly. He opposes this on the grounds that it "would make the Senate like Congress," that is, like the House. Senators would be "the mere Agents and Advocates of State interests and views, instead of being the *impartial umpires and Guardians of justice and general Good* [emphasis added]."[75]

Madison sees the Senate as a quasi-judicial body that serves a dual role. It is at the same time a neutral arbiter promoting justice and a means of representing property. Madison is somewhat clearer about the latter function in the secret proceedings of the Philadelphia conventional although, it should be emphasized, there is no necessary conflict between representing property and promoting justice so long as the former is justly acquired. In any case, Madison believed throughout his life that the Senate would tend to attract respectable persons who would protect rights of property. If such respect is taken to be a civic virtue in liberal regimes, it is fair to say that the Senate would consist in large measure of the most virtuous members of the political community.

It should be remembered that Madison's discussion of the dangers of a "levelling spirit," the symptoms of which were already beginning to trouble him, was brought up at the convention in the course of discussing the role of the Senate and the length of a senator's term of office. He argued that this "danger" was to be guarded against in part by "the establishment of a body in the Govt. sufficiently respectable for its wisdom & virtue, to aid on such emergencies, the preponderance of justice by throwing its weight in that scale."[76]

The "virtue" of senators is largely a function of the size of their statewide districts. "Large districts," Madison argued, "are manifestly favorable to the election of persons of general respectability, and of probable attachment to the rights of property, over competitors depending on the personal solicitations practicable in a contracted theater."[77] Large districts promote civic virtue, since the opportunities for corruption in the form of, say, personal favors or nepotism, which may be requirements to get elected in a smaller compass—are simply less significant. The vote of a small block of individuals simply counts for less—and can be catered to less—when the district size is expanded.

Here, too, the virtue of even this "disinterested" body of senators is reinforced, if indirectly, by a dose of self-interest. In discussing the dangers of a "levelling spirit" Madison set forth quite clearly the reasonable view that people's attachment to property rights depend in large measure on how well they are faring under the rules of distributive justice in place. Madison presumes that senators, more than representatives, are drawn from a class of persons who are faring rather well. This prudential motive toward duty cannot fail to stabilize the political system and, at the same time, make it more just.

In the Pennsylvania debates over the ratification of the 1787 Constitution, the staunch Federalist Jasper Yeates offered these observations.

> What, Mr. President, has hitherto been the effect of tender laws, paper money, and the iniquitous speculations these excrescences of weak government naturally engendered? I wish not, Sir, to afflict you with a painful recollection upon this subject; but it will be well to remember how much we have suffered, that we may properly estimate the hand which rescues us from poverty and disgrace. *If virtue be the foundation of republican government*, has it not been fatally sapped by these means? The morals of the people have been almost sunk into depravity; and the government of laws has been almost superceded by licentious anarchy [emphasis added]."[78]

The very conditions for a virtuous citizenry are undermined by the social and political conditions brought on by weak central government under the Articles of Confederation. For Yeates, the cure for the disease of licentiousness and loss of virtue, a strong central government, is what the Anti-Federalists see as the cause of these horrors.

Moreover, like the authors of *The Federalist*, Yeates finds implausible the fear of the Constitution's opponents that powers granted to the new government will almost certainly be abused. "Is it fair, is it liberal, that every presumption should impute to Congress an abuse of the powers with which they are entrusted? We might surely, on the ground of such extravagant apprehensions, proscribe the use of fire and water—for fire may burn, and water may drown us."[79]

These observations are more than a little "Madisonian." Madison too had derided the Confederation for its tendency to promote too "mutable" a policy and saw this tendency as undermining the "reverence" the people should come to feel for their political community.

> The most deplorable effect of all is that diminution of attachment and reverence which steals into the hearts of the people towards a political system which betrays so many marks of infirmity, and disappoints so many of their flattering hopes. No government, any more than an individual, will long be respected without being truly respectable; nor be truly respectable without possessing a certain portion of order and stability.[80]

Indeed, one can trace the threads of this argument back to Hobbes. Hobbes had formulated the problem of moral action under conditions of uncertainty with his typical perspicuity. No one, he argued, could reasonably observe the laws of nature in the absence of a coercive authority as each presented an innocent threat to every other individual.[81]

The Federalist position is somewhat less dramatic than Hobbes's, although its point is much the same. Instability *discourages* virtue for several reasons. First, mutable policy allows the "sagacious," those aware of the quick-breaking changes in law, to barter on their insider information and reap the benefits therefrom. Second, such specific virtues as honesty and industry are discouraged, if, for example, a contractor has little reason to believe that the disadvantageous contract he entered into yesterday will be legally enforceable tomorrow. Industry is further discouraged if the speculator expects to reap the labor-free rewards of inflation.

Alexander Hamilton and James Madison believe that adoption of the Constitution is necessary to create an orderly polity and that doing so is essential to fostering a loyal even virtuous, citizenry. Their conception of virtue—and keeping officials to it—is, to be sure, less exalted than classical republican conceptions of that term. Yet it should not be dismissed lightly. Madison in particular is defending fair dealing in politics as well as honesty and industry in society. These virtues are required to sustain a reasonably just polity and are in accord with the American spirit. His goal is to help foster a political society that is both worthy of respect and respected. Moreover, Madison's belief that political stability is a necessity for the exercise of such virtues is not easily refuted.

This last view was also shared by other supporters of the Constitution. Thus, Edmund Pendleton, the president of the Virginia ratifying convention, put the point as follows: "There is no quarrel between government and liberty; the former is the shield and protector of the latter. The war is between government and licentiousness, faction, turbulence, and other violations of the rules of society, to preserve liberty."[82] Governmental power and political stability are required to preserve liberty. But they are equally important to curb the vice of "licentiousness," the misuse of liberty in the name of doing whatever one pleases. This vice gives rise to political turbulence as factions compete for power. When laws are excessively "mutable," when politics becomes overly factious and loses sight of public good, men lose a considerable motive to virtue and a real threat to their liberty exists.

The cast of argument the authors of *The Federalist* use in claiming that the Constitution will sustain sufficient virtue to avoid these problems is decidedly empirical. The social, psychological, and political conditions that foster virtue are observed from experience. In this and in much of the content of their particular psychological observations on the complex interplay of interest, duty, and habit in forming loyal citizens and dutiful public officials there are decided Humean parallels and even indications of direct Humean influence.

The particular liberal statesmen who wrote *The Federalist* were clearly concerned with civic virtue and offered a compelling conception of it. Let us conclude, however, with a cautionary note. We need not assume that they offer the only, or even the best, understanding of the appropriate civic virtues for all liberal societies. Indeed, as we have suggested and will again in the last chapter, there are good reasons for liberal, as well as communitarian and neorepublican critics of *The Federalist*, to be dissatisfied with Publius's pessimistic assessment of the desirability of broad-based political participation and its effects on the stability of the regime. However, the task of the next chapter is to examine the principles of justice and the conception of civic virtue offered by Publius's opponents, the Anti-Federalists.

7

The Anti-Federalists and Civic Virtue

Characterizing differences between Federalists and Anti-Federalists either in terms of social background or political doctrines has been an enterprise wrought with controversy in American historiography. There has been a pronounced absence of consensus as to how to understand the Anti-Federalist opposition to the Constitution. Are we to view this debate, for all its rhetorical fire, along the lines of the controversies between political parties in established polities? In such controversies, there is much disagreement over *policy*, while there is substantial consensus over *principles*, which keeps the policy debate in moderate bounds. Or do the two sides in the founding debates offer competing conceptions of political regimes with inclusive conceptions of human nature, society, and government? This type of conflict is generally associated with revolutionary situations.

As problematic as this question has proven for historians and political theorists, it also raises difficulties for the accepted, heroic images of the American founders. If we answer in the first sense, we imply that not all that much was at stake in the set of debates that produced some of the finest moments in American statesmanship as well as the Constitution itself. By viewing the Constitution against the background of a broad consensus on principles, it appears to be one possible political compromise among many, and its drafters appear less as great innovators than as skillful politicians purveying commonly accepted political wisdom. If, on the other hand, we accept the regime-conflict interpretation, and value the Constitution, we are left to conclude that many of the founders, including Revolutionary war heroes like Patrick Henry, were dangerously wrong in their political opinions. Even if we resist the tendency to paint these figures as black, as we paint the drafters and supporters of the Constitution white, the pool of national heroes has been reduced. Further, whoever offers the second answer needs to explain the peaceful and rapid acceptance of the Constitution by its former enemies and their ready incorporation into postratification American politics.[1]

Of course, the terms *historian* and *political theorist*, on the one hand, and *icon venerator* and *iconoclast*, on the other, are not mutually exclusive. The overlap between them explains in part the continuous, cyclical conflict between consensualist and "progressive" interpretations of the founding. This is merely to restate the truism that historians generally, and students of the founding in particular, write about the past with one eye focused on the

129

present. Thus, progressives such as Charles Beard found allies for their disputes with the powers that be in their day in the Anti-Federalists, whom they portrayed as agrarian democrats overmatched by the wealthier, urban, and elitist Federalists. And the consensualists in the 1950s and early 1960s either pronounced an end to ideology or suggested that it never existed in American politics.[2] The consensus school position was used by some to criticize the American political tradition for its parochialism and its inability to recognize the claims to legitimacy of nonliberal capitalist forms of government and society.[3] For others, it served as a vehicle for minimizing the significance of regional, class, or ideological tensions in American political thought and life and emphasizing the extent to which Americans are one, united people.[4]

Republican-revisionist readings of the founding have tended to present Anti-Federalist thought as the last or next to last gasp of old-style republicanism confronting the cold realities of liberal modernity. Thus Gordon Wood, whose magisterial book, *The Creation of the American Republic*, has done more to stimulate a rethinking of the critical period than any other recent work, emphasizes the deep rifts between Federalists and Anti-Federalists. To the Anti-Federalists, he argues, "the Constitution represented a repudiation of everything Americans fought for" in the Revolutionary War.[5] It required a "startling strengthening of the ruler's power at the expense of the people's participation in government" and thereby threatened to weaken the conception of the "unitary public good" that arose from virtuous civic participation undertaken in light of perceived common interests.[6] The Federalists, in contrast, offered a "new conception of society" that could accommodate greater size and diversity of interests. They offered a "new science of politics" that "looked to mechanical devices and institutional contrivances as the only lasting solution for America's ills" rather than to "moral reform and the regeneration of men's hearts."[7]

Wood suggests that this fundamental difference in political ideologies is sometimes obscured by the fact that Anti-Federalists had to engage Federalists on the latter's terms. Differences over first principles were doomed to irrelevancy, he suggests, since the Constitution's opponents had no choice but to deal with the more restricted issue of the powers and structure of the proposed national government.[8] This position cannot be sustained, however. Debates over the powers and structure of the national government did not preclude—indeed, they rested on—deeper philosophical justifications of the nature, scope, and limits of political power in general.

John Pocock, in his synthesis of Wood and other primary researchers, differs over the extent to which the Federalists break with the civic-humanist paradigm. He notes, however, a similar pattern of ideological divergence. Thus, "old-guard" Anti-Federalists like Patrick Henry are led out of an "austere sense of virtue" to criticize the Constitution for "making too many concessions to self-interest and empire."[9] Pocock differs from the progressives—and from many of their fellow revisionists—in not attaching any great opprobrium to the Federalists, and especially to Publius, for this (partial?) rejection of republicanism. He credits Publius for his greater perspicacity in recognizing impending "modernity" (that is, the era of large commercial states) and the changes it would bring. Pocock goes so far as to suggest that, given the onerous demands of the civic virtue required to sustain true republics, a little "corruption" of the sort Publius seems to legitimize may not be a bad thing.[10]

Such stark drawings of the differences between Federalist and Anti-Federalist political perspectives are not generally supported by a close reading of the best texts expounding each position or set of positions. The Federalist and Anti-Federalist spokesmen considered in this book agree, with one interesting exception, on the fundamental political principles derived from the liberal-contractarian tradition. However, this consensus on deep ideological principles exists side by side with differences over the desirability of certain institutions, policies, and civic character traits. The Anti-Federalists, for all their internal variations, tend to differ from Federalists over such questions as the most desirable locus of power in the political system, the adequacy of the checks and balances in the Constitution, the role of representative political institutions, and the social and moral requisites of free government. The last two are an especially cogent test of our ability to account for differences within consensus where citizenship and allegiance issues are concerned.

Federalists and Anti-Federalists disagree, based on different psychological and social assumptions, about the necessary conditions for fostering a bond of allegiance between citizen and state, and the fidelity of rulers to constitutional duties. Three of the Anti-Federalists discussed—the Federal Farmer, Cato, and Brutus—share with Publius a sense of the importance of maintaining political legitimacy. They recognize that political institutions, no matter how firmly grounded in principles of justice, are rendered unstable if the citizenry is not sufficiently virtuous to sustain them. Also like Publius, their conception of civic virtue is largely grounded in an affective bond between citizen and state. The Anti-Federalist conception can with some poetic license be described as Hutchesonian rather than Humean in structure. The role played by benevolence as a bond holding political society together is given greater place in Anti-Federalist thought than in that of the Federalists. Publius, like Hume, doubted the utility of such a bond in political societies the size of most American states, much less the nation as a whole.

Therefore, unlike Publius, Anti-Federalists often contend that the *size* of the polity is a necessary condition for fostering a sense of allegiance. Much of their critique of "consolidated government" rests on this claim. They want to establish that state governments can generate popular support by appealing to the interests and affections of citizens while a national government could not.

Also unlike Publius, the Anti-Federalists tend to subscribe to what I have called a version of "weak republicanism." There is in these writings a sense, not expressed by Madison or Hamilton, that political participation is valuable for the type of character it produces. The weakness of this variant of republicanism emerges from two considerations. First, this value is *not* the primary justification for the small-state–small-district polity the Anti-

Federalists offer as the more stable alternative to "consolidated government." Such democratic institutions as rotation in office, recall, and annual elections are far more frequently defended as what Madison might call "auxiliary precautions." They are not primarily valuable, that is, for promoting the "virtue" of citizens but for checking potential abusers of power. Second, Brutus, Cato, and the Federal Farmer all sense the inevitability of the waning of civic virtue over time. The "weakness" of their republican commitments comes through in their conviction that this waning, though regrettable, is not a legitimate cause for action. Liberal rights constrain what can be done to maintain republican goods.

There is, however, one pamphleteer about whom the above generalizations do not apply. He calls himself "A Farmer from Maryland" and his republican commitments are beyond question. He writes among the most interesting pamphlets produced in the constitutional period. He is something of a voice in the wilderness. An examination of his thought—and the gap between it and more conventional Anti-Federalist critiques of the Constitution—gives a sense of both the range and the limits of political discourse in this period.[11]

Liberty, Society, and the Locus of Power: Arguments of Brutus, Cato, and the Federal Farmer

Brutus, Cato, and the Federal Farmer accept, as did Publius, that a political system must have the capacity to generate sufficient virtue among its citizens so that they will voluntarily support the government most of the time. That the so-called consolidated government being proffered by the Federalists fails this test is a central contention of these writers. However, before we fix the conception of civic virtue they rely on, two analytically prior tasks are in order. First, as with Publius, we must specify in broad outlines at least the political principles as realized by institutions of government to which the citizen is expected to be loyal. Are these principles liberal, republican, or some combination thereof? Second, the *process* and the *motivations* for becoming "virtuous" must be examined in some detail. Are the people virtuous for the "perfectionist" reasons we identify with republicanism or for from some other cause yet to be specified?

The most general ground for Anti-Federalist attacks on the Constitution is the charge that the document represents a move toward consolidated government, which is inimical to the liberties fought for in the Revolutionary War. What then is the Anti-Federalist understanding of the nature of the liberties being lost? And, a question as important, why does an extended republic lead so directly to these losses?

Fortunately, the pamphleteers under examination define the liberty they believe consolidated government would deprive them of quite explicitly. They do so in the context of a general theory of the origins and purpose of political power. It is worth quoting an explicit rendering of this theory, that of Brutus, at some length. After noting that the "mutual wants of man" dictate the formation of societies, Brutus considers the origins of government.

> In a state of nature every individual pursues his own interests; in this pursuit it frequently happened [sic] that the possessions and enjoyments of one were sacrificed to the views and designs of another; thus the weak were a prey to the strong ... every individual was insecure; common interest therefore directed that government should be established, in which the force of the whole community should be collected, and under such directions; as to protect and defend everyone who compose it. The common good, therefore is the end of civil government, and common consent the foundation on which it is established.[12]

There is no basic difference in this exposition between Brutus and Publius on the purpose of government. To paraphrase Brutus, the purpose is to protect through legitimate use of force the pursuit of possessions and enjoyments by each from the designs of others. Brutus sees government as conventional, not natural, in the civic-humanist sense. Moreover, the convention requires that citizens surrender only those natural rights that are incompatible with any form of social cooperation. To establish government, Brutus argues that

> it was necessary that a certain portion of natural liberty should be surrendered, in order that what remained should be preserved. ... But it is not necessary for this purpose, that individuals should relinquish all their natural rights. Some are of such a nature that they cannot be surrendered. Of this kind are rights of conscience, the right of enjoying and defending life, etc.[13]

Brutus's argument is neither lucid nor complete in its account of the distinction between the origins of society and the founding of government, the full content of natural rights and other such philosophical issues. It is clear, however, that at the heart of his presentation are the following common liberal-contractarian assumptions. First, individuals, prior to the existence of plans of cooperation among them, are fully developed persons with their own conceptions of enjoyment, their own possessions, their own opinions. Second, the threat each poses to others' possessions and enjoyments justifies the establishment of government. Finally, the legitimacy of government diminishes if it usurps any more of these natural rights than are necessary to maintain public order.

Further, like Publius, the Anti-Federalists frequently suggest that citizens appeal to just these criteria when deciding on ratification. Thus, Cato follows Brutus in noting the consensual basis of political power. It was, he argues, the "freedom, equality and independence which you enjoyed by nature, induced you to consent to political power." He then suggests that the central question concerning the Constitution was "whether it will answer the ends for which ... all men engage in political society, to wit, the mutual preservation of lives, liberties, and estates."[14] The Federal Farmer similarly notes that the end of government is the provision of the necessary "security to enjoy the effects of our honest industry and labours, in a free and mild government, and personal security from all illegal restraints."[15] He offers a variety of reasons why the proposed national government can be neither free nor mild. Among these are its insufficient checks on abuses of powers by rulers, the inadequacy of its system of representation, and its incapacity to appeal to the interests and affections of its citizens. Yet, ironically, the criteria he uses evaluate the prospects of constitutional government are provided by much the same set of principles Publius uses to criticize the activities of state governments under the Confederation.

Gordon Wood differentiates the Anti-Federalists from their opponents by portraying the former as "fervent defenders of the traditional assumption that the state was a cohesive organic entity with a single homogeneous interest."[16] He may mean to suggest, as the word *organic* implies, that the Constitution's opponents saw the state as a community within which fundamental conceptions of justice were embedded, in some sense, in a perceived natural order. In this case, Wood would be offering a viable description of classical republics, or even medieval polities, within which the distribution of political power and material rewards reflected a "natural" distribution of rational, moral, and/or spiritual qualities among persons. This distribution determined the manner in which each would contribute to the common good. Yet the arguments of the Anti-Federalists legitimizing political power through consent, and their understanding of the principles independent and equal rational beings *would consent to*, offer little support for understanding their thought in these terms.

Moreover, Wood's characterization does not accord with the form of argument the Anti-Federalists use in expressing their most fundamental concern, the abuse of governmental power under the proposed constitutional system. The Anti-Federalists acknowledge that powers to raise taxes and to provide for defense and internal order "must be lodged somewhere."[17] They recognize, in other words, that power is required to preserve liberty. But they fear that rulers will abuse these requisite powers. Brutus exemplifies this concern in terms drawn directly from liberal contractarian theory. "But rulers," he argues, "have the same propensities as other men" and thus are as likely to use their power for "private purposes, and to the injury and oppression of those over whom they are placed, as individuals in the state of nature are to injure and oppress one another."[18]

Thus, Brutus argues that the untenability or, at best, the inconveniences of the state of nature dictate the establishment of a coercive mechanism to enforce rules of conduct, which, despite their claim to justice, would not generally be acted upon without this mechanism. This can be presumed given the observable propensities of men that impel them to violate the laws all persons require in order to act on their life choices. Rulers are given to the same predilections as others and, given the powers vested in them, are more a threat to the personal freedoms of each citizen than citizens generally are to each other in settled polities. Without adequate checks on the uses of their power, rulers are likely to pursue their own interests to the detriment of the rest of society. In the absence of these checks, no citizen can be assured, within reason, that rulers will not violate their trusts and effectively dissolve political society. Citizens lose their main incentive for voluntary compliance with laws and society degenerates either into tyranny or anarchy.

Brutus contends that the proposed constitutional government cannot sufficiently bind rulers and thus supply the necessary assurances to citizens to inspire law-abiding conduct on their part. The explicit use of contractarian justifications for the exercise of and restraints on political power indicates that Brutus's disagreement with Publius cannot be explained by the regime-conflict interpretation advanced by Wood. And the use of contractarian justification is not restricted to the three figures we focus on here. Thus, Republicus writes in the *Kentucky Gazette* that natural freedom is the power to perform "all our actions agreeable to our own will; or in plainer terms, . . . doing as we please," within the constraints of reason and—an echo of Locke—natural law. On this is founded a "right of *equality*" in the enjoyment of life, liberty, and property. No other person nor even a "community of men can have a right to deprive him" of these goods so long as he extends like freedoms to others. The fact that men are "more generally actuated by their passions and appetites, than by their reason," necessitates civil government to "restrain, controul, or at least counteract those passions." Far from arguing that government is a vehicle for fostering civic virtue, Republicus concludes that "civil government becomes a *substitute* for moral virtue: and that instead of infringing the rightful liberties of mankind, it tends to secure them."[19]

Agrippa of Massachusetts, who is unusual among Anti-Federalists in his unreserved use of commercial progress as the measure of the well-being of a nation, argues in a similar vain. The main vice of the Constitution is its regulation of commerce, which shackles investment and productivity. "When business is unshackled," he argues, "it will find out the channel which is most friendly to its course." We ought, therefore, be very "cautious about diverting it or restraining it." Agrippa is not unusual in using social-contract reasoning in opposition to the proposed Constitution. In particular, by failing to adequately protect local interests, the Constitution's supporters ignore the reason that induces men to form political societies. "It is vain to tell us that we ought to overlook local interests. It is only by protecting [them] that the interest of the whole is preserved. No man when he enters into society, does it from a view to promote the good of others, but he does it for his own good." The apparent selfishness of his view is ameliorated by the consideration that all men, "having the same view are bound equally to promote the welfare of the whole."[20]

Vox Populi, an opponent of the Constitution from Massachusetts, expresses the same point in a mocking way. A Federalist calling himself Examiner had suggested in print that it was a new idea that government originates from "*jealousy and distrust*." Vox Populi responds as if this point is not much more controversial than asserting that the sun sets in the west. What other principle, he asks, "could induce a *rational* person to make himself subject to civil government[?] . . . Are not all the advantages which a person can expect to derive from entering into a state of civil government (or at least all he ought to expect) of a negative nature?" They are all comprehended in this one general idea: "*a prevention of injury from others.*"[21]

The tendency of Anti-Federalists to use classical liberal-contractarian arguments as grounds for opposing the constitution is widespread. Government is largely conceived as an instrument for preserving natural rights and such rights are discovered by reason, since they form a part, as Republicus observed, of natural law. The constricted role perceived for civil government should not indicate to us that Anti-Federalists were the radical individualists we encounter in caricatures of liberal theory. It does indicate, however, that their first principles are far from the classical republican conception of man as a political animal. Institutions, and practices that could conceivably be defended on republican grounds (for example, that having more representatives allows more people to serve in public office and therefore to develop their faculties and their public spirit) are rarely defended in these terms. If man is a social being, these writers seem to be saying, this social nature is best expressed in other than political forums.

Why Small Is Better (I): Allegiance and Interest

Despite their harmony on first principles, Federalists and Anti-Federalists are divided by significant political differences that cannot be ignored. In particular, the Anti-Federalists' defenses of the small state and small electoral districts are so at odds with Publius's advocacy of a large federal republic that some explanation of this difference is in order. Its scope suggests that, although it does not emerge from as deep a level as foundational ideological commitments, it does come from a fairly well-developed conception of the requisites of legitimate government.

Publius had two main objections to the Anti-Federalist characterization of the social and political structure of the individual states and the uses to which his opponents put their peculiar sociology. First, he suggests that they overstate the homogeneity within states, noting that regional and economic diversity within large states such as Virginia and Massachusetts were as great as differences among states. Moreover, all the states had already surpassed in size and population the ancient republics, which, Publius contends, were not themselves the model of stable, amicable polities. Second, Publius claims that the Anti-Federalists overstate the dangers of abuses of power in the new government. There is no reason to suppose that just because power is increased in the central government the likelihood of its abuse is increased proportionately. In fact, Publius offers a variety of reasons for supposing the opposite relation.

Publius knows that, if these claims convince his readers, he has undermined the central pillar of the Anti-Federalists' *principled* opposition to the Constitution. If we accept the explicit avowals of Brutus, Cato, and others who define the ends of government as the protection of life, liberty, and estate, we conclude that their defense of some looser form of confederation derives from the fact that it better conduces to those ends. That it does so depends on a proposed relationship between the social structure of the states and political stability. If Publius can show either that the states themselves do not meet the Anti-Federalists' social requisites of stability (among them homogeneity and uniformity of interest) or that these criteria are not necessary conditions of stability, the critical part of his exposition has succeeded. In fact, Publius largely succeeds in both these demonstrations. He does so because he can exploit weaknesses in the Anti-Federalist conceptions of the relation between civil society and the state.

Brutus begins his criticism of consolidated government by drawing the viable distinction between authoritative government and rule by force. Any government which cannot count on citizens' recognition of its authority must rely on force for its edicts to be obeyed. Thus, Brutus writes, men are motivated to obey laws from "affection for government or from fear." In the absence of affection, governments become "nerveless and inefficient" and this increases the need to rely on compulsion.[22] While Cato, after citing Montesquieu in noting that "political liberty . . . consists in security, or at least the opinion we have of security," claims that only "moderate governments," which "beget a confidence in the people" produce this security and the opinion of it.[23] Immoderate governments, by definition, fail to generate in citizens the will to comply with laws voluntarily and, as for Brutus, the alternatives become an illegitimate rule of fear or anarchy.

These observations form an objection to "consolidated" government if and only if, as Cato claims, the moderation of governments depends "in a great measure on their limits."[24] This is clearly the Anti-Federalist claim. The Federal Farmer exemplifies it when he writes that the "laws of a free government . . . never can extend their influence very far" as these laws "must be executed on the principles of fear and force in the extremes."[25] The position that the effectiveness of rules which require some element of self-sacrifice (a description that subsumes most laws) bears some relation to the size of the community bound by those rules is neither an incoherent nor an uncommon one.[26] The problems for the Anti-Federalists are to show that small size is a necessary condition for the promotion of effective dispositions to comply with laws and that the states meet this size requirement. Then they can argue that state governments can avoid the cycle of decline to which a federated national government is so prone.

The arguments Brutus, Cato, and the Federal Farmer use are neither internally consistent nor consistent with each other in making this claim. Nonetheless, they can be classified into two general categories that illuminate a shared approach even as particular arguments vary. All three claim that the states are particularly well-adapted to generate in citizens a sense of approbation grounded in *prudential* sources on the one hand and in *natural* sentiments or primary affections on the other. The prudentially based sentiment is engaged since only citizens of small states can have confidence that political institutions are so constituted as not to violate rights and to effectively promote prosperity. That the latter source comes into play is explained less by a particular political theory than by a psychological notion of the ties that bind collectivities together generally. These are thought to be affective bonds which grow naturally among persons with similar "manners, sentiments and interests."[27]

In order to show how these sources give rise to a sense of allegiance toward state governments that would be denied consolidated government, it is useful to focus on a specific—and most essential—institutional critique the Anti-Federalists offer, the alleged inadequacy of the plan of representation in the Constitution. The utility of focusing on an institutional critique of this sort is that it enables us to distinguish between the rhetorical "packaging" and the substance of Anti-Federalist argumentation. Such criticisms call for a greater theoretical explicitness than do the general denunciations of the "corrupt," power-hungry aristocracy that characterize the weaker Anti-Federalist pamphlets. An institutional focus suggests to us that the Anti-Federalist characterizations of the state and society, which seem to show a pronounced civic humanist influence, actually diverge from this tradition in fundamental ways.

The Anti-Federalists criticize the Constitution's plan of representation on a number of grounds. The two that bear most directly on the problem of allegiance are their charges, first, that there are too few legislators in the national assembly to represent adequately the diversity of interests in American society and, second, that public confidence in government decreases in proportion to the distance between representative and represented. They use the term *distance* in both social and geographic senses and argue that it will be too great in both senses for constitutional government to generate sufficient support among citizens.

In order to make the first criticism, the Anti-Federalists must offer a characterization of American society. They must address the question of *who* is to be represented as well as *how* this is to be done. Specifying the relation between these two questions is, however, complicated by ambiguities in their conception of society, readings of which can provide grist for a variety of mills, including a republican one. Thus, the Federal Farmer begins his discussion of representation by offering a theory that society is composed of two primary classes in a manner reminiscent of classical mixed government theory. These classes are a "natural aristocracy" consisting of large property owners, high office-holders and "eminent professional men," and a "natural democracy" made up of subordinate officeholders and professionals, mechanics, traders, small merchants, and similar citizens.[28] He notes their fundamental differences in a way that recognizes the contribution of each to the good of the polity. He does so by invoking the mixed-government ideal of balance between these two classes with equally legitimate claims to power. He suggests that the role of representation is the "uniting, and balancing [of] their interests, feelings, opinions, and views in the legislature."[29]

This seed of mixed-government theory is quickly abandoned, however, suggesting that the Federal Farmer doubts its suitability for American soil. This is seen when he adds to these "two great parties" other categories of citizens that cut across the class distinction and that are presumed to have interests at least as disharmonious as those of Madison's factions.

> Not only the efforts of these two great parties are to be balanced, but other interests and parties also, which do not always oppress each other *merely for want of power*, and for *fear of the consequences*. . . .[S]uch are their general views, that the merchants alone would never fail to make laws favorable to themselves and oppressive to farmers & c. The farmers would act on like principles; the former would tax the land, the latter the trade [emphasis added]."[30]

The consequences of this understanding of the basic units of society on the Federal Farmer's theory of representation are as follows. If we presume, as we surely must, that all these parties are entitled to adequate representation, and we doubt the capacity of citizens of any class or group to disinterestedly perform the duties of public office, representative assemblies must reproduce in all essentials the interest structure of society at large. This is, in fact, the conclusion the Federal Farmer draws. He claims that in "every period of society, and in all transactions of men . . . those classes which have not their centinels in the government, in proportion to what they have to gain or lose, most infallibly be ruined."[31]

This defense of representation as a means to protect interests is widespread in Anti-Federalist writings. It is echoed by the noted Virginian Richard Henry Lee, who displays even more clearly the antimajoritarian tendency in Anti-Federalist thought.[32] Lee argues that the number in the House of Representatives is dangerously low and this makes it too easy for a majority faction to assemble. "A bare majority," he argues, "may be seduced by strong motives of interest to injure and oppress the minority of the community."[33]

Ironically, Lee's call for a larger House is quite similar to Madison's defense of extended electoral districts. Both make it more difficult for majority factions to assemble and exercise power effectively. It is worth remembering, however, that Publius, despite a similar assessment of the tendencies of interests, was spared Lee's conclusion by his more complex understanding of political psychology. It allowed him to claim that dispositions to rule justly could, and in all likelihood, would be fostered at least among those likely to hold power in post-ratification American politics.

Rejecting this argument opened to the Anti-Federalists a wealth of practical and theoretical objections to the Constitution. The first—that there are too few representatives in the national legislature to make it "like the people" in its composition—is argued with frequency and force. If legislators do not "bear a just resemblance to the several classes of people" of society, that is, to "farmer, merchant, mecanick" and other occupational groups, they will not "be intimately acquainted with the wants" and interests of these groups, nor will they "feel a proper sense and becoming zeal to promote their prosperity."[34] It follows in Brutus's and the Federal Farmer's arguments that this acquaintance and zeal can exist only on state and local levels of government.

The Anti-Federalists argue that a government which does not represent all interests equally is unjust.[35] They also note that such a government is likely to be unstable. It is not able to promote the fidelity of rulers nor the allegiance of citizens. The former is, of course, a necessary condition for the latter. Citizens cannot be expected to feel allegiance toward a government whose leaders are able (and, presumably, disposed) to violate the terms of the social contract. It is not a sufficient condition, however, since, even assuming its existence, it still makes sense to ask two further questions. To what rules of cooperation ought leaders be faithful, and why do these rules give rise to feelings of allegiance and civic virtue?

There is a considerable overlap between the Anti-Federalists' and Publius's understandings of the relationship between principles of justice and the dispositions of citizens to act justly. Publius, in fact, borrowed one of the Anti-Federalists' most frequently expressed positions on this relation in order to reassure his opponents of the continued viability of the states under the proposed Constitution. State sovereignty would be protected not only by constitutional provisions, but also by the strong hold states would have on the affections of their citizens. The prudential basis for this hold was that the affairs of state governments were more palpably connected with the preservation of rights and the promotion of prosperity of individual citizens than were those of the national government. This position is essentially the one the Federal Farmer takes in the following remarks: The detailed administration of affairs, in the mixed republics, depends principally on the local governments; and the people would be wretched without them: and a great proportion of social happiness depends on the internal administration of justice, and on internal police."[36] He argues that the goods provided by these agencies—the provision of security of rights and goods—is the true cause of the "happiness of the subject," not "splendor of the monarch" nor "power of the government." He then echoes Publius's contention that the best-administered state is the best state, so that the soundness of administration takes precedence over the form of government.

> My uniform federal attachments [i.e., the recognition that some form of national union is required], and the interest I have in the protection of property, and a steady execution of the laws, will convince you; that, if I am under any biass at all, it is in favor of *any general system* which shall promise these advantages. . . .A wise and honest administration, may make people happy under any government; but necessity only can justify even our leaving open avenues to the abuse of power, by wicked, unthinking, ambitious men [emphasis added]."[37]

That the Federal Farmer places the policing functions of the state at the core of his concept of sound administration and gives priority to this good should not imply indifference on his part to the other goods the state provides. These lower-ranked goods could conceivably include a republican-inspired idea that recognizes the intrinsic value of civic participation as a developer of human capacities. Yet the provision of this good is clearly not the essential criterion by which government is to be evaluated. The Federal Farmer does not generally contend that the function of representation is to perfect faculties nor that this good is an authoritative one in the sense of the classical tradition. It is not one all citizens capable of understanding their own good ought to desire or, conversely, one for which the absence of desire indicates a defect of personality.

The Federal Farmer's ideal of free government leaves us with quite a different impression of what he conceives citizens to desire, the proper role of government in relation to these desires, and the relation between this role and the allegiance of citizens. "In free governments the people, or their representatives, make the laws; their execution is principally the effect of voluntary consent and aid; the people respect the magistrate, follow their private pursuits, and enjoy the fruits of their labour with very small deductions for public use."[38] This Anti-Federalist is well aware of the sort of free rider problems that make the unconstrained pursuit of private ends destabilizing. He notes in a passage characterizing the motivations of citizens and rulers alike that, if "on a fair calculation, a man will gain more by measures oppressive to others than he will lose by them, he is interested in their adoption."[39] He suggests, however, that as long as citizens have a sense that government is so constituted as to promote their interests and thus advance their happiness, a generally effective disposition to comply with laws will emerge. Moreover, this "opinion of interest" will be sufficiently strong in most circumstances to override natural, narrowly self-interested motives toward defection.

The vulnerability of the Anti-Federalist critique of "consolidated" government to Publius's two-pronged attack now begins to emerge. The case of the Constitution's opponents depends in large measure on their being able to establish a relationship between certain basic characteristics of the states and legitimate government. A feature of states frequently used to differentiate them from the nation as a whole is the greater similarity within their borders of mores, habits and sentiments. Yet, when the Federal Farmer and Brutus discuss the nature of society in general terms they emphasize the diversity and mutual antagonism of interests within it. Moreover, the types of interests they discuss, primarily occupational groups including large and small merchants and farmers, professionals, and others—are found in all complex societies. Thus, they are found within individual states as well as being distributed in varying proportions among states.

Further, the argument that popular support for government is largely a function of its capacity to appeal to prudentially based sentiments weakens a political theoretical defense of small republics. In utilizing this argument, the Anti-Federalist case does not rest on any claim for the intrinsic merits of small states (such as civic humanism could theoretically provide). Rather, it rests on a set of empirical generalizations pertaining to the dispositions of citizens and public officials and the requisites for fostering state-supporting dispositions. It is not even clear what theoretical objections could be made to consolidated government. For the Anti-Federalists, as much as for Publius, the most powerful justification for any government is that it enables citizens to pursue possessions and enjoyments within a legal framework. And a consolidated government could arguably provide this framework as effectively as could the individual states.

The theoretical defense of the small state is made no stronger by the arguments that, first, citizens' confidence in government varies in direct proportion to the distance between the locus of power and the citizen and, second, the size of the states define the limits of acceptable distance. These claims rest on the presumption that the sole basis of trust in government is an "intimate acquaintance" between representative and represented. Their effect is to reject the position that citizens can have confidence in the virtue of their rulers on such other grounds as tradition (in the Burkean sense according to which rulers and citizens perceive themselves bound by habits and practices shared over generations) or a meritocratic faith that those best qualified to rule will rule best. That is, he rejects as grounds of confidence just the sort of reasons Publius stresses.

Brutus traces the likely effects of the increase in social and geographical distance under consolidated government to the usual extremes of government by force or anarchy, each resulting in the "total destruction of liberty."[40] These dire consequences emerge from the tendency of large electoral districts to favor the election of members of the "natural aristocracy" who, like members of any particular interest group, cannot speak for the other diverse interests in the community. The large-district–few-representatives combination found in the Constitution falls short of the desired goal of "full and fair" representation and cannot provide "reasonable ground for public trust" in government among the full range of classes of citizens who constitute American society.[41]

Brutus argues that when the plan of representation is full and fair, "those to whom the power [of government] is committed shall be subject to the same feelings, and aim at the same objects as the people do who transfer to them their authority."[42] The lesson he draws from this is similar to that drawn by the Federal Farmer. Representative assemblies should be like the people virtually in the sense of being a statistical sample of the various occupational interests in society. Only then will elected officials be disposed sufficiently to take into account the interests of all citizens such that citizens can have adequate grounds for trust in government.

For Brutus, the antithesis of the confidence people have in government is suspicion or jealousy. Suspicion is the direct function of the distance between government and governed. It will, therefore, increase as consolidated government increases this distance. Under the Constitutional government, representatives "will not be viewed by the people as parts of themselves, but as a body distinct from them with separate interests to pursue" with the result of a "perpetual jealousy" between ruler and ruled.[43] Jealousy is the natural result when one must rely on a stranger to act as a trustee for one's interests.

If the person confided in, be a neighbour with whom his employer is intimately acquainted . . . his honesty and fidelity [are] unsuspected, and his friendship and zeal for the service of this principal unquestionable, he will commit his affairs into his hands with unreserved confidence. . . . But, if the person employed be a stranger, whom he has never seen, and whose character for ability and fidelity he cannot fully learn, . . . he will trust him with caution and be suspicious of all his conduct.[44]

Brutus applies this understanding of trustee relationships in general to the problem of representation by suggesting that a majority of state residents will have "no persons so immediately of their choice so near them, of their neighbors and of their own rank in life, that they can feel themselves secure in trusting their interests in their hands."[45] Citizens, lacking this security, will then have lost a considerable motive for complying with laws. Their practices will accord with their dispositions and anarchy or tyranny is the outcome.

The main thrust of Brutus's position is clear. Friends make better representatives than strangers, since friends can be trusted not to put their own self-interest first upon assuming power. Intimate acquaintance fosters a willingness to comply with laws both because the citizens have a natural affection for those who write them and because they can be reasonably confident that their representatives are promoting their interests. Representatives are likely to "feel a proper sense and becoming zeal to promote [the] prosperity" of constituents because, given a full and fair representation, they are acquainted with and share the concerns of the locality. This zeal will be matched by the affection the citizens feel for things which advance their ends, and this affection will take the form of a sense of allegiance toward government and a corresponding willingness to be good citizens.

Moreover, insofar as we can cull a theory of political allegiance from Brutus's critique of consolidated government, it bears a strong resemblance in several essential regards to that of Publius. Both suggest that dispositions to act as good citizens are requisites of stable government, thereby rejecting the notion that institutional checks and balances are sufficient to advance this end. They also agree, by implication, that these dispositions are likely to emerge only if it is widely perceived that supporting government does not regularly require self-abnegatory actions. There is no ethos of heroic or saintly self-sacrifice in either's conception of "civic virtue," although both are aware that stable liberal democracy depends on citizens' contributing to the public order even when such contributions can be avoided. The propensity to contribute in both active and passive ways, although always vulnerable to prudential reasoning of the narrowest form, is more likely to emerge if citizens are reasonably assured that their interests are being preserved and promoted within a stable legal order.

The Anti-Federalists and Publius also generally agree that this opinion of interest must be supplemented by something else if regulative dispositions are to emerge to restrain the narrow egoism of citizens and public officials. They disagree sharply, however, about just what this something else is. I have already suggested that Publius saw as a stabilizing necessity the emergence of a "habitual sense of obligation" (Hamilton's words) among citizens and a web of rational and nonrational dispositions among rulers. These functioned to fill the cracks between the general sense of the advantages of government and the narrowly prudential desire to let others pay for them. For the Anti-Federalists, sentiments of benevolence play a similar role, although, I will suggest, at the considerable cost of theoretical inconsistency.

Why Small Is Better (II): Allegiance and Benevolence

Cato, who shares with Brutus and the Federal Farmer a liberal conception of the ends of government and an interest-group conception of society, perhaps goes furthest in criticizing the Constitution for its failure to take into account the importance of natural benevolent sentiments. He uses what can be described as a *circle-of-affections* argument to suggest that *The Federalist's* advocacy of a large republic disregards the "principles which bind them together" and is inherently unstable for this reason.[46] "These principles are in their exercise, like a pebble cast on the calm surface of a river, the circles begin in the center and are *small, active and forcible*, but as they depart from that point, they lose their force and vanish into calmness [emphasis added]."[47] He implies that the decline in sentimental attachment felt for members of the same state ("where acquaintance, habits, and fortunes, nourish affection, and attachment") and in the attachment felt for members of the same nation (toward whom we acknowledge little more than the "same national denomination") is not so much a change in degree as one in kind.[48] "Is it therefore, from certainty like this, reasonable to believe, that inhabitants of Georgia, or New Hampshire, will have the same obligations toward you as *your own*, and preside over your lives, liberties, and property, with the same care and attachment? Intuitive reason, answers in the negative [emphasis added]."[49]

Cato's approach is indeed an intuitive one. He is not interested in providing the rigorous criteria of similitude and difference that would allow him to draw the line between state and national attachments as sharply as he wants it to be drawn. This is not surprising given the frequent imprecision in dealing with thorny philosophical issues we find in these works of political persuasion. It is, however, no less significant for this fact. If the effective force of affections is not dissipated until we reach the national level, Cato's state-national distinction blurs into non-existence. If, on the other hand—as I think more consistent with the whole of Cato's political theory—the ties of benevolence are too weak to provide regulative dispositions within social units the size of the states, his circle-of-affections argument meets the same end, but with an added complication. This eliminates the utility of appeals to benevolence as a tie that binds any but small localities where the possibility of face to face contact with other members remains possible.

Cato suggests that sentiments of benevolence (in his terms, ties of friendship and trust nourished by personal acquaintance) can provide a motive for allegiance and fidelity over as broad a sphere as a state. This is a odd suggestion in that, at the same time, he posits as a trait of rulers "in all governments" a desire to "erect an interest separate from that of the ruled, which will have a tendency to enslave them."[50] The lessons he draws from this are, first, the need to establish "the principles of distrust" in constituents and, second, the need for explicit constitutional barriers to power, "the want of which induced men to engage in political society."[51]

The validity of these lessons rests on supposedly eternal verities concerning the tendencies of power. Cato advances no argument to suggest that the attitude of distrust or constitutional barriers is rendered nugatory by bonds of benevolence within any specified territorial boundary, much less one the size of any of the states. In fact, it is perhaps the best known of the Anti-Federalist critiques of the Constitution that it does not include enough of those checks that the states have deemed necessary to preserve liberty, foremost among them a bill of rights.

Cato's notion of the attitudinal and institutional requirements for maintaining liberal-contractarian principles of justice suggests a Humean understanding of the relationship between justice and benevolence. Essentially, justice begins where benevolence ends. Thus, rules of justice are unnecessary in families and small communities in which one's concern for the well-being of others is presumed to be sufficiently strong to override the temptation to do them harm even when one would benefit greatly from doing so. But Cato wants to have it both ways. He also expresses the more generous, "Hutchesonian" notion that primary, benevolent sentiments are motives for action not just in families or neighborhoods but in more extensive political communities. It is surely unusual, however, to suggest that benevolence helps generate in citizens feelings of friendship and trust, while also suggesting that those citizens deemed worthy to represent their peers ought not to be trusted.

It is possible to restore some coherence to Cato's critique of consolidated government with an argument along the following lines. It could be suggested, that, in order to be consistent, Cato does not have to show that benevolence *overrides* self-interest in the states such that constitutional barriers are rendered unnecessary. He merely has to show that a balance between these motives is reached so that a disposition not to inconvenience unjustly or oppress others emerges that is generally, but not always, effective. Constitutional checks and balances are then required for those instances when benevolent affections are overcome by strictly personal temptations. Thus, it could be claimed that even within families it is not inconsistent with the notion of benevolence for rules of cooperation complete with sanctions to be set up where divisions of costs and benefits are concerned. In fact, such rules (as those allocating household chores) are common in families, even though, there exists a strong concern for others' well-being.

This point, when taken in the abstract, is fair, but it still does not respond to criticisms of Cato's application of the circle of affections argument to the problem of consolidated government. Madison presents the form of such a critique in *Federalist* 55 when he rejects the notion that there is any necessary relationship between the size of electoral districts, or of the whole polity, and dispositions toward civic virtue. "Nothing," he writes, "could be more fallacious than to found our political calculations on arithmetical principles."[52]

Clearly, Cato (and Brutus as well in his reliance on "intimate acquaintance" as a source of confidence in government) wants to suggest that, at some point, quantity transforms into quality. Thus, his political calculations are grounded in fundamental, intuitively recognized facts of human experience—the ties that "bind men together"—and are not a simple matter of head counting. But even the most coherent reading of Cato's argument does not help us in locating this point. He does not provide criteria of difference to distinguish between affections for state and national government in as clear a fashion as he desires.

Perhaps a more important flaw in Cato's approach is that the very logic of the circle-of-affections argument points to the need for some other binding principle if a just state or national government is to be sustained. If benevolent sentiments tend to dissipate as the regularity of personal contacts diminishes, we meet the following problem even if the government's plan of representation is full and fair by Anti-Federalist criteria. It can be presumed under these circumstances that the great Anti-Federalist fear, that legislators' will establish themselves as a separate interest from the people, has been assuaged. Annual elections, rotation in office, recall procedures, and other provisions ensure that the sole objective legislators will be willing or able to act on is the advancement of their constituents' ends. It is also presumed that members of any one district are essentially similar in interests. Benevolence in this context clearly plays the role of binding representatives to their constituents. What it does not do, however, is to explain how these representatives function as *one legislative body* harmonizing competing interests and distributing equitably the costs of collective goods.

It is at least plausible that benevolence will impel a representative to advance the ends of constituents with whom he shares bonds of personal acquaintance by seeking to shift their share of the costs of cooperation to relative strangers in other parts of the state. This point is behind Hamilton's position in *Federalist* 15 that "predilections" naturally felt for local objects are a probable source of injustice because they encourage resistance to the loss of local power and benefits however much this loss is warranted according to criteria of justice. Clearly, if Hamilton's critique holds any weight, something beside benevolence is required to explain why any legislator would be disposed to look after the rights and interests of persons whom he does not know personally. And the dependence of this "something else" on the size of the polity, and thus its standing as a critique of consolidated government, would have to be defended with arguments very different from the circle-of-affections argument Cato and Brutus employ.

Brutus, Cato, the Federal Farmer, and Weak Republicanism

The reconstruction and critique of arguments just presented points to some of the difficulties in trying to distinguish Federalists from Anti-Federalists in terms of preferences for "mechanical devices" or "moral regeneration," following Wood, or self-interest versus virtue, following Pocock. Neither is there any compelling philosophical reason to perceive these pairs as dichotomous choices, nor does the textual evidence indicate that this was the perception of the participants in the debate over ratification. Remarks by Anti-Federalists akin to that of Patrick Henry's criticism of the Federalists for their naive confidence in the virtue of public officials, and even of citizens, are common.[53] In contrast, Publius comments on the necessity of virtue to sustain the commonwealth on several occasions and states his confidence that citizens will possess a sufficient degree of virtue at least to choose virtuous public officials.

However, just as there are differences in institutional preferences between the two camps of debaters, there are differences in their conceptions of a virtuous citizenry, which a modified consensualist approach should not ignore. These differences, I will suggest, could justify a weak-republican interpretation of Anti-Federalist thought, although even here I would place a few caveats. Weak republicanism does not contain a perfectionist argument for civic participation as a regulative conception of the good on which all persons seeking moral and rational fulfillment ought to act. It does entail, first, some recognition of the satisfactions of public service; second, a preference that these satisfactions be spread over a large segment of the civic population; and (possibly) third, a desire to expand the size and the range of activities of this population. Storing has something like this in mind when he describes the Anti-Federalists as "reluctant" liberals.[54] It is now important to get some sense of the sources of this "reluctance."

There should be little question that when the Anti-Federalists speak of the role of popular participation in government, they do so with an instrumental purpose in mind. The metaphors they use to describe the function of government are those of "guarding," "preserving," "securing," and soon. The objects government guards are private interests and personal liberties, and they are to be guarded against the usurpations of bad rulers. The Anti-Federalists place a relatively greater stress on this danger and less on the dangers of faction than does Publius. Thus, Cato argues that the more "complete" representation is, "the better will your interests be preserved, and the greater the opportunity you will have to participate in government, one of the principle securities of a free people."[55] And the Federal Farmer argues for rotation in office, claiming that in employing it, "we guard against the pernicious connections, which usually grow up among men left to continue long periods in office . . . . [H]ence a balance of interests and exertions are preserved, and the ruinous measures of factions [among rulers] rendered more impracticable."[56] Brutus's argument for intimate acquaintance between representative and represented takes this form as well.

But in each of these cases, there are arguments, or hints of arguments, that, as citizens are acting to preserve their interests against the designing few, they also are contributing to the development of a civic spirit, which is an *admirable* as well as a *useful* quality. Thus, in what is perhaps the purest example of a civic-humanist-inspired remark of any of the three Anti-Federalists discussed in this chapter, Cato favors annual elections at least in part because they afford to many "the opportunity to be advanced to the supreme command." The honors that public service brings "fill them with a desire of rendering themselves worthy of them; hence this desire becomes part of their education, is matured in manhood, and produces an ardent affection for their country."[57] Similarly, the Federal Farmer advocates rotation in office, claiming that, in addition to its primary purpose, it has the collateral advantage of "spread[ing] information, and preserv[ing] a spirit of activity and investigation among the people."[58]

Storing is probably overstating the case in claiming that the Anti-Federalists thought "of the whole organization of the polity as having an educative function," seeing the small republic "as a school of citizenship as much as a scheme of government."[59] But the preceding comments and other evidence he presents, particularly on the educative role played by an explicit declaration of rights, do point to an Anti-Federalist desire that states perform an educative function. This objective is far removed from Publius's goal of keeping the people in their collective capacity out of government. It also articulates an understanding of a necessary connection between the institutional requisites of good government and civic dispositions. It does so by relating a civic spirit to specific institutional structures such as rotation and annual elections. The Anti-Federalists avoid the tendency, shared by Hume and Publius, to divorce these concerns by developing a virtually contentless conception of allegiance in terms of habitual obedience.

It is an irony of Anti-Federalist thought and, I think, a particularly damaging point for a republican revisionist interpretation of it, that so few of the Anti-Federalists' criticisms of the Constitution revolve around these concerns. The primary focus of their attacks on the institutional inadequacies of the Constitution employ classical liberal-contractarian arguments and arguments from the affections. To be sure, much of the reactive character of their works can be explained by the historical fact that they were presented with the Constitution as a fait accompli. But this cannot explain the terms in which they chose to ground their critique of the document. I, therefore, would not accept Pocock's claim that a "neoclassical politics . . . accounts for the singular cultural homogeneity of the Founding Fathers and their generation." And that though "not all Americans were schooled in this tradition . . . . [T]here was (it would almost appear) no alternative tradition in which to be schooled."[60] Much of the weakness of the Anti-Federalist critique of Constitutional government, in fact, derives from its inability to articulate these weak republican concerns in any other than a liberal-contractarian framework. This is seen in the Anti-Federalists' thoughts on the public's attentiveness to politics, and on the relation between civic virtue and impending socioeconomic change.

The Federal Farmer frequently rebukes the Federalists for what he sees as their naive and perhaps disingenuous faith that the peoples' "virtue" and "manly habits" will be effective guardians of their liberty under the constitutional system.[61] He suggests two reasons for downplaying reliance on the peoples' virtue. First, even at present, the people are only sporadically attentive to the impact governmental decisions have on their rights and interests. Second, this cautionary attention will become even less reliable in the future.

He notes that, although during the Revolution, American's tried "our ability as free men in a most arduous contest," it has since been discovered that the "main spring of our movements were the love of liberty, and a temporary ardor."[62] The Federal Farmer would not want to recommend that this ardor be maintained at the feverish revolutionary pitch in normal times. But even against the background of more moderate expectations, the level to which he believes this attentiveness is likely to fall is striking.

This Anti-Federalist presents his own version of the propitious moment argument developed by Madison. This is seen, for example, in his contention that the people should not rely on the amendment process to correct defects in the Constitution. In fact, this process will more likely be used to make those defects more pronounced.

> There will be danger that the people, after the system shall be adopted, will become inattentive to amendments. Their attention is now awake . . . but [the] vigilance of the people is not sufficiently constant to be depended on—Fortunate it is for the body of a people, if they can continue attentive to their liberties long enough to erect for them *a temple, and constitutional barriers* for their permanent security [emphasis added]."[63]

It is a bit odd that the Federal Farmer should express this concern in a series of letters aimed at exposing the tyrannical tendencies of the Constitution. If the consequences of constitutional government were likely to be as harmful to the rights and interests of the majority of Americans as he writes, it would seem that the "love of liberty" would suffice to rekindle the ardor to remove the oppressors just as the British had been removed. That he notes the dangers of inattentiveness at several points suggests that he did not believe the Constitution to be as incompatible with a reign of "normalcy" as he argues elsewhere in his letters. Or he wants to claim, even more remarkably, that citizens will lack sufficient vigilance *even when* their rights and goods are subject to serious threats.

In either case, we have learned something of interest about the Anti-Federalists' conception of the requirement of virtue. The public vigilance that is associated with civic virtue is awakened only under conditions of severe systemic strains. When these periods of tension pass, so does the "temporary ardor" that produced mass participation in defense of liberty. This is why "when the people are attentive, they ought cautiously to provide for those benefits, those advantageous changes in the administration of their affairs, which they are often apt to be inattentive to in practice."[64] They ought, in other words, to erect that temple of constitutional barriers that "serve as centinels for the people at all times, and especially in those unavoidable intervals of inattention."[65]

The Federal Farmer would not want to contend that during these intervals the people are "unvirtuous." Rather, he seems to have in mind merely that their attention is turned to private affairs. It can be presumed that under most circumstances these affairs are conducted by the majority of artisans, small merchants and farmers, and others with a high degree of propriety such that laws are regularly obeyed, contracts honored, and the other requirements of civility observed. These are moral qualities citizens must have in order to sustain a polity in which each is free to tend to his own affairs with minimal external restraints. They are also *passive* virtues in that they entail no great participatory effort or high level of self-sacrifice. The Federal Farmer observes, but does not attach disapprobation to, the fact that the active virtues are more rarely encountered. The Anti-Federalists may want to see tendencies toward privatism offset by such institutions as state militias and annual elections, but they nonetheless see these tendencies as embedded in the natural course of things.

A final indication of and caveat to a weak republican interpretation concerns the Anti-Federalist conception of impending socioeconomic change and its effect on civic character traits. Pocock has identified as one of the defining features of neoclassical politics a dread of modernity that takes several forms. Among them, and of central interest here, is a fear that the transformation from an agricultural to a commercial society will undermine the basis of autonomy in property for the small farmers and petit bourgeois classes and thus, deny their capacity to act as free citizens.[66] In fact, the Anti-Federalists express this fear at various points. Thus, Cato criticizes the Federalists for claiming that "the opinions and manners" of the American people "are capable to resist and prevent an extension of prerogative or oppression." The Constitution's supporters are naive in this regard. They ignore the fact that "opinions and manners are mutable, and may not always be a permanent obstruction against the encroachments of government."[67] He cites as a cause of this unfortunate mutation "the progress of commercial society," which "begets luxury, the parent of inequality, the foe to virtue, and the enemy to restraint."[68] Given the inevitability of "progress" in this regard, the key point for Cato is that a constitution founded on equitable principles should be established now. Moreover, it should be so explicit in its demarcation of rights and powers that citizens have to rely neither on the good will of rulers nor on their own continuous virtue to secure their freedoms.

The Federal Farmer criticizes the Federalists on much the same grounds in a passage rich in ambiguities.

> Instead of checks in the formation of government, to secure the rights of the people against the usurpations of those they appoint to govern, we are to understand that the equal divisions of land among the people, and the strong arm furnished them by nature and situation, are to secure them against these usurpations. If there are advantages in the equal divisions of our lands, and the strong and manly habits of our people, we ought to establish governments calculated to give duration to them, and not governments which never can work naturally, till that equality of property, and those free and manly habits are destroyed; these evidently are not the natural basis of the proposed constitution. No man of reflection, and skilled in the science of government, can suppose that these will move on harmoniously together for ages, or even for fifty years.[69]

There is a sense in this passage of the dread of modernity to which Pocock refers. The passage also claims that a relationship exists between socioeconomic changes (pertaining both to land distribution and the virtues associated with agrarian societies) and the proposed Constitution, although the nature of this relationship is not clear. The Constitution is criticized both for an overreliance on civic virtue to maintain stability and for undermining the requisite virtue. The Federal Farmer could be interpreted as viewing the Constitution as a *cause* of the destruction of "manly habits" and, thus, its defenders as internally inconsistent if not disingenuous in claiming to rely on them to prevent abuses of power. In this interpretation, he criticizes the Constitution for relying on virtues while not specifying institutional means of giving permanence to them. The irony in this criticism is that the Federal Farmer nowhere adequately specifies these means himself.

Annual elections, rotation in office, and small electoral districts ensure that the yeomanry's interests are represented. But these mechanisms would affect the distribution of land and other forms of wealth only peripherally for two reasons. First, they do not presuppose any particular conception of distributive justice. Second, neither the Federal Farmer nor other participants in the ratification debates suppose that legitimate government, whatever its internal structure, either could or should alter in any fundamental way the economic distributions produced by market interactions.[70]

The Federal Farmer recognizes also that the cultural and especially religious homogeneity that promotes mild government is not likely to last forever. Though "we are not disposed to differ much, at present, about religion," this will not always be the case. Therefore, "for ages and millions yet unborn, why not establish the free exercise of religion, as a part of the national compact."[71] The solution to this loss of homogeneity is *not* to resist trends against it but to assure that a constitutional bulwark is in place that protects religious minorities.

Cato too describes the progress of commercial society as inevitable, at least as essentially independent of political structures and choices. Neither Cato nor the Federal Farmer suggests that government can or ought to act to preserve the roughly equal distribution of land that gives rise to republican virtues. Rather, they argue for designing a government that is *better able to function in their absence* than is that of the proposed Constitution.

Postscript: The Wistful Republicanism of a Farmer

A Farmer from Maryland, of all the Anti-Federalists, displays the best—and most wistful—commitment to republicanism in the American setting. He is deeply imbued in the classical republican tradition and writes one of the most learned pieces of the founding period. He distinguishes with great subtlety the varieties of the republican tradition and questions tellingly their applicability in the United States. Ironically, his arguments cut so deeply into American character and institutions that they are not terribly relevant to the concrete choice faced by his readers of whether to support or oppose the proposed Constitution. Both Federalist and Anti-Federalist proposals fall far short of his vision of good government. A Farmer is, if not a voice in the wilderness, certainly a voice against the wind.[72]

Like his fellow Anti-Federalists, A Farmer builds upon the premise that persons have rights prior to joining a political community and that the role of that community is to preserve these rights. He departs from his fellows in the rather odd claim that any system of representation is deleterious to the preservation of rights, so that direct democracy becomes an essential ingredient of any stable, rights-based system of government. His considerations begin with a discussion of the origins of inequality reminiscent of Rousseau's discourse on the subject. Let a people choose fairly, he argues, and they will "establish the *law of equality*" to govern their relations. However, "almost as soon as society is formed . . . this equality is materially injured if not destroyed" by growing inequalities in the division of property. Equality is only reasserted "in the advanced stages of government" by equality of law. The "great" and the "humble" are then compelled to submit to the same law and it is this "most perfect state of liberty" to which the mind aspires.[73]

Yet Americans since the Revolution had made a fateful mistake. Essential among the rights of man is a right to self-governance. A Farmer is not unusual in this view. He is unusual in seeing that a failure to engage in self-government directly leads to threats to *all* of one's rights. "Alas!," he sighs, "I see nothing in my fellow-citizens, that will permit my still fostering the delusion, that they are now capable of sustaining the weight of SELF-GOVERNMENT." A *few* among them will govern and government of the few is by "*force* only,—where men *relinquish part* of their natural rights to secure the *rest*, instead of a union of will and force, to protect *all* their natural rights, which ought to be the foundation of every rightful social compact."[74] Social inequalities become legitimated in law and the happiest early state of civil equality is lost. In A Farmer's more colorful language, "Laws are cobwebs, catching only the flies and letting the wasps escape."[75]

For reasons that are never spelled out clearly, A Farmer believes that representation per se leads to a bias in government toward the interests of the great.[76] This would be so, he suggests, even with such popular controls as rotation in office and recall. Rotation can be pernicious, in fact: "if virtue gets into office, rotation wheels it out, hated and despised."[77] It is thus not sufficient for him, as it is for most other Anti-Federalists, that sturdy checks be built into the plan of representation to prevent abuses by those in power.

If A Farmer would not accept Publius's praise of representation as a way of filtering the best society has to offer into government, he is more sympathetic to the argument that party divisions are a useful constraint on factious majorities even in true republics. However much he follows a Rousseauian path in his conception of the exercise of popular sovereignty, he leaves it where it points toward the general will. Rousseau had claimed that, if there are private interests in the polity, there should be many, so that they counterbalance each other *but* that it is better if there are none at all. A Farmer is closer to Madison on this score. The preservation of public liberty, he argues, depends on "the preservation of parties." For "wherever men are unanimous on great public questions, . . . freedom ceases and despotism commences. The object of a free and wise people should be so to balance parties, that *from the weakness of all you may be governed by the moderation of the combined judgments of the whole, not tyrannized ever by the blind passions of a few individuals.*"[78] In fact, given the power of majorities in democratic systems of government, and given that "the rights of individuals are frequently opposed to the apparent interests of the majority," not only parties but such constraints on power as a bill of rights are *more* essential in democracies than in other forms of government.[79] Even this model republican shows the powerful liberal influences on his thought; threats to individual rights are the paramount concern and they place constraints on the political institutions we ought to choose.

Nonetheless, what is clearer in A Farmer's presentation is that direct democracy is intrinsically valuable for all the reasons republicans have always claimed it to be. Moreover, this intrinsic value is essential to A Farmer's— unlike Brutus's, Cato's, and the Federal Farmer's—political vision. His models are historical and philosophical. He admires the Swiss example, where every man is a legislator, with as much passion as Rousseau. Like Rousseau, he praises the misunderstood Machiavelli as a closet republican who, with "the greatest human discernment, . . . delivers his deliberate opinion in favor of the body of the people, as the only safe depository of liberty and power." "He prefers the people to the aristocracy or the Prince" and "does not disgrace the inquiry by mentioning representation."[80]

The virtue of direct democracy is the cultivation of the faculties of those who participate in it. This becomes clear in A Farmer's critique of the Constitution for not requiring jury trials for civil offenses.

> Men no longer cultivate, what is no longer useful,—should every opportunity be taken away, of exercising their reason, you will reduce them to that state of mental baseness, in which they appear in nine-tenths of this globe—distinguished from brutes, only by the form and articulation of sound—*Give them power and they will find understanding to use it.*[81]

Trial by jury is not defended as a better protection of the rights of the accused, although it does provide this. Rather, it is good for the opportunities it provides jurors to reason and talk with others in an important public activity.[82] This line of argument makes all the more poignant A Farmer's disenchantment with the decided lack of capacity exhibited by Americans for self-government under the Articles of Confederation.[83]

A Farmer faces the same chicken-and-egg problem encountered in Rousseau, Lenin, and others, who believe that their fellow citizens are failing to act in their own best interests. Citizens could be made better by good institutions, but those institutions will not be established unless the people demand them. Such a conundrum led Rousseau to call for a legislator who would "remake human nature" fitting a people for self-rule and Lenin to advance the idea of a vanguard party.

A Farmer is not so bold to call for either but the paradox plagues him. Thus, he argues,

That the people are not at present disposed for, and are actually incapable of, governments of simplicity and equal rights, I can no longer doubt—But whose fault is it? We make them bad, by bad governments and then abuse and despise them for being so. Our people are capable of being made anything, that human nature was or is capable of, if we would only have a little patience and give them good and wholesome institutions; but I see none and very little prospect of such.[84]

It is not clear who "we" refers to in this passage. If the people do not favor direct democracy, if too many among them are prone to "indolence" and are indifferent to forms of government as long as they are left undisturbed, who do the people—"we"—have to blame but themselves?[85] Or, does the pronoun refer after all to some legislators who are failing their duties by not forming institutions to make the people better? In either case, A Farmer's lament is starker and more poignant than those of Brutus, Cato, and the Federal Farmer, who consider the gradual decline in "virtue" among the people as a liberal political economy develops. A Farmer is as helpless as they are in coming up with means to counteract this trend in a generally liberal culture, where people are free to choose their own conceptions of the good life, but he is more devastated by it, since the classical republican value of self-development through political participation is more important to him.

Given such a pessimistic view, A Farmer is led to consider "second-best" forms of government and the one he favors is a mixed government modeled on the British constitution. Under any system of government short of direct democracy, representatives of the people are drawn from the great rather than the humble and show little respect for the latter. This bias is mitigated by a permanent distinction of ranks in society and, he argues, by an executive "sacred from impeachment" and a senate also appointed for life. These officers are presumably disinterested enough, given their permanent positions, to "hold the balance" in society among social orders and must "have the power of adding weight and influence to the lightest scale."[86]

However consistent this analysis is with classical mixed-government theory (and A Farmer's analysis of the vicissitudes of power and cycles of decline through class conflict would be familiar to Aristotle or Polybius), it is not a terribly effective counterpoise to the Federalist case for the Constitution. A Farmer directly undermines key criticisms made by many other Anti-Federalists, for example, that the Constitution grants too much power to the executive, grants too long a term in office to the Senate, and invests the Senate with executive powers.

A Farmer makes little functional distinction between executive and Senate and, more important, it could reasonably be argued that, having ruled out "simple government" in America, the proposed Constitution better approaches second-best mixed government than anything the Anti-Federalists have to offer. In fact, A Farmer seems to throw up his hands at the prospect of devising any suitable form of government. The Constitution represents an attempt "to patch up the ruined fabric of the British Constitution for our use" and neglects that we lack the "distinctions of rank which preserve that government."

Simple, or direct-democratic, government is ruled out, on the other hand, by poor choices Americans have made and by their singular lack of virtue.[87]

However intriguing A Farmer's observations are, they are not relevant to the choice on the proposed Constitution. Nor are they consistent with the fundamental political principles of Brutus, Cato, and a Federal Farmer, much less Publius. He recognizes that most of his compatriots reject his philosophy, which places self-development through political participation at its core. He is not so brazen as to offer a platform for addressing this problem (though he goes some way toward this, for example, by favoring sumptuary laws). Rather, he meets this gap between his political commitments and American political practices more with the resignation of the martyr than the fire of the prophet.

In sum, the Anti-Federalists did not lack a republican rhetoric, nor did republican language wholly lack content. The language of virtue and its corruption is quite effective as a rhetorical device to better accuse their opponents and mobilize their supporters.[88] Such rallying language is to be expected in works of political persuasion, however self-consciously theoretical they are or claim to be. However, when one forces the Anti-Federalists to answer the questions of not only what is wrong with the Constitution, but what political theory underlies the identification of its faults, the republican-revisionist thesis becomes less compelling for most of their leading spokesmen. This is seen in the issues of distributive justice just discussed. For Brutus, Cato, the Federal Farmer, either republicanism is unable to provide criteria of distributive justice such that the market allocation of resources could be effectively criticized, or the Anti-Federalists rank the continued existence of republican virtues lower than maintaining liberal capitalist standards of just acquisition and entitlement, so that the latter should not be tampered with whatever the price to be paid by the former. A Farmer, who ranks this republican good more highly, is largely out of step with his compatriots and not terribly responsive to the issue of constitutional choice. In either case, a modified consensualism that recognizes institutional and dispositional differences in Federalist and Anti-Federalist political theories but grounds both in liberal-contractarian premises concerning the person, society, the state—but that also recognizes that consensus does not mean *complete* agreement on first principles—offers the most satisfactory account of the political ideas found in the constitutional ratification debates. What these debates have to teach us about the nature of citizenship in American society today is our last concern.

8

Conclusion: American Citizenship Viewed from the Founding

I began this study with a statement of Rousseau's problem—how to balance the competing demands of civic and private life on our time and energy—and attempted to provide some sense of the constitutional founders' response to it. Though I have rejected the revisionist view that classical republican notions of civic virtue played a large role in shaping the constitutional founders' thought, I have supported the revisionists to at least this extent: both Federalists and Anti-Federalists considered in some depth the social and psychological bases of civic motivations. They debated whether the national government could generate and sustain the support of citizens. They also disagreed over the role citizens should play in political decision making, with Anti-Federalists committed to variants of what I call weak republicanism. Neither Federalists nor Anti-Federalists believed institutional checks and balances to be enough to stabilize society without at least some degree of motivation of citizens to undertake civic duties. In making this case, I have attempted to give due weight to the differences within the broadly liberal consensus that has set the terms of debate in American politics.

Not all readers will be convinced by this "modified consensualist" position I have taken on the constitutional debates and I have little new in the way of persuasion to add here. Rather, I want to return to the normative concerns first addressed in chapter 2 and ask a "what if" question. What if there were a strong republican tradition for Americans to recover and to take as a guide in orienting civic practices today? Would we be wise to do as a recent scholar has suggested and reappropriate that tradition to provide us with a stronger conception of the common good? What, if anything, of political value would we be asked to sacrifice if we attempted to do so? I suggest that though there are many advocates of a revived republicanism, the force of their reasons have not matched the power of their convictions. What I call "neorepublicanism" remains essentially undefended. This critique does not imply, however, an endorsement of the rather passive notion of citizenship expounded by Publius. Liberal philosophy demands a full dialogue justifying political power to free and equal citizens, a much richer dialogue than Publius thought wise.

These questions will not take us far from the main concerns of this book. A great many Americans today believe that we as a people have not achieved the appropriate solution of the Rousseauian equation. And it will not surprise anyone that both scholars and others observing the American scene often invoke the founders' thought as a vehicle for expressing this concern. We have tilted, it is often suggested, too much in a privatistic direction and have grown apathetic about public affairs.[1] We encounter this concern among scholars and citizens from a range of political perspectives. The extent to which a revived republicanism is a solution for a widely perceived problem needs to be explored. In addressing this question, I point to several affinities in the debates between Federalists and Anti-Federalists and disagreements today over the proper role of the citizen in the American polity. Hence, I offer some last reflections on the *meaning* of the founding debates regarding citizenship for our own times.

Neoconservative and Neorepublican Citizenship

Criticisms of the civic spirit prevailing in the American polity have been made from both the political right and the left. Yet the nature of these criticisms differs sharply, especially concerning the appropriate levels and kinds of political participation in American life. Thus, the "neoconservative," Daniel Bell has written passionately on the loss of *civitas* in American life and has traced this loss to a cultural contradiction endemic to liberal capitalist societies. Those critics on the left who advocate a more participatory democracy have likewise decried what they see as an inability to articulate common concerns in a shared language grounded in common goals. One such critic of note, Robert Bellah, calls on Americans to revive a "republican" and biblical past when, presumably, conceptions of public virtue were more in force.[2]

The concern expressed about the weakness of civitas in American liberal democracy is certainly not a new one in the American context. Tocqueville noticed the sharp pull of American society toward an excessive concern with material success and, indeed, toward a narrow egoism more than one-hundred and fifty years ago. To be sure, democratic societies yield "fewer splendid deeds" than aristocratic ones, whether of the classical republican or later Christian European type.[3] But more important for our purposes, a democratic people feels less connected to other parts of the social whole as they lose a sense of society as an organism whose parts each make a unique (though not equally valuable) contribution to the good of the whole. We may feel, Tocqueville suggests, a sense of community at the level of neighborhood or township, but we have less of a sense of society *as a* community with a shared sense of common good.

Yet Tocqueville was equally profound in his diagnosis of those aspects of American life that counteract this trend. Americans, he noted, are joiners. We do get involved over issues of immediate and local concern. Moreover, we take pride in our democracy and if it at times this gives rise to a prickly defensiveness about our institutions and beliefs, it also manifests itself in a well-founded pride in what a free, democratic people can accomplish without direction from above. Tocqueville recognized, in short, that the same egalitarian and democratic beliefs that give rise to the worst within us also give rise to the best. Even if it were possible to eliminate democracy's "ills," Tocqueville's analysis hints that a price may be paid in doing so. We may risk losing as well the "blessings" democracy bestows.

Whether Americans are less civic minded today than in the late eighteenth or nineteenth centuries is difficult to ascertain. There is no easy way to measure civic mindedness, and political scientists who study even the readiest measure of civic participation, voting in national elections, come to widely divergent conclusions whether they are explaining participation rates in the United States as compared to other countries or those in the United States over time. Some emphasize cultural factors, others the effects of registration laws and the level of interparty competition.[4] And, even if this is the case, I doubt that a fundamental shift from a predominant republican to a liberal ideology is the explanation for it.[5]

It is worth remembering that the authors of *The Federalist* considered the active patriotism of the revolutionary era to be the result of a "temporary ardor," not long sustainable in periods of normal politics. And, among the Anti-Federalists, no less a figure than the Federal Farmer, who also speaks of the temporary ardor of the revolutionary era, was equally sure that the public's concern would shortly be redirected to private affairs and thus recommended the creation of "constitutional barriers" to protect the people as they grow less vigilant.[6]

I do know that many perceptive social critics of contemporary American society from the left and the right at least perceive a loss of *civitas* and try to explain it. Thus, Bell describes a crisis in our civic culture and suggests that a new public philosophy is needed for our age. "The difficulty is that the public household of the twentieth century is not a community but an arena, in which there are no normative rules (other than bargaining) to define the common good and adjudicate claims on the basis of rights. The question again is: what can be the political philosophy of the public household?"[7]

Bell is as emphatic as any radical in his understanding of "bourgeois appetites which resist curbs on acquisitiveness" as a source of tension in liberal societies.[8] The sum of his critique of the public household today is that these appetites are decreasingly restrained in a polity that is increasingly democratic. Thus, its members demand "more and more social services as entitlements" while their "individualist ethos" impels them to "at best [defend] the idea of personal liberty, and at worst evade the necessary social responsibilities and social sacrifices which a communal society demands."[9]

If the public had been more willing in the nineteenth and early twentieth centuries to meet these responsibilities (and this is a big if), the explanation for Bell lies largely in the historical conjoining of capitalism and the Protestant ethic. The latter had provided capitalism with a religious legitimation for those virtues that capitalism requires and ostensibly rewards (diligence, honesty, and other forms of delayed gratification). The demise of the Protestant ethic, argues Bell, exposes a cultural contradiction at the heart of capitalism itself. While the production of wealth and political order require those bourgeois virtues, consumption—in an era when the output of fully utilized productive resources cannot find available markets—requires an ethos of self-gratification.[10]

The political spillover of this sociocultural change is an "entitlement revolution," in which citizens make numerous demands on government for specific programs as matters of "right," and a corresponding disinclination on the part of citizens to moderate their own claims to scarce resources to accommodate the claims of others. Bell states this more starkly: "The major consequence of this crisis . . . is the loss of *civitas*, that spontaneous willingness to obey the law, to respect the rights of others, to forego the temptations of private enrichment at the expense of the public weal . . . . Instead, each man goes his own way, pursuing his private vices, which can be indulged only at the expense of public benefits."[11]

Bell's analysis is seconded by Samuel Huntington, another friendly critic of American democracy from the political right. Huntington's understanding of the loss of *civitas* is, however, less cultural and more directly political. "The effective operation of a democratic system," he argues, "usually requires some measure of apathy and noninvolvement on the part of some individuals or groups." The problem is that certain groups that were marginal and generally uninvolved in politics in the past, including blacks and women, are now involved in politics and making demands for government resources. This risks overloading the democratic process. "Less marginality on the part of some groups," Huntington argues, "needs to be replaced by more self-restraint on the part of all groups."[12] Like Bell, Huntington leaves open the question of whether—or how—this ethos of self-restraint can emerge in the late twentieth century.[13]

If critics of American citizenship from the right have tended to focus on the instabilities created by citizens participating *too much* (read also as demanding too much), many on the left have bemoaned the harmful effects of a body of citizens who do not participate *enough*. These "neorepublican" critics suggest that American liberal democracy fails its citizens in areas having to do with fellowship and, more broadly, the "meaning of life." Benjamin Barber, who expresses these concerns as well as anyone today, puts it as follows:

> "Thin democracy" . . . yields neither the pleasures of participation nor the fellowship of civic association, neither the autonomy and self-governance of continuous political activity nor the enlarging mutuality of shared public goods—of mutual deliberation, decision, and work. . . .[T]hin democratic politics is at best a static politics of interest, never a politics of transformation; a politics of bargaining and exchange, never a politics of invention and creation; a politics that conceives of women and men at their worst (in order to protect themselves), never at their potential best (to help them become better than they are).[14]

The metaphor of thinness is encountered with some frequency among neorepublicans, and in all cases they use it to suggest that liberal democracy leaves its citizens psychically (perhaps even spiritually) malnourished. It suggests that Americans lack a robust conception of the public good and that this lack distorts the manner in which they choose to lead their private lives as well. Sheldon Wolin develops the first theme by pointing to a "thin theory of legitimacy" and a "thin theory of consent" as pathologies of American political culture.[15] The centralization of political power in the administrative state of the twentieth century and great concentrations of economic power have contributed to the "delegitimization of democratic man" and the replacement of the very notion of citizen by that much studied specimen, the American voter. "A state that needs only formal legitimization," he writes, reduces "the citizen to such a negligible consideration that all the burning issues of political theory—participation, equality, civic virtue, and justice—no longer seem to matter."[16]

Politics is reduced to symbolic behavior. Citizens vote and thereby relegitimize the regime but have little effect on political outcomes, which are determined by interest group politics. More importantly, absence of opportunities for effective participation deprives citizens of such goods as "moral autonomy" and "political agency," goods that are the essence of the good life.[17] Public life becomes divided between ritualized reaffirmations of national identity and an arena for competition among possessive individuals.

Generalizing from a recent series of interviews with a wide cross section of Americans, Robert Bellah and his co-authors phrase a similar point somewhat differently. Bellah describes the "limitations in the common tradition of moral discourse," which deprive the Americans interviewed (and believed to be representative) of a language with which to articulate their commitments to social and political ideals. Their "first language," the one that comes most naturally to them, is radically individualistic. It is adequate to articulate conceptions of fair procedures for getting what one wants (that is, conceptions of equal opportunity), but not to identify "exactly what we should want."[18] It is in offering public conceptions of the latter that Bellah finds Americans especially inarticulate. The thinness of shared conceptions of the public good, he suggests, leads citizens to assume that "there is something arbitrary about the goals of the good life." Thus, it is not clear how the good life can come to be defined in terms of the substantive values Wolin identifies as the core valudes of the Western political tradition or how these values could come to regulate the conduct of citizens. There is simply no consensus on the meanings of these terms. Bellah writes that there is a "thin theory of consensus limited largely to procedural matters."[19] It is natural, therefore, for Americans to seek purposes in their lives in the private sphere and to conceive of their choices as arbitrary ones that do not have to be (and perhaps cannot be) defended in a court of public opinion.

Barber, Wolin, and Bellah all contend that participation is somehow good for us and that the absence of effective channels for it in the American polity is regrettable.[20] And, while they seem to place a higher value on participation than do most Americans, a weaker version of the types of concerns they express is encountered in editorial pages and television commentaries across the nation, especially at election time. At the same time, efforts to increase participation (largely for its own sake) have characterized many of the institutional and procedural reforms in party and electoral politics, at least through the 1980 presidential election.[21] These theorists do not, therefore, speak for a set of values that places them far outside mainstream concerns of practicing politicians and decision makers.

Whether we look at neoconservative or neorepublican critics today, the arguments of each sound eerily familiar to students of the American founding. Like Huntington, the authors of *The Federalist* expressed deep concerns about the sorts of demands, especially redistributive ones, that an actively participating citizenry might make. These concerns gave rise both to a strong defense of representative, as opposed to direct, democracy and to a Humean reluctance to disturb habitual, customary attachment to government by calling attention to its real or imagined defects.

This is not to say that either Publius's or the neoconservative position regarding civic participation bears up all that well under scrutiny. Certainly, our society has withstood the strains of a much broader electorate than Madison or Hamilton would have endorsed. And the neoconservative complaints of Bell and Huntington, developed in the 1970s, already seem dated. Politicians of the Reagan and Bush era have resisted importunings for new social programs—especially ones conceived as entitlements—quite successfully if not always beneficially. Budget pressures have been a frequent rationale for such resistance among both Democrats and Republicans. The "entitlement revolution" described by Bell and the dangers of overloaded democracy expressed by Huntington are, at least, in abeyance.

Another, if weaker, affinity can be located in the current neorepublican position(s) and some of the arguments made by the Anti-Federalists in favor of local democracy. The neorepublicans mentioned echo—and restate in sronger terms—Anti-Federalist republican concerns in their more self-conscious call for a revival of republicanism in contemporary American life. I have suggested that relatively few of the Anti-Federalist arguments against "consolidation" and even for democratic practices that kept government closer to the people (for example, large legislative assemblies, short electoral terms, and rotation in office) grew out of a fully articulated republican philosophy. Not the least important reason for this was a firm commitment to Lockean liberal natural rights and a belief that the primary role of government is to secure them. Yet, we found that some Anti-Federalists expressed a conception of civic participation as valuable for fostering a sense of community and creating more civic-minded persons. In contrast, while the Lockean liberal commitments of such neorepublicans as Barber and Bellah are much more ambivalent than were those of their weak-republican American predecessors, the importance of the republican perfectionist theory of civic participation as essential to the good life is much stronger.

Apart from the historical claims on which they rely, neorepublicans raise an intriguing normative question. Would the United States have been a better place if classical republican commitments had played a stronger role in our founding debates? Here I am skeptical. This is so in part because neither the Anti-Federalists nor contemporary neorepublicans provided adequate guidance on how liberal and republican values can or should be conjoined. They offer a politics more of aspiration than of culmination, making it difficult for the observer to see what we risk losing, or what we stand to gain, if we took republicanism seriously.

One ought to recognize, as did Tocqueville—and as neorepublicans do— the potentially corrosive effects liberal democracies can have on notions of public good and a sense of community. I discussed some of these effects in chapter 2. If, however, one is being asked to abandon aspects of liberalism in order to foster community, then a strong case ought to be made for doing so. In this case, we are entitled to know what "blessings," to borrow Tocqueville's phrase, we thereby put at risk. This case, by and large, has not been made. Neorepublicanism today remains as little defended as was the weak republican synthesis of the Anti-Federalists.[22] This is a strong charge and it requires some explaining.

The Neorepublican Case Considered

Embedded in each of the contemporary advocacies of participatory politics discussed is some form of a perfectionist, Aristotelian theory of the good. Barber's critique of thin democracy shows this quite explicitly. It rests on the notion that each person has a best possible self that is realized in civic context and that liberal democracy's inability to promote this route to personal development is the greatest indictment of it. The political system should some- how enable citizens to become "better than they are."

Bellah's theory of citizenship is implicitly perfectionist as well. His con- cern with the lack of substantive, as opposed to procedural, areas of consensus in American politics and with the lack of a "common moral vocabulary" to articulate common goals indicates this. Also indicative is his doleful observa- tion of the extent to which Americans sense an arbitrariness about their ideas of the good life. They sense, that is, that the good life is good because they chose it rather than because of its intrinsic merits. This concern can imply only that this sense of arbitrariness is avoidable, that Americans would come to a consensus on how best to live if they had the moral language in with to do so. In fact, Bellah describes the main purpose of his work as aiding Americans in reappropriating traditions of American political discourse (bibli- cal and republican ones) that are better equipped to generate a "thick consen- sus" than the unmitigated individualism that is currently dominant.

Barber's and Bellah's perfectionism raises epistemological and ethical questions that are beyond the scope of this chapter (for example, what is the good and how do we come to know it?).[23] I will restrict myself to two points. First, I suspect that their conception of the good life as centered around civic participation has an intuitive appeal to many readers, even those whose conduct does not conform to their intuitions. It is not unusual to hear people say that they would like to be better informed about issues and more active in political causes (that is, they would feel *better* about themselves if they were more informed) but that they simply do not have the time. A firmer empirical indication of this is the fact that a substantial number of citizens tell pollsters that they are registered voters and *did* vote in elections who did not actually do so. Much as La Rochefoucauld said that hypocrisy is the homage vice pays to virtue, claiming to vote when one has not is a recognition of the validity of the social norm defining voting as the sort of thing one should do.[24]

But, second, this intuitive appeal has its limits and becomes even more restricted upon reflection from the point of view of liberal first principles. If Barber and Bellah want to claim a special and privileged status for the political life among competing conceptions of the good life, the appeal of their position becomes more suspect on liberal grounds. One cannot maintain this position without implying that those who do not act on this conception of the good are somehow defective either cognitively or morally. Perhaps they are unable to see where their good lies. Worse, perhaps they do see it but do not act upon it.[25]

It is this last implication that is potentially troubling. Aristotle could make such a claim quite directly, since his political theory was avowedly perfectionist. Given the premise that the role of the state is to enable citizens to realize the good life for man, it was incumbent on him to theorize about the nature of the good life. That it was to some significant degree a political life (we should not forget that Aristotle recognizes, as did Plato, the virtues of the contemplative life) can best by explained in reference to the nature of the small, homogeneous Greek city-state. The plausibility of this conception lost force as the Greek polis was replaced by the Hellenistic and then Roman cosmopolis.

It is perhaps not inevitable that life in more cosmopolitan societies tends to draw us away from Aristotle's notion of the political nature of the good life, but at least it is understandable. Oscar Wilde captured this non-Aristotelian point with characteristic wit in his critique of socialism—it takes too many evenings, that is, too many committee meetings, a point with which most of us in the academy can readily empathize. I do not know any arguments that Barber provides that would persuade Wilde that his time would indeed be better spent in committee meetings than writing at his desk or exchanging witticisms in the shadow of the Eiffel Tower. Moreover, I am reasonably sure that posterity has been better served by having access to Wilde's unique sensibilities through his works than it would have been knowing that he did not write as much or as well because of his political activities.

I have not even raised for objection the potentially more troubling position of coercing Wilde and others with his preferences to become more political. Yet even at the current level of discussion, the question arises about the compatibility of Bellah's and Barber's civic ideals with liberal ideology and, to the extent that disharmonies exist between them, over what adjustments must be made to preserve the best of both ideals. Neither writer is oblivious to this question. Neither altogether denies that liberal societies have their virtues. Yet, it is also true that neither offers us much practical guidance in combining the blessings of liberalism and republicanism while diminishing their respective ills. That being the case, the political preferences of each remain essentially unsupported by argument.

To illustrate this point, let us look at one area of possible tension between liberal and republican commitments. Bellah advocates a "new social ecology," that is, the redrawing of relations among persons, and between man and nature, that would take place in a civic world he would prefer. One element of this change is that people would learn to place greater value on the intrinsic rewards of their activities and less on the trappings of success that these activities bring. The distinction is between, let us say, a musician who practices in order to develop her craft and one who practices—and does whatever else it takes, to become a superstar. More attention to intrinsic rewards, Bellah argues, will not only make us happier; it also forms the basis for a "more genuinely integrated societal community."[26]

> The satisfaction of work well done, indeed "the pursuit of excellence," is a permanent and positive human motive. Where its reward is the approbation of one's fellows more than the accumulation of private wealth, it can contribute to what the founders of our republic called civic virtue. Indeed, in a revived social ecology, it would be a primary form of civic virtue.[27]

Bellah suggests that this form of civic virtue would require changes in the relationship between government and economy and in the very relations of production. Government would, for example, encourage efforts in economic democracy though it would not nationalize industries. These two points are, however, essentially all the practical guidance Bellah provides on how America's methods of doing business will be affected by the changes he endorses. And, while it would be unfair to expect a blueprint or even a party platform for the future from him, it is curious that certain realities of the capitalist mode of production and the constraints they impose on implementing institutional reforms conducive to his civic vision are left unexplored. Not the least of these constraints is that, as Bell notes, economic expansion requires that consumers and producers want those external rewards that are so bad for us.

One need not be a neoconservative, or a Marxist, to recognize that abandonment of dreams of private success would erode incentives for production. Perhaps we would be better off with less, as many have argued. But we would still have to deal with those workers displaced by changes in consumption patterns, and with the question of whose responsibility it would be to retrain them and for what. There would surely be redistributive consequences of Bellah's new social ecology and it is certainly a point of interest where the burdens and benefits would fall. In fact, I do not see how the *justice* of his proposed reforms can be evaluated without considering these consequences.

Further, Bellah recognizes that there is some relation between a capitalist economy and the desires persons within it have for external goods. It does not matter for this recognition whether base determines superstructure, as Marx might say, or vica versa, as Weber might argue. It is enough that some non-random relation exists between the two.[28] Since Bellah is especially concerned with acquisitiveness and its political consequences, it is reasonable to ask how the link between the two is to be broken. It is not clear, for example, that the piecemeal implementation of economic democracy within individual firms is adequate to the sort of transformation of values he advocates. Economic democracy within firms may alter how owners, management, and labor share profits, and it will allow for more worker input in the production process. But, given that firms operate in a competitive economy, democratic ones are subject to the same market forces as autocratic ones and it does not follow that the motives of their managers and employees will differ. It is as reasonable to assume that they will be as dedicated to dreams of private success, although, of course, other members of the firm gain from it in proportion. Once again, the radicalness of Bellah's social vision is not done justice by the paucity of reforms he offers for realizing it.

Much of the same ambivalence is found in Barber's recommendations for changes in the political process to facilitate strong democracy (SD). Barber is aware of potential incompatibilities between strong and liberal democracy and devotes the bulk of his book to exploring them. Further, his recognition of the commitment most Americans have to liberal democracy leads him to recommend gradualism to the strong-democrat reformer. The strong democrat must assuage "Madisonian" fears about the consequences of opening up participatory opportunities, for example, that doing so will encourage parochialism, that pressures for social conformity will arise, and sub-rosa manipulation of votes in small assemblies will occur. Not the least reason for recommending gradualism is that these fears are, in large measure, justified.[29] Thus, the strong democrat should stress that participatory reforms complement constitutional rights of minorities and representative democratic institutions.

> The strong democrat who says, "Let us experiment with neighborhood assemblies, with an initiative and referendum process, . . . with local participation in neighborhood common work, and with national participation in legislative decision-making," speaks a language liberal democrats can respect even when they disagree with its recommendations. The strong democrat who says, "Let us tear down our oligarchic representative institutions and shove aside the plodding Constitutional safeguards that mire the sovereign people in a swamp of checks and balances . . . " subverts his democratic faith in the rush to achieve his democratic goals. He is not to be trusted. Strong democracy is a complementary strategy that adds without removing and that reorients without distorting. There is no other way.[30]

Barber is surely correct to suggest that given the commitment most Americans have to liberal democracy, the strong democrat would make little headway with a frontal assault on it. A gradualist policy that stresses complementary goals is indicated if he expects to be effective. Yet, passages like the one just cited do leave some doubt about where the balance lies between liberal and strong-democratic virtues and vices.

Barber offers a set of concrete reforms for institutionalizing strong democracy that range from neighborhood to national levels. He advocates establishing neighborhood assemblies for local decision making and discussion of broader issues, citizens' groups to do neighborhood common work, experiments in institutions of lay justice for misdemeanor offenses, and some choosing local office holders by lot. Nationally, he supports initiative and referendum procedures, publicly funded civic information services, electronic balloting (using an interactive television system) that provides immediate tabulation of public responses to multichoice survey questions, compulsory universal public service on the VISTA or Peace Corps model, and experiments in workplace democracy.[31] Barber stresses the necessity of implementing the whole package of reforms in its entirety despite the practical difficulties involved, among them the incremental nature of the American political process and the fact that some reforms would clearly be more offensive to liberal democrats than others.

Some of the reforms would almost certainly be the subject of litigation and some of the litigation would focus on alleged violations of constitutional rights. At one point, Barber argues that the "inertial force" of the Constitution is the "best check" on the excesses of strong democracy.[32] This check would, of course, be too strong if it killed the program. Recent judicial experience with draft registration laws suggest that universal public service would be a matter of constitutional dispute, even with a nonmilitary option. Some citizens will find compulsory "do-gooder" service as or more offensive than serving in the armed forces. Given the primacy of politics for Barber, would this belief serve as grounds for conscientious objection? The constitutionality of many other reforms would depend on precisely what activities the institutions would undertake. What is the range of decisions that neighborhood assemblies will be permitted to make? The same question can be asked of workplace assemblies and community action groups. Can neighbors be "forced to be free" if they do not cut their crabgrass or do whatever else meets neighborhood standards of decorum?

The range-of-decision problem is central to Barber's thesis on the complementarity of liberal and strong democratic ideals. In order to do justice to the perfectionist strains in his advocacy of strong democracy (as a practice that *transforms* citizens, making them "better than they are"), the range of decisions would, I think, have to be broader than the Constitution would allow. It is not clear that individuals would be transformed into Rousseauian citizens if, for example, the decision-making powers of neighborhood assemblies were restricted to writing zoning laws. There may be justifications for allowing citizens direct participatory input into this process, but it is difficult to see that it would make them better persons. At least, it is not evident that it would do so any more than would *any other* form of public activity, such as planning the company picnic or coaching the local Little League team.

The above example of limits on local assemblies' powers may be overly restrictive. It does, however, point out the types of constraints liberalism must place on strong democracy. The essence of rights in the liberal tradition is that they function as constraints on state power *whether or not* this power is constituted democratically. Rights, such as those embodied in the first eight Amendments to the Constitution, restrict the range of issues subject to normal democratic procedures.[33] Moreover, areas are off limits to democratic determinations precisely because they are conceived to be most essential to each person's pursuit of her chosen good. This notion is captured in the familiar Lockean triad of rights to life, liberty, and property.

A persistent problem in liberal democratic theory and practical politics has been to locate the boundaries of these restricted areas. Federal courts are frequently asked to decide boundary disputes, as, for example, the extent to which the distribution of pornography can be restricted by local laws. Strong democrats, however, cannot afford to be indifferent to this issue any more than liberals, especially if they advocate conjoining strong- and liberal-democratic practices. In the absence of deliberation, they simply do not offer reasons for accepting their vision of the well-ordered polity (and personality) to those of us who do not accept them intuitively. To the extent that I place a value on the right to free expression or freedom of contract, I will want to know whether, and to what degree, democratic reformers are willing to subject this right (or its exercise in concrete cases) to the outcomes of democratic deliberation. I will want to know this for reasons of self-interest. Will I be compensated for restrictions on the exercise of an erstwhile right? But I will also want an answer to evaluate the *justice* of strong-democratic practices. Participation is not the only political good and considerations of justice require an evaluation of the trade-offs justice may demand between "negative freedoms" and entitlements to material goods.

In sum, the two critiques of Barber's notion of strong democracy are virtually mirror images of each other. First, taking liberalism seriously leaves too narrow a range of decision for democratic processes to satisfy the perfectionist claims made for strong democracy. Second, taking strong democracy seriously may so broaden this range as to violate constitutionally guaranteed liberal freedoms. In either case, Barber's complementarity thesis is called into question. Barber is too competent a political thinker to be unaware of these tensions and of the radical reconceptualization of the way Americans do politics that strong democracy would require. A sense of this awareness is indicated in the following remark:

> If democracy is popular government in the name of and for the benefit of individual liberty (the classical Lockean formulation), collective coercion in matters political and economic will always appear as illegitimate . . . On the other hand, if democracy is popular government in the name of equality and

social justice, collective coercion will appear not only as a necessity but as an essential aspect of legitimacy. The legitimate common will will be manifested as the community in action, exerting itself as a decisive instrument in shaping the common future.[34]

The latter understanding is, of course, strong democracy although Barber has little to say about either social justice or equality in his exposition of it. In any case, the Rousseauian ring of the passage just cited is likely to give liberals pause—and for good reason. For liberals, the future is shaped by the "tyranny of small decisions" of many (government-regulated) individual and group actors. For strong democrats, it is the product of the common will that plans it. Barber is correct to note that liberals tend to resent the exercise of governmental power even if it is democratically constituted. But to say that strong democrats will accept "collective coercion" more readily does not relieve one of the need to provide criteria for the legitimacy of the uses to which this power can be put. In the absence of some such criteria—of a theory of justice—strong democracy remains essentially undefended as an ideal or as a practice.

I have called into question the historical claim that republicanism was as vital an intellectual influence during the debates over the Constitution as the revisionists have suggested. I have also questioned the desirability of republicanism as a guiding ideology, at least as it has been formulated by its best contemporary exponents. Liberal citizenship is not, however, necessarily Madisonian citizenship. In challenging the revisionist case I have not endorsed Publius's implicit advocacy of a passive, habitually loyal citizenry—or his assessment of the dangers of a more active one.

There are good reasons for committed liberals to be troubled by the normative implications of Publius's notion of civic involvement. I suggested in chapter 2 that liberalism is not only compatible with but *demands* a full public dialogue on the justification of political power over free and equal individuals.[35] When Publius suggests that recourse to "first principles" of government ought not be encouraged, as Madison did in his response to Jefferson's call for periodic constitutional conventions, modern liberals must ask why.

The debate over what liberal principles require can never be settled once and for all if only because technological changes open up new possibilities for state control (for example, in surveillance techniques) and new spheres of personal choice (for example, genetic engineering). Liberals must be willing to reconsider what principles require in light of new social possibilities, and respect for persons dictates that all have an opportunity to participate in political dialogue. This entails the absence of formal restrictions on participation, such as poll taxes or literacy tests. It also entails, I think, some degree of substantive equality, the absence of which inhibits political participation by those with insufficient time for politics.

The liberal ideal demands that governmental policies be justified from the standpoint of the individual, a condition that can be met only if opportunities exist to shape outcomes of policy debate. It is an ideal imperfectly met, to be sure. Our society has not only excluded groups historically on grounds of race and gender; it has allowed and continues to allow unequal access to the political process through campaign financing and lobbying. Such practices are of concern for liberals in that they confer privilege on given interests and hinder others in the public arena for morally arbitrary reasons.

As Ronald Dworkin has suggested, sacrifices (as those imposed through a government austerity program) can be asked legitimately of members of a community if and only if they have a real voice in public decision making. He writes that "If people are asked to sacrifice for their community, they must be offered some reason why the community which benefits from that sacrifice is *their* community. . . . [An individual] can . . . accept present deprivation as sacrifice rather than tyranny, only if he has some power to help determine the shape of that future [emphasis added]."[36]

Dworkin is right to claim that membership in a liberal political community should presuppose a capacity to make one's political preferences known. Yet people will differ over the time and effort they wish to attach to politics as opposed to other activities, and a liberal society should see to it that those who choose to pursue other ends are not effectively punished for doing so. This would likely be the case if all of our political institutions were built on a participatory-democratic model, which would bias policies toward the interests of the activists, who often do not represent the preferences of the public at large.

Like any political philosophy, liberal democracy offers a conception of the public good. It must, however, accept that fundamental rights constrain the pursuit of private conceptions of the good when they run afoul of others' rights. Thus, however valuable practices like prayer in school or restrictions on disruptive speech may be in generating a richer sense of community, they are suspect if they require restricting individual expression of religious or political commitments. Neither social utility nor conceptions of public virtue ought to be allowed to determine social choices if they violate the rights of persons. When they do so is, of course, a matter for legislative and judicial determination.

Now Madison and Hamilton were extremely doubtful that liberal rights to life, liberty, and property could be respected given a highly mobilized citizenry. Their pessimism, it seems to me, has little to do with the core liberal commitments that Madison in particular expressed. It is, at least, not entailed by those commitments. Moreover, each time we have expanded the electorate by including previously excluded groups, such as blacks and women, we have effectively suggested that a liberal-democratic system can tolerate a larger, more diverse civic body than either Madison and Hamilton thought possible. There is no reason to doubt that it could tolerate a more participatory public as well, neoconservative arguments notwithstanding. There is also no reason to give these constitutional founders the final word on what our civic commitments can or should be. The common American practice of seeking a pedigree for one's values in the founders' thought is not always fruitful, and especially not on this issue.

We should also, however, keep sight of what is most valuable and still viable in the constitutional founders' politics: a commitment to liberal justice that recognizes the moral worth of each person and embodies it politically in a commitment to fundamental rights. Contemporary republicans should recognize the dangers, as the constitutional founders did, of asking more classical republican virtue from the American republic than it wants—or could stand— to give.

Appendix: A Note on Method

The view has become common in recent years that political theory is history or it is nothing. This view takes various forms but essential to all of them is the notion that the meaning of texts can be captured only in the context of their times.[1] Whatever one makes of this view—and I think it has been over-done—political theorists, even those commonly designated as historians of political thought, are not generally well-trained to be intellectual historians. We tend to want to test our wits, to paraphrase Matthew Arnold, against the best that has been thought and said. There is, to be sure, some egoism in this since there is little satisfaction in interpreting and criticizing weak arguments. But there is a point of principle as well.

The great books that define the Western tradition of political theory are great precisely because they offer the most profound reflections on the human condition. On one view, they clarify ideas that members of society hold in-choately. Thus, Aristotle presents a somewhat idealized view of the practices of the Athenian city-state (even as he criticizes aspects of the practices). But the great books do more than this; we do not need theorists only to explicate dominant ideologies. Political theorists are, in fact, moderately more useful in criticizing them and offering alternatives. This criticism needs some starting point and it is often provided by the intuitions widely shared in one's political culture. The depth of criticism depends at least in part on the extent to which the theorist shares these intuitions. Though inconsistencies among intuitions, or in their ordering, become apparent to any competent theorist, a minimal task is to test them against rational criteria of consistency and coherence. The aim of this project is to assess which of our intuitions remain acceptable to us upon reflection.[2]

Theorists tend to want to draw lessons from the great books for their own societies or, failing that, their own souls. This concern is fraught with dangers, however, from the historian's point of view. The present-day or personal focus of theorists can elide into the historical vice of anachronism. One is lead to suspect that the secularization of Locke, for which the works of Macpherson and Leo Strauss have been rightly criticized, is a case in point. Locke is taken by each to be a precursor of certain contemporary vices, whether bourgeois appropriation of capital or a nihilism inherent in "modernity." It is not surpris-ing that given these practical concerns, the "premodern" aspects of Lockean thought get lost.

Indeed, the very notion of a western tradition of political thought is something of a fiction. It is, at least, a strange notion of tradition that allows us to
pull great books from such diverse social settings.[3] We perpetuate this fiction
by thinking of the great books as engaged in a "great dialogue." In fact,
reconstructing this dialogue by fitting individual thinkers into the tradition has
been the primary task of many twentieth-century historians of political
thought, including Strauss, Eric Voegelin, and Sheldon Wolin.

The notion of a tradition, even of a great dialogue, can be defended because
the political philosophers who are taken to constitute it did address each other
frequently and directly. One need only think of Hobbes's barbs against the
medieval "schoolmen," or Locke's attempts to differentiate his views, not only
from Filmer's, but from those of Hobbes. Yet, by stressing this we risk making
the great political thinkers into more "bookish" sorts than they actually were.
The exiles of Machiavelli, Locke, Marx, and others indicate that their ideas
mattered enough to contemporaries to be seen as threats to some of the most
powerful among them. Their ideas mattered not because kings or parliaments
were particularly concerned with such theoretical questions as the nature of
the right and the good but because of the political challenges their works
posed. Thus, abstracting the great books out of their context to promote the
notion of a great dialogue exacts a price. We lose a sense of how political
ideas could have mattered so much to contemporaries engaged in politics.

Indeed, there is probably no more intractable bone of contention between
contemporary historians and political theorists than how great political ideas
come to influence political practitioners and future generations of thinkers.
When we political theorists tackle this historical problem, we often tend to
assume that the best ideas are the most influential. We do not usually articulate
so crude a view, but it comes through in our choice of subject matter. I think
it is undeniable that a tracing of the American founders' thought to Locke is
more plausible to most theorists, perhaps to most general readers, than being
traced to, say, Burlamaqui, or even to putting Locke on a par with Burlamaqui.
The problem is that it cannot be presumed a priori that historical personages
are most impressed by the best ideas available to them. I leave aside the question of whether our judgment of which ideas are best can be defended without
anachronism.[4] We know, for example, that Ronald Reagan found more inspiration in the conservative *Reader's Digest* clone, *Human Events*, than he did in
Edmund Burke or Adam Smith.

As with the notion of a tradition, the theorist's bias need not be historically
indefensible, although it certainly can be. A strong case could be made that
the ideas found in *Human Events* are inchoate versions of notions better expressed by Burke and/or Smith and, therefore, that we can make most sense
of Ronald Reagan in the context of a modern conservative tradition even if
he himself is waiting for the movie versions of *The Wealth of Nations* and
Reflections on the Revolution in France. I am prejudging not the documenta-
tion of this claim, merely its intelligibility.

This solution replaces the question of influence or, at least, reinterprets it
in terms of *correspondence*. I use this term to cover cases in which an author

or speaker is appropriating ideas available in his political culture whether by assenting to them or implicitly rejecting them. It stipulates as the main concern *our* understanding of Ronald Reagan and puts on the back burner the question of how he came to have the ideas he has. We would not want to say that someone has been influenced by books he has not read. At the same time, this is not cause to surrender a key tool for our understanding his thought, its correspondence to and explication in the thought of a clearer, deeper thinker.

Yet, the elision of these concerns, call them the *historical* and the *practical*, is bound to cause—and has caused—confusion between intellectual historians and political theorists. The claim, for example, that Locke is a Hobbesian can make perfectly good sense to the one group and very little to the other. Historians remind us that Locke, and his circle of religious dissenters, explicitly rejected such parentage. Political theorists, on the other hand, might deny Locke the last word on the subject and argue, as Macpherson does (though in some essential regards, wrongly), that Locke shares but moderates essential Hobbesian assumptions about human motivation and political cooperation. Whether he does so or not can be debated. The point here is that the outcome of this debate need not depend on Locke's self-understanding or the understanding of him by his contemporaries.

If the disciplinary bounds found in most universities between political theorists (including historians of political thought) and historians pose problems in communication and interpretation, there are as severe interpretive conundrums within each approach. The question of tracing the influence of ideas raises serious problems for the intellectual historian. Taking an example close at hand, the Federalists and Anti-Federalists cite a plethora of names in developing their arguments. They were rather like intellectual scavengers finding support where they could, much as, although more self-consciously than, politicians do today.

One useful though limited approach to sorting out the question of influence is a content analysis of writings yielding numbers of citations of various sources.[5] The same method can be applied to particular terms or concepts. As useful as this approach might be, it is hardly adequate to the task, as even its proponents recognize. Influence is too ambiguous a notion and there are too many possible relations between a text or concept and the person using it for the citation alone to explain much.

The conceptual—as opposed to the empirical—difficulty of establishing the historical influence of ideas is not to be minimized. Most of us are likely to be persuaded by ideas we are already at least somewhat disposed to accept. Those who doubt this should consider which opinion journals they subscribe to and the editorial writers they find most convincing. It is often difficult to ascertain even for ourselves whether the idea or argument we have read has influenced our views—if we mean by this an alteration in our convictions that would not have occurred in the absence of reading or experiencing this or that—or has reinforced or strengthened prior convictions. It is more difficult to make this determination about a third party, for whom we must suppose much more about the types of experiences and knowledge that are brought to bear on a problem. Thus, conclusive cases of direct and traceable influence of one person's ideas on another, especially on political questions where prior convictions play such a strong role, are going to be fairly rare. These are issues that call for more explicit theoretical consideration than is possible here. Although of primary concern to historians, a theory of influence would have to draw on research in other fields, particularly cognitive psychology, that explore the ways in which people's beliefs are changed by the introduction of new information.[6]

Moreover, as Quentin Skinner has observed, it is not enough to focus on political language per se to recover the author's intentions; rather, we must look at the uses to which language is put.[7] Among these uses could be the legitimization of some new practice by describing it in old commending terms. The authors of *The Federalist* were masters of this tactic as in their appropriation of the term *federalism*, formerly reserved for what we would call confederacies, to describe the more centralized government they proposed.

Another use of language is to neutralize the condemnation formerly attached to a term by deploying it in commendatory contexts. Albert Hirschman shows how this occurred in the seventeenth and eighteenth centuries with the notions of ambition, commerce, and interest. Interest tamed the passions as men engaged in the peaceful process of making themselves rich through commerce. Former hurrah-words such as *glory* and *honor* were correspondingly delegitimized and seen as sources of medieval violence and strife.[8]

Other examples of uses of language in political argument abound, but one we might call indirection is worth special mention. In this case, an author's ideas are appropriated though his name is not mentioned because it evokes condemnatory associations. Madison's use of Hume, at times to the point of paraphrase, is a particularly relevant case. When we find this strategy deployed, we have good reason to believe we have located a case of genuine influence. It is risky because disclosure of the source can discredit its user. It thus points to a sincerity on the part of the user. Hume's ideas were used, we can conclude, because they were the truest expressions of Madison's beliefs.

Knowledge of prevailing social and linguistic conventions is central to the task of tracing historical influences. We cannot know why, for example, Hume is rarely mentioned by name while Montesquieu is frequently without knowing more of the roles of these two thinkers in prevailing belief systems. And without this knowledge, we are hard-pressed to distinguish citations showing genuine influence from strictly strategic deployments.

Such knowledge is relevant but, I suggest, less central to satisfying our practical concerns, which rest on a *correspondence* between the ideas of one thinker and another. Noting correspondences can be illuminating, although they must be noted case by case. It is easy to think of cases where attempts at this sort of approach have led to some very bad social analysis indeed. I think particularly of recent works drawing connections between contemporary subatomic physics and ancient Buddhist understandings of being (and non-being).[9] Given the vastly different cultures from which such notions spring, it is unlikely that a correspondence tells us much of interest about either contemporary physics or Buddhism, however curious it may be. Another example is drawn from the gap between the "two cultures" of science and the humanities. It has been fashionable, for example, for humanistic social scientists favoring participant-observer approaches to call upon Heisenberg's uncertainty principle—that the motion of electrons cannot be observed without being altered by the observer—to argue their case.

It is beyond my scope to set ground rules for the utility of drawing correspondences, of using one text as a device for clarifying or challenging another, here. It is fair to conclude that doing so will be most useful where cultural and epistemological differences are minimal. Thus, in the Heisenberg example, the difference between the type and extent of interference the observer causes and between the objects observed (electrons and persons) is so great that no analogy is going to be persuasive except at the most metaphorical level. In the tradition of western philosophy, on the contrary, it can be very fruitful to use the ideas of one philosopher to illuminate those of another. Doing so can improve our understanding of both so that, insofar as this is our aim, even the charge of anachronism carries little weight.

It would not matter to the contemporary philosopher, for example, whether she learns from Kant's criticism of Hume's notion of personal identity in forming her own or whether Hume's empiricism not only resists but points out weaknesses in Kant's transcendental metaphysics. What matters is the force of the two arguments, not their historical ordering.

In sum, different methods of analysis and types of evidence are appropriate to different problems. Where historical influence is asserted, the reader can expect quite rightfully that it be demonstrated by pointing to some causal chain between the ideas of the relevant parties. This is no easy task as the chain can take many forms (*a* influenced *b*, *a* and *b* were jointly influenced by *c*, and so on) and, as in the case of Madison and Hume, an author may have an interest in covering his tracks. Nonetheless, the types of evidence that can be appealed to are reasonably clear (library holdings, college course curricula, as well as specific textual references), however difficult any given attribution may be to ascertain.

The test of correspondence has to do with its utility in clarifying the thought of both parties. If Madison is a "Humean" in some sense, how does knowing this help us to understand Madison and, insofar as we live in a "Madisonian" polity ourselves? This practical question and related ones regarding the Anti-Federalists have been of primary interest to me as a political theorist and are dealt with throughout this study. Concern about historical influence has been the limiting condition and not the end of my analysis.

Notes

Chapter 1

1. Jean-Jacques Rousseau, "Discourse on the Sciences and Arts (First Discourse)," in *The First and Second Discourses*, trans. Roger D. Masters and Judith R. Masters, ed. Roger D. Masters (New York: St. Martin's Press, 1964), p. 59.

2. As a matter of terminological shorthand, I sometimes refer to the people engaged in the constitutional framing and ratification controversies simply as the "constitutional founders." Clearly, the founding encompasses a much broader time frame and variety of thought than I cover in this book and I do not intend to treat the writers I discuss as representative of the whole.

3. Quoted in Don Herzog, "Some Questions for Republicans," *Political Theory* 14 (August 1986): 483.

4. The phrase is Gordon Wood's. See his *The Creation of the American Republic, 1776-1787.* (Chapel Hill: University of North Carolina Press, 1969), p. 428. Robert Dahl's *A Preface to Democratic Theory* (Chicago: University of Chicago Press, 1956) is a classic example of a work focusing on the role of governmental and social checks and balances in promoting political stability to the exclusion of civic dispositions.

5. The main revisionist works discussing republican influence in early America include the following: Bernard Bailyn, *The Ideological Origins of the American Revolution* (Cambridge, Mass.: Harvard University Press, Belknap Press, 1967); idem, *The Origins of American Politics* (New York: Vintage Books, 1968); Lance Banning, "Jeffersonian Ideology Revisited: Liberal and Classical Ideas in the New American Republic," *William and Mary Quarterly*, 3d ser., 43 (January 1986): 3-19; Drew McCoy, *The Elusive Republic: Political Economy in Jeffersonian America* (Chapel Hill: University of North Carolina Press, 1980); J. G. A. Pocock, "Between Gog and Magog: The Republican Thesis and the *Ideologica Americana*," *Journal of the History of Ideas* 48 (April-June, 1987): 325-46; Pocock, *The Machiavellian Moment* (Princeton, N.J.: Princeton University Press, 1975); idem, *"The Machiavellian Moment* Revisited: A Study in History and Ideology," *Journal of Modern History* 53 (March 1981): 49-72; Gerald Stourzh, *Alexander Hamilton and the Idea of Republican Government* (Stanford, Calif.: Stanford University Press, 1970); and Wood, *The Creation of the American Republic, 1776-1787.*

For a more comprehensive review and criticism of various aspects of the republican thesis, see, for example, Joyce Appleby, "Republicanism in Old and New Contexts," *William and Mary Quarterly*, 3d ser., 43 (January 1986): 20-34; James T. Kloppenburg, "Christianity, Republicanism, and Ethics in Early American Political Discourse," *Journal of American History* 74 (June 1987): 9-33; Isaac Kramnick, "Republican Revisionism Revisited," *American Historical Review* 87 (June 1982): 629-64; idem,

Republicanism and Bourgeois Radicalism: Political Ideology in Late Eighteenth-Century England and America (Ithaca, N.Y.: Cornell University Press, 1990); Robert E. Shalhope, "Toward a Republican Synthesis: The Emergence of an Understanding of Republicanism in American Historiography," *William and Mary Quarterly*, 3d ser., 29 (January 1972): 49–80; Jean Yarborough, "Representation and Republicanism: Two Views," *Publius* 9 (Spring 1979): 77–98; idem, "Republicanism Reconsidered: Some Thoughts on the Foundation and Preservation of the American Republic," *Review of Politics* 41 (January 1979): 61–95.

6. For a critical view of liberalism essentially as a justification for bourgeois property arrangements, see C. B. Macpherson, *The Political Theory of Possessive Individualism*, (New York: Oxford University Press, 1962). The revitalization and defense of liberal political thought in recent works by John Rawls, Ronald Dworkin, Robert Nozick, and others has not altered in any significant way the understanding of liberalism employed in contemporary scholarship on the founding. Although there is a danger of anachronism in using contemporary writers as a guidepost for our understanding of liberalism, each of these authors offers a rich moral conception of liberal social contract theory as conceived by the key figures in the liberal tradition from Locke through Kant. They invite, therefore, a reconsideration of classical liberalism and not just its contemporary manifestation. As much as the notion that the founders were "possessive individualists" is questioned, the essential correctness of Macpherson's identification of core liberal principles has not been widely challenged. Indeed, as Pocock has noted, not only republican revisionists but even many who defend the view that the founders were liberals do so the better to excoriate them. Such critics see liberal political commitments to be the cause of much of the materialism and egoism many find at the heart of American life. See Pocock, "Between Gog and Magog," pp. 338–39.

7. Hartz's thesis is developed in *The Liberal Tradition in America: An Interpretation of American Political Thought Since the Revolution* (New York: Harcourt, Brace and World, 1955).

8. Alexander Hamilton, James Madison and John Jay, *The Federalist Papers*, ed. Clinton Rossiter (New York: New American Library, 1961), p. 78. Madison's analogy, taken quite literally, suggests only that liberty is an enabling condition for faction as air is an enabling condition for fire. The context makes clear that he accepts the stronger claim that where liberty is respected, faction follows. I use the conditional *could* in this context not to weaken Madison's claim but to leave open for the moment the question of whether he therefore believed liberalism to be a "selfish" philosophy as some have argued and whether, even if this is the case, we are compelled to accept his conclusion. Since these matters are discussed in detail in chapter 2, I will merely suggest here that *Federalist* 10 should not be taken as a complete statement of Madison's political philosophy.

9. One ought not to conflate present-day communitarian concerns with classical republicanism or republicanism as it was understood in the eighteenth century. It is nonetheless true that many major communitarian critics of contemporary liberalism including Michael Sandel, Mark Tushnet, Benjamin Barber, Robert Bellah, and Wilson Carey McWilliams (discussed later) appeal explicitly to republicanism in the founding era and call for Americans to come home to civic values lost in the eventual triumph of liberalism. Sandel is as explicit as anyone in this regard arguing that the American republican tradition leaves open the prospect of "revitalizing our public life and restoring a sense of community" to contemporary American society (quoted in Kramnick, *Republicanism and Bourgeois Radicalism*, p. 39).

10. Thomas Hobbes, *Leviathan*, ed. Michael Oakeshott (New York: Macmillan, 1962), p. 36.

11. Max Farrand, ed. *The Records of the Federal Convention of 1787*, rev. ed. in 4 vol. (New Haven, Conn.: Yale University Press, 1966), 3: 560.

12. Karl Marx, "The Eighteenth Brumaire of Louis Bonaparte," in *The Marx-Engels Reader*, 2d ed., ed. Robert C. Tucker (New York: W. W. Norton, 1978), p. 595.

13. Benjamin R. Barber, "The Compromised Republic: Public Purposelessness in America," in *The Moral Foundations of the American Republic*, ed. Robert H. Horwitz (Charlottsville: University Press of Virginia, 1977), pp. 20-21.

14. Jeffrey C. Isaac makes a similar point though he formulates it quite differently. Isaac argues that "liberalism incorporates Aristotelian republican values of individual independence and patriotism in its understanding of the good life" (p. 375). This view recognizes that liberal societies also have their public sphere and that "republican" virtues are essential to its functioning if for no other reason than provide a language of legitimation. Such virtues, that is, do not allow us to distinguish a fundamentally liberal from a fundamentally republican worldview. Isaac's treatment of the dichotomization of liberalism and republicanism is interesting and persuasive. My one quibble would be to stress that *some* readings of Aristotelian republicanism, what I call strong republicanism below, are not compatible with core liberal values. His larger point, that a language and practice of civic virtue is required by liberal regimes as much as by others is nonetheless well taken. See "Republicanism vs. Liberalism? A Reconsideration," *History of Political Thought* 9 (Summer 1988): 349-77.

15. Pocock draws the first distinction; see his *Machiavellian Moment*, pp. 531-32. Cass R. Sunstein treats public deliberation and political equality as two distinguishing features of republicanism; see his article "Beyond the Republican Revival," *Yale Law Journal* 97 (July 1988), especially pp. 1548-53.

16. This distinction is developed by Ronald Dworkin in "Constitutional Cases," in his *Taking Rights Seriously* (Cambridge, Mass.: Harvard University Press, 1978), p. 134.

17. My use of the term *ideology* is derived from David Gauthier. A person's ideology is inferred from her words and activities and provides the most economical explanation of them. It is not required that the person to whom we attribute an ideology actually express its most basic premises or be fully consciously aware of them. Nor is there reason to suppose that what she does actually express is always consistent with her ideology (although if this was not generally the case one would suspect that we identified the ideology incorrectly). There must be, however, coherence among the principles that constitute the ideology such that its containing a particular conception of rationality precludes its containing some principles of cooperation and political institutions. And, while this concept of rationality may not *necessitate* any given institution, it at least limits the range to some set of possible institutions. If this were not the case, if, in other words, an ideology consisted of a more or less ad hoc, or random set of political judgments, it is not clear how competing claims over rights or goods in a given community could ever be resolved in principle. Nor is it clear how, or whether, members of the community could communicate the bases of their claims to each other. See David Gauthier, "The Social Contract as Ideology," *Philosophy & Public Affairs* 6 (Winter 1977): 131.

18. J. G. A. Pocock, "Civic Humanism and Its Role in Anglo-American Thought," in his *Politics, Language and Time* (New York: Atheneum, 1971), p. 85.

19. Pocock, "*The Machiavellian Moment* Revisited," pp. 75-76.

20. Pocock, *Machiavellian Moment*, p. 507.

21. The legal scholar Frank Michelman offers a similar characterization. "In the strongest versions of republicanism," he writes, "citizenship—participation as an equal in public affairs, in pursuit of a common good—appears as a primary, indeed, constitutive, interest of the person." See "Law's Republic," *Yale Law Journal* 97 (July 1988): 1503.

22. See Wood, *Creation*, pp. viii, 59-60. In a more recent piece, however, Wood revises his earlier view on the true bearers of the republican tradition. Now he treats the Federalists as representing a republican ideal of a disinterested elite who make decisions in light of the public good versus the Anti-Federalists who have become the precursors of a modern, interest-oriented liberal politics; see "Interests and Disinterestedness," in *Beyond Confederation*, ed. Richard Beeman, Stephen Botein, and Edward C. Carter II (Chapel Hill University of North Carolina Press, 1987), pp. 69-109.

23. The phrase is borrowed from John Rawls, "The Priority of the Right and Ideas of the Good," *Philosophy & Public Affairs* 17 (Fall 1988): 272-73. There he draws a distinction between what he describes (somewhat idiosyncratically) as classical republicanism and civic humanism. The former "take[s] the view that if the citizens of a democratic society are to preserve their basic rights and liberties, including the civil liberties which secure the freedoms of private life, they must also have to a sufficient degree the political virtues ... and be willing to take part in public life." Civic humanism, on the other hand, is incompatible with liberalism because it follows Aristotle in treating political participation as "the privileged locus of the good life."

24. Pocock, *Machiavellian Moment*, p. 507.

25. Wood, "The Intellectual Origins of the American Constitution," *National Forum* 64 (Fall 1984): 6.

26. Pocock, "*The Machiavellian Moment* Revisited," p. 53. This quite understandable change of heart has not prevented Pocock from taking to task critics who impute to him the view that their was "no available alternative" to classical republicanism for the founders, his explicit avowal of this view in *The Machiavellian Moment* notwithstanding. See "Between Gog and Magog," p. 342.

27. Wood, review of *The Lost Soul of American Politics* by John Patrick Diggins, *The New York Review of Books*, 28 February 1985, p. 30.

28. See Banning, "Jeffersonian Ideology," p. 12.

29. Mark Tushnet displays an interesting variant of this problem in his understanding of liberalism and its weaknesses as a political theory. In his important work, *Red, White and Blue: A Critical Analysis of Constitutional Law* (Cambridge, Mass.: Harvard University Press, 1988), he explains that what he calls the liberal tradition in that work had in an earlier draft been called "Lockean liberalism." He makes this change to accommodate recent scholarship that discusses the importance of traditional notions of natural law in Locke's largely theological conceptions of politics (pp. 4-5). Locke no longer fits into his definition of liberalism and, rather remarkably, is excluded from Tushnet's liberal tradition, Locke's explicit endorsements of religious tolerance, limited government, natural rights, and other goods traditionally associated with liberalism notwithstanding. I would suggest that if an understanding of the liberal tradition fails to account for Locke, it may be the understanding that is at fault. Rethinking it seems a more reasonable approach than the exclusionary one taken by Tushnet. Tushnet also claims that his understanding of the liberal tradition derives from C. B. Macpherson's *The Political Theory of Possessive Individualism* and Louis Hartz's *The Liberal Tradition in America*. Macpherson's Locke is a fully secular representative, indeed propagandist, for the capitalist class and of bourgeois property relations. In Macpherson's terms,

he is fully a liberal. The new Locke scholarship Tushnet endorses takes Macpherson quite explicitly as its bête noire.

30. It is debatable, of course, whether these Scots can properly be described as liberals. Certainly, Smith and Hume rejected Lockean notions of natural rights and, with some ambivalence in Hume's case, the social contract. We will return to this issue in chapter 4. It is adequate to say for now, first, that there are elements of a classical liberal political philosophy, especially with respect to property relations and limitations on state power, among the Scots even if these are not justified in Lockean terms. Second, much of the Humean political psychology seeks to explain why allegiance develops toward almost *any* state regardless of its guiding principles. A liberal like Madison could absorb much of this understanding, even if Hume and he were to differ, as they did to some degree, in their fundamental political values.

31. For further discussion of the methodological issue, see the appendix to this study.

Chapter 2

1. Jonathan Elliot, ed., *The Debates in the Several States on the Adoption of the Federal Constitution*, 5 vols. (Philadelphia: J. B. Lippincott, 1901) 3:489.

2. See, for example, Benjamin R. Barber, *Strong Democracy* (Berkeley: University of California Press, 1984); Robert N. Bellah et al., *Habits of the Heart: Individualism and Commitment in American Life* (Berkeley: University of California Press, 1985); Michael J. Sandel, *Liberalism and the Limits of Justice* (New York: Cambridge University Press, 1982).

3. For example, on Diggins's motives see Benjamin Barber, review of *The Lost Soul of American Politics* by John Patrick Diggins, *The New York Times Book Review*, 13 January 1985, p. 9; On Pocock's motives, see Cesare Vasoli, "The Machiavellian Moment: A Grand Ideological Synthesis" *Modern History* 49 (December 1977): 661-70. For the motives both of Pocock and contemporary communitarians in reviving republican readings of the founding, see Kramnick, *Republicanism*, pp. 37-40. For Pocock on the discrediting motives of Kramnick, Diggins, and just about everyone who disagrees with him, see "Gog and Magog," especially p. 339.

4. This contrast is drawn by many including Barber, "Compromised Republic"; Wilson Carey McWilliams, "Democracy and the Citizen: Community, Dignity, and the Crisis of Contemporary Politics in America," in *How Democratic Is the Constitution?*, ed. Robert A. Goldwin and William A. Schambra (Washington, D.C.: American Enterprise Institute, 1980); Wood, *Creation*, p. 428; Pocock, *Machiavellian Moment*, especially pp. 516-17, 531; and Banning, "Jeffersonian Ideology," p. 12.

5. Sandel, *Liberalism*, p. 1.

6. I describe this as a more important feature because the first mentioned—for example, the elite bias of perfectionist theories including classical republicanism ones— is amenable to change by expanding the notion of who counts as a citizen. Yet, "modern republicanism" as, for example, in Rousseau, is more egalitarian but not necessarily more pluralistic. The role of a virtuous elite is emphasized less or not at all, that of a culturally homogeneous political community, more.

7. As Schneewind has argued, classical virtue theory, offers little to show how one virtuous person could convince another who disagrees with him about the very criteria of virtue and thus about the best form of political and social life. By Aristotle's account at least, we are led to believe that one of the agents is not really virtuous at

all and is, in fact, morally defective. See J. B. Schneewind, "The Misfortunes of Virtue," *Ethics* 101 (October 1990): 62.

8. See Charles Larmore, "Political Liberalism," *Political Theory* 18 (August 1990): 339-60; and John Rawls, "The Idea of an Overlapping Consensus," *Oxford Journal of Legal Studies* 7 (1987): 1-25.

9. For particular attention to the dialogic nature of liberalism see Bruce A. Ackerman, *Social Justice in the Liberal State* (New Haven, Conn.: Yale University Press, 1980); especially pp. 70-75; and Larmore, "Political Liberalism."

10. Ronald Dworkin, "What Rights Do We Have?" in his *Taking Rights Seriously*, p. 271.

11. See *Roth* v. *United States*, 354 U.S. 476 (1957); and *Miller* v. *California*, 413 U.S. 15 (1973). Brennan asserts in the majority opinion in Roth that "all ideas having even the slightest social importance—unorthodox ideas, controversial ideas, even ideas hateful to the prevailing climate of opinion—have the full protection of the guarantees [of the First Amendment] unless excluded because they encroach upon the limited area of more important interests." Obscenity is not protected speech as it is "utterly without redeeming social importance." p. 1507.

12. Kathryn Abrams, "Law's Republicanism," *Yale Law Journal* 97 (July 1988): 1591. No less than ten articles in this volume deal with republicanism and its implications for constitutional interpretation. See also Richard H. Fallon, Jr., "What Is Republicanism and Is It Worth Reviving?," *Harvard Law Review* 102 (May 1989): 1695-1735.

13. Cass R. Sunstein, "Beyond the Republican Revival," *Yale Law Journal* 97 (July 1988): 1540. Sunstein, Fallon, and Abrams are each cautious in their assessments of the promise of republican theory for constitutional interpretation. I do not mean to suggest any simple endorsement of the value of republicanism on their part, though none question its influence on early American political thought. I am concerned here with the ways in which Sunstein draws the distinction between liberalism and republicanism. Although he wants to claim that liberalism and the four republican goods he cites are compatible, and that the founders were "liberal republicans," I must wonder why he understands these goods to differentiate liberalism from republicanism in the first place. My view is that they lack the differentiating content to instantiate any ideology in particular. For a work in constitutional theory that explicitly criticizes liberalism from a republican viewpoint, see Mark Tushnet, *Red, White and Blue.*

14. Sunstein, "Beyond the Republican Revival," p. 1540, n. 4.

15. Ibid., pp. 1540-41.

16. Ibid., p. 1554.

17. Ibid., pp. 1567-68.

18. Ibid., pp. 1549, 1551. Mark Tushnet also regards treating wants and desires as "prepolitical" to be one of the defining features of liberalism. See his *Red, White and Blue, pp. 270-72.*

19. This view is argued by Robert Nozick in *Anarchy, State and Utopia* (New York: Basic Books, 1974).

20. For a contrasting view that denies the dialogic potential I ascribe to liberal politics, see Mark Tushnet, "The Constitution of Religion," *Review of Politics* 50 (Fall 1988): 628-58.

21. See Jon Elster, *Sour Grapes: Studies in the Subversion of Rationality* (New York: Cambridge University Press, 1983), p. 38. As Elster puts it, "Even assuming unlimited time for discussion, unanimous and rational agreement would not necessarily ensue. Could there not be legitimate and unresolvable differences of opinion over the nature of the common good? Could there not even be a plurality of ultimate values?"

22. For a discussion of the extension of liberal tolerance from the religious into the sexual sphere see Ron Replogle, "Sex, God and Liberalism," *Journal of Politics* 50 (November 1988): 937-60.

23. For a recent treatment of the importance of Calvinism in early American political thought, see John P. Diggins, *The Lost Soul of American Politics: Virtue, Self-Interest and the Foundations of Liberalism* (New York, Basic Books, 1984).

24. See Sandel, *Liberalism and the Limits of Justice*, for a thorough discussion of this notion of the self and its consequences for liberal theory.

25. Allen E. Buchanan, "Assessing the Communitarian Critique of Liberalism," *Ethics* 99 (July 1989): 857.

26. As Buchanan has pointed out, communitarians have not always been clear whether the intrinsic value claimed for community is a psychological or a normative claim. Is it something we happen to desire given our psychological makeup (and supposedly feel the absence of which in some fashion) or something we should desire for moral or other normative reasons?

27. Will Kymlicka, "Liberal Individualism and Liberal Neutrality," *Ethics* 99 (July 1989): 904.

28. Ibid.

29. Tocqueville's discussion of the important role played by civic associations in American society is a case in point. It is no coincidence, his analysis suggests, that a liberal democratic society such as the United States encourages high rates of voluntarism. That cooperation is uncoerced and based on premises of equality gives a vibrancy to popular political activity that was to Tocqueville one of the most frequently observed—and most salutary—aspects of life in American democracy. See Alexis de Tocqueville, *Democracy in America*, ed. J. P. Mayer (Garden City, N.Y.: Doubleday, 1969), especially pp. 513-17.

30. For a particularly good social history of the civil rights movement that captures both the rivalries and the solidarity among civil rights activists, see Taylor Branch, *Parting the Waters: America in the King Years, 1954-63* (New York: Simon and Schuster, 1988).

31. For an interesting discussion of states, including community, that are essentially achieved as by-products, that is, not through a conscious aiming at the goal, see Elster, pp. 43-108.

32. This point is discussed in greater detail in the next chapter. When Locke describes the obligations of parents toward their children, he does not do so in terms of an obligation to respect children's rights. That is, the right of the child to be provided for derives from the prior duty of the parents to so provide. This responsibility derives from a more general obligation to preserve God's workmanship. Locke's strictures against spoilage in his discussion of property in the *Second Treatise* is another case in point. Neither of these duties is formulated in terms of the rights of children, or the rights of nature, against parents or people in general. See John Locke, *The Second Treatise of Government*, pars. 31 and 58, in John Locke, *Two Treatises of Government*, with introduction and notes by Peter Laslett (New York: Cambridge University Press, 1960), pp. 332, 348-49.

33. Judith Jarvis Thomson's article adds an interesting wrinkle to the usual debate in arguing that, even conceding a fetus's right to life, an *obligation* is not imposed on the mother to bring the fetus to term in all instances. See "A Defense of Abortion," *Philosophy & Public Affairs* 1 (Fall 1971): 47-66.

34. For an illuminating discussion of differences between American and European laws concerning abortion, see Mary Ann Glendon, *Abortion and Divorce in Western*

Law (Cambridge, Mass.: Harvard University Press, 1987). Glendon argues that the public debate about these issues is much more constricted in the United States than in Europe largely because of our tendency to formulate these problems in terms of rights. Continental European discussions, she contends, are set in the context of broader considerations of what is good for the society and for individual family members. They still, as a rule, respect the right of the individual to make choices regarding reproduction and proceed in terms consistent with liberal principles, although certain states, like France, impose more restrictions than are permitted under *Roe* v. *Wade*. Thus, Glendon is careful not to overstate the differences between Anglo-American and European approaches, but she makes a compelling case that the European debate is richer in part because it is not almost exclusively centered on the language of rights. See especially pp. 112–42.

35. Tocqueville, *Democracy*, p. 508.

36. John Locke, "The Reasonableness of Christianity, as Delivered in the Scriptures," in *The Works of John Locke*, 10 vols. (London: Thomas Davison, 1823), 7:145.

37. Tocqueville, p. 508.

38. Mandeville comes to mind as the most likely eighteenth-century example of this extreme. See Bernard Mandeville, *The Fable of the Bees: or Private Vices, Publick Benefits*, with an essay by F. B. Kaye (Oxford: The Clarendon Press, 1924)

39. Locke, quoted in Nathan Tarcov, *Locke's Education for Liberty* (Chicago: University of Chicago Press, 1984), p. 77.

40. John Rawls, *A Theory of Justice* (Cambridge, Mass.: The Harvard University Press, Belknap Press, 1971), p. 455.

41. See, for example, Mancur Olson, *The Logic of Collective Action* (Cambridge, Mass.: Harvard University Press, 1971). It is not necessarily the case, of course, that free riders are morally deficient. This depends on the manner in which the public good is decided upon and the reason for one's not contributing to it. A conscientious objector could arguably be a free rider (assuming he enjoys an advantage because of the security the state provides) for highly moral reasons. If, however, a person deems this decision process fair and has no compelling ethical reason not to do her share, then moral blame is justified.

42. The example is, of course, Hume's. See David Hume, *An Enquiry Concerning the Principles of Morals*, ed. J. B. Schneewind (Indianapolis: Hackett 1983), p. 95.

43. I use the somewhat awkward italicized phrase to avoid characterizing these responses as "moral." That implies a certain conscientiousness that I do not want to presume at this stage.

44. Thomas Hobbes, *Leviathan*, ed. Michael Oakeshott (New York: Macmillan, 1962), p. 114.

45. Ibid., p. 115.

46. Ibid., p. 120.

47. Ibid., p. 119.

48. Ibid., p. 249.

49. Ibid., p. 122.

50. Ibid., p. 122. For a telling critique of the commonplace interpretation of Hobbes as the apostle of asocial individualism, see Ron Replogle, "Personality and Society in Hobbes's *Leviathan*," *Polity* 19 (Summer 1987): 570–94. Much of the analysis presented above finds its origins in this piece.

51. For a discussion of a "common sense" morality attributed to citizens of liberal polities, see James Fishkin, *The Limits of Obligation* (New Haven, Conn.: Yale University Press, 1982).

Chapter 3

1. The underlined phrase is drawn from Nathan Tarcov's illuminating work, *Locke's Education for Liberty* (Chicago: University of Chicago Press, 1984).

2. See note 58 below.

3. John Dunn, who has done so much to correct our understanding of Locke's political thought, would dispute the influence of Locke's major political work, the *Two Treatises*, on American thought in the eighteenth century. The *Treatises*, he suggests, were not widely read before 1750 and thereafter only by a small intellectual elite. See "The Politics of Locke in England and America in the Eighteenth Century," *John Locke: Problems and Perspectives*, ed. John W. Yolton (New York: Cambridge University Press, 1969), pp. 45-80. Dunn does not deny, however, Locke's renown as an epistemologist prior to this time, and few who read his *Essay Concerning Human Understanding* fail to notice how political a work it is. Moreover, Dunn may be understating Locke's influence by focusing largely on works in private libraries. There is ample evidence that Locke's political ideas were spread secondhand through political pamphlets and, perhaps more importantly, through sermons by the clergy in the revolutionary period. On the former, see Donald Lutz, "The Relative Influence of European Writers on Late Eighteenth-Century American Political Thought," *American Political Science Review* 78 (March 1984): 189-97. On the latter, see Steven M. Dworetz, *The Unvarnished Doctrine: Locke, Liberalism and the American Revolution* (Durham, N.C.: Duke University Press, 1990). In chapters 5 and 7, I demonstrate the Lockean character of Federalist and Anti-Federalist thought. This is more important to me than the problem of tracing influence, a problem left in the more capable hands of intellectual historians. On the methodological problem of influence, see the appendix.

4. A brief chronology of the major works by Locke cited here may be helpful. The *Essays on the Law of Nature*, which Locke never published, although he lectured on the subject as Censor of Moral Philosophy at Oxford, were apparently written shortly after 1660 while Locke was in his late twenties. Both the *Essay Concerning Human Understanding* and the *Two Treatises of Government* were first published in 1690, although it is virtually certain that the *First Treatise* and most of the *Second Treatise* were written prior to the Glorious Revolution of 1688. *Some Thoughts Concerning Education* was published in 1693. That work began, however, as a series of letters Locke wrote (beginning in 1683) to his friend, Edward Clarke, who requested advice on the education of his son. Finally, *The Reasonableness of Christianity as Delivered in the Scriptures* appeared in 1695, nine years before his death.

5. Richard Ashcraft, *Revolutionary Politics and Locke's Two Treatises of Government* (Princeton, N.J.: Princeton University Press, 1986), especially p. 127.

6. James Tully, *A Discourse on Property: John Locke and His Adversaries* (New York: Cambridge University Press, 1980), p. 39.

7. Locke, *The Second Treatise of Government*, in *Two Treatises*, par. 6, p. 311.

8. For a statement on Locke's consistent rationalism in morals, see Jeremy Waldron, "Property and Locke's Method of Natural Law," paper presented at the Northeastern Political Science Association's annual meeting, Providence, 1988. See also John Dunn, *The Political Thought of John Locke* (New York: Cambridge University Press, 1969), p. 92. Dunn takes the somewhat weaker position that Locke at least had good reasons to suppose his political ideas consistent with the epistemology of the *Essay*. The claim that the reliance on natural law in the *Two Treatises* is inconsistent with Locke's empiricism in the *Essay* is made by Laslett in his introduction to the *Two Treatises*, p. 98.

9. Richard Ashcraft, "Faith and Knowledge in Locke's Philosophy," in *John Locke: Problems and Perspectives*, ed. John W. Yolton, pp. 200-201.

10. Locke, *The First Treatise of Government*, in *Two Treatises*, par. 86, p. 242.

11. John Dunn, *The Political Thought of John Locke*, p. 219.

12. Locke, *First Treatise*, in *Two Treatises*, sec. 86, p. 243.

13. Quoted in W. von Leyden's Introduction to John Locke, *Essays on the Law of Nature*, ed. and introduction by W. von Leyden, (Oxford: Clarendon Press, 1954), p. 71.

14. Ibid., p. 183. See also *The Reasonableness of Christianity*, in *The Works of John Locke*, 10 vols. (London: Thomas Davison, 1823) 7:143. For a good discussion of Locke's synthesis of "voluntarist" and "rationalist" views on the binding force of natural law, see Tully, especially p. 41. Locke, Tully argues, "accepts the rationalist tenet that natural laws are discovered by reason, are wise and good by independent criteria, but he denies the inference that this is the source of their binding force." Rather, this force derives from their being expressions of God's will.

15. Leyden, in Locke, *Essays on the Law of Nature*, p. 75.

16. *Second Treatise*, chap. 5, in *Two Treatises*, pp. 327-44.

17. Dunn, *Political Thought*, p. 191.

18. Leyden, in Locke, *Essays on the Law of Nature*, pp. 71-72.

19. Ibid., p. 71.

20. Ibid., pp. 72-73.

21. John Locke, *An Essay Concerning Human Understanding*, ed. with an introduction by John W. Yolton (New York: E. P. Dutton, 1961), pp. 213-14.

22. Ibid., p. 209.

23. Ibid., p. 226.

24. Ibid., p. 227.

25. Ibid., p. 222.

26. *Reasonableness of Christianity* in *Works*, 7:161.

27. *Essay*, p. 222.

28. Ibid., p. 211.

29. Quoted in Ashcraft, *Revolutionary Politics*, p. 55.

30. Ibid., p. 49

31. *Reasonableness in Works*, 7:140.

32. Ibid., 7:146.

33. Ibid., 7:158.

34. For a counterargument that sees Locke as deploying religious language for purely strategic purposes, see Pangle, especially pp. 150 and 234 and Thomas L. Pangle, *The Spirit of Modern Republicanism: The Moral Vision of the American Founders and the Philosophy of Locke* (Chicago: University of Chicago Press, 1988).

35. Quoted in Tarcov, *Locke's Education for Liberty*, p. 77.

36. Quoted in ibid., p. 82.

37. Ibid., p. 91.

38. John Locke, "Of the Conduct of the Understanding," In *The Educational Writings of John Locke*, ed. John William Adamson (London: E. Arnold, 1912), p. 187.

39. Ibid., p. 197.

40. Ibid., p. 187.

41. John Locke, "Some Thoughts Concerning Education," in *The Educational Writings of John Locke*, ed. James L. Axtell (Cambridge: Cambridge University Press, 1968), sec. 146, p. 253.

42. Quoted in Tarcov, *Locke's Education for Liberty*, p. 149.

43. "Some Thoughts," in *Educational Writings*, ed. Axtell, sec. 66, p. 158.

44. Ibid., sec. 66, p. 159.

45. Ibid., sec. 81, p. 181.

46. Ibid., sec. 103, p. 207.

47. Ibid., sec. 35, p. 139.

48. Ibid., especially sec. 74, pp. 173-74.

49. Ibid., sec. 54, p. 152.

50. Ibid., sec. 56, pp. 152-53.

51. Ibid., sec. 61, pp. 155-56.

52. Ibid., p. 156.

53. On the former point, see secs. 158 and 159, Axtell, in *Educational Writings*, pp. 261-62. On the latter, see sec. 136, ibid., p. 242.

54. Locke, *Essay*, vol. 2, chap. 28, sec. 12

55. This is the approach taken by Pangle. See *Spirit*, esp. p. 205.

56. Leyden, in Locke, *Essays on the Law of Nature*, p. 76.

57. Ibid.

58. Identifying classical conceptions of the virtues is a complicated task and one I do not intend to explore in great depth. Let me discuss briefly, however, two important classical accounts of the virtues, one Greek and one Roman, which are quite distinct from that of Locke. First, Aristotle in the *Nicomachean Ethics* contends that only a life that practices the virtues can be a truly happy life. This view rests on a teleological conception of man and rejects a subjectivist view that defines happiness as just what anybody might call it. Only the good man can understand what happiness is, and only he can be truly happy though others experience "corrupt" and "abnormal" pleasures. "What seems pleasant to a person in such a condition is not," Aristotle says, "really a pleasure at all." (see *The Ethics of Aristotle*, trans. J. A. K. Thomson (Baltimore: Penguin Books, 1956), p. 300. The answer to the question, why be virtuous?, including virtuous in the civic sense, is essentially that only in this way can one be truly happy and reach the fullest perfection of human nature.

Contrast this to the Stoic conception of virtue shared by Polybius and Marcus Aurelius. The Stoics abandoned a notion of a *telos* for man and any internal link between virtue and happiness. Virtuous action was action that conformed to a standard of right embodied in a natural or cosmic law that applied equally to all rational beings regardless of kingdom, city, or state. See Alasdair MacIntyre, *After Virtue* (Notre Dame, Ind.: University of Notre Dame Press, 1981), p. 157. This standard, needless to say, does not vary with custom or fashion, and conduct determined by a desire for esteem could not be described as virtuous at all. Virtue is a matter of *will* brought into conformity with law. The Stoic understanding bears a family resemblance to modern conceptions of civic virtue as a willingness to abide by laws. Yet Locke's account of civic virtue differs from both classical theories. He differs from Aristotle in his lack of a teleological view of human nature and in ruling out the internal connection between virtue and happiness by giving a subjectivist account of the good. He differs from the Stoics in his account of moral motives and the goal of the moral life, which for the stoics, is to produce a self-sufficient character living in harmony with nature.

59. Here I agree with Alasdair MacIntyre, who also distinguishes modern virtue from a classical Greek view, the presupposition of which is that "there exists a cosmic order which dictates the place of each virtue in a total harmonious scheme of human life." See *After Virtue*, p. 133.

Chapter 4

1. David Hume, "Of the First Principles of Government," in *Political Essays of David Hume*, ed. Charles W. Hendel (New York: Bobbs-Merrill, 1953), pp. 24-25.

2. Ronald Hamowy, *The Scottish Enlightenment and the Theory of Spontaneous Order,* (Carbondale and Edwardsville: Southern Illinois University Press, 1987).

3. Edmund Burke, a friend and admirer of both Hume and Smith, is perhaps the best known exponent of the non-reactionary sort of conservatism we are describing. Burke did not seek a return to some premodern "golden age." Rather, he criticizes those who seek to design a society according to rational principles. Much the same thought is expressed by Hume in the weight he places on customary attachment to government and the dangers of shaking it, in his reluctance to change institutions for marginal gains in utility, and in his unwillingness to endorse anything more than a "hypothetical" theory of the social contract. "Spontaneous," that is, undirected, order has both a descriptive and normative component in Scottish Enlightenment thought. See also Hamowy, *The Scottish Enlightenment,* p. 5.

4. Among the works I have found useful in establishing the importance of Scottish Enlightenment thought in early America are the following. First, dealing especially with Hume: Douglass Adair, *Fame and the Founding Fathers* (New York: W. W. Norton, 1974); Earl Burk Braly, "The Reputation of David Hume in America" (Ph.D. diss., University of Texas, 1962); James Conniff, "The Enlightenment and American Political Thought: A Study of the Origins of Madison's *Federalist* Number 10," *Political Theory* 8 (August 1980): 381-402; Diggins, *The Lost Soul of American Politics*; Geoffrey Marshall, "David Hume and Political Scepticism," *The Philosophical Quarterly* 4 (July 1954): 247-257; James Moore, "Hume's Political Science and the Classical Republican Tradition," *Canadian Journal of Political Science* 10 (December 1977): 809-39; Ernest Campbell Mossner, *The Life of David Hume,* 2d ed. (Oxford: Clarendon Press, 1980); Morton White, *Philosophy, "The Federalist," and the Constitution,* (New York: Oxford University Press, 1987); Garry Wills, *Explaining America: The Federalist* (New York: Penguin Books, 1981). Hutcheson's influence, especially on Jefferson, is argued for in Garry Wills, *Inventing America: Jefferson's Declaration of Independence* (Garden City, N.Y.: Doubleday, 1978). Works that stress the influence of Reid include Daniel W. Howe, "The Political Psychology of *The Federalist*," *The William and Mary Quarterly,* 3d ser. 44 (July 1987): 485-509; and Conrad, "Metaphor and Imagination," Perhaps the best general survey of Enlightenment ideas in early America, including extensive discussions of Scottish influence, is May, *The Enlightenment in America.* See also Roy Branson, "James Madison and the Scottish Enlightenment," *Journal of the History of Ideas* 40 (April-June 1979): 235-50; James Kloppenburg, "Christianity, Republicanism and Ethics in Early American Political Thought," *Journal of American History* 74 (June 1987): 9-33; and Donald S. Lutz, "The Relative Influence of European Writers on Late Eighteenth-Century American Political Thought," *American Political Science Review* 78 (March 1984): 189-97.

5. Wills, *Inventing America,* p. 194.

6. May, *Enlightenment,* p. 38; Wills, *Inventing America,* p. 201.

7. Ralph L. Ketcham, "James Madison and Religion—A New Hypothesis," in *James Madison on Religious Liberty,* ed. Robert S. Alley (Buffalo, NY: Prometheus Books, 1985), p. 179.

8. See discussion of Reid, below.

9. James McCosh, *The Scottish Philosophy* (New York: Charles Scribner's Sons, 1890), p. 185.

10. Ibid., p. 188.

11. Quoted in Ketcham, James Madison, p. 189.

12. See chapter 5, pp. 96-97.

13. Other Scots included on Witherspoon's reading list were Adam Smith, Lord Kames, and Thomas Reid. May, p. 63.

14. Ibid.

15. Braly, "The Reputation of Hume," pp. 41–42.

16. For a thorough discussion of the availability of Hume's works in colonial and revolutionary America see Braly, "The Reputation of Hume," pp. 21–37.

17. Morton White has written the most extensive and useful treatments of the epistemological presuppositions of the American founders, first in his *Philosophy of the American Revolution* and more recently in *Philosophy, "The Federalist" and the Constitution*. In the former work, he discusses the central importance of the notions of "self-evident truths," in the revolutionary period and as expressed in the Declaration of Independence. It is not surprising, given the pervasiveness of this widespread reliance on rational intuitionism, that Reid's "common sense" philosophy was later to become so popular in the late eighteenth and early nineteenth century. Yet, as White shows in his work on *The Federalist*, Madison and Hamilton were quite able to rely on a Humean empiricist psychology, particularly in addressing motivational concerns, even as they remained committed to an "*un*Humeian, rationalistic view that all moral principles and even some propositions about matters of fact can be rationally 'demonstrated.'" See *Philosophy, "The Federalist," and the Constitution*, p. 3.

18. James Wilson was one founder who expressed concern over the potentially corrosive skepticism of Hume and appealed to Reid as a corrective, See Conrad, "Metaphor and Imagination," p. 17.

19. Braly, "The Reputation of Hume," pp. 47–48.

20. Madison's responses to Smith in this particular correspondence are lost. However, Smith's responses reveal an assumption that Madison is aware of the arguments on liberty and necessity in Locke, Samuel Clarke, and David Hume, among others. See Ketcham, "James Madison," p. 182.

21. Conrad, "Metaphor and Imagination," p. 17.

22. On the warm personal relation between Franklin and Hume, and also on several proposals Franklin offered at the Federal Convention of 1787 drawn directly from Hume's essay, "Idea of a Perfect Commonwealth," see Hendel's introduction to Hume's *Political Essays*, pp. liii–liv. See also Braly, "The Reputation of Hume," pp. 5–16.

23. Quoted in Braly, "The Reputation of Hume," p. 103.

24. Thomas Jefferson, *The Papers of Thomas Jefferson*, ed. Julian F. Boyd, vol. 13 (Princeton, N.J.: Princeton University Press, 1955), p. 1228.

25. Quoted in Hume, *Political Essays*, ed. Hendel, p. lii; and Braly, "The Reputation of Hume," p. 16.

26. Jefferson, *Papers*, 16:448.

27. Ibid., 11:291.

28. Alexander Hamilton, James Madison, and John Jay, *The Federalist Papers*, ed. Clinton Rossiter (New York: New American Library, 1961), p. 526–27. The passage is taken from Hume's essay, "Of the Rise and Progress of the Arts and Sciences," *Political Essays*, p. 117.

29. Wills, *Explaining America*, p. 66.

30. Hume, "Of the Independence of Parliament," in *Political Essays*, p. 68.

31. Quoted in Braly, "The Reputation of Hume," p. 44.

32. Francis Hutcheson, *An Essay on the Nature and Conduct of the Passions and Affections*, 3d ed. (Gainseville, Fl.: Scholars' Facsimiles and Reprints, 1969), p. 221.

33. Hutcheson, *Essay*, p. 226.

34. Hutcheson ordinarily refers to both benevolence and self-interest as calm desires because they include a cognitive element in the consideration of one's own and other's long-term interests. These desires are species of what he generally describes as "affections" which are contrasted with "passions." The former emerge from some notion

of good or evil, pleasure or pain, which are to be avoided. The latter are "brutal impulse(s) of will" and are closer to what we call instincts, including hunger, the sex drive, and the urge to seek company. For a thorough discussion of this point see Henning Jensen, *Motivation and Moral Sense in Francis Hutcheson's Ethical Theory* (The Hague: Marinus Nijhoff, 1971), pp. 10-11.

35. See Jensen, *Motivation*, especially p. 112. Also see William Frankena, "Hutcheson's Moral Sense Theory," *Journal of the History of Ideas* 16 (June 1955): 366-67.

36. Quoted in Frankena, "Hutcheson's Moral Sense Theory," p. 367-68.

37. Although David Hume does not posit the existence of a separate moral sense, any theory that argues for the affective basis of morals runs into this chicken-and-egg problem. For a discussion of it in Hume's work, see Jonathan Harrison, *Hume's Moral Epistemology* (Oxford: Clarendon Press, 1976), pp. 120-25.

38. Hutcheson, *Essay*, p. 319.

39. Ibid., pp. 319-20.

40. Adam Smith, *The Theory of Moral Sentiments*, with an introduction by E. G. West (Indianapolis: Liberty Classics, 1976), p. 19.

41. Anthony Flew, *David Hume: Philosopher of Moral Science* (New York: Basil Blackwell, 1986), p. 11.

42. Neither Hume nor Smith are committed to Lockean natural rights, but such a commitment is not a defining feature of liberalism. Such rights play no role, for example, in contemporary liberal theories such as those of Rawls and Dworkin. What is essential, and what Hume and Smith share is a role for "government conceived of as 'artifice' coordinating (when necessary) the actions of independent centers of decision and exercising limited authority through laws" as the solution to "guaranteeing individual freedom and security." See Frederick G. Whelan, *Order and Artifice in Hume's Political Thought* (Princeton, N.J.: Princeton University Press, 1985), p. 357-58.

43. For a similar list of affinities, see Eldon J. Eisenach, *Two Worlds of Liberalism* (Chicago: University of Chicago Press, 1981), especially pp. 142 and 146-50.

44. For a good discussion of Hume's political thought in general and his aversion to religious enthusiasms in particular, see David Miller *Philosophy and Ideology in Hume's Political Thought* (Oxford: Clarendon Press, 1981), especially p. 117.

45. Smith, *Moral Sentiments*, p. 506.

46. Ibid., p. 505. Of course, induction is also a rational process, but there is still a sharp distinction between Smith on the role of reason in morals and the intuitionism of Clarke or Wollaston.

47. This judgment is not irrelevant to understanding Hume's guiding philosophical principles. He did not blame the public for rejecting this great work if they derived little pleasure in reading it. Thereafter, he paid much more attention to form and became a fine stylist. Also, see Hume's essay, "The Sceptic," for a discussion of philosophy as amusement. David Hume, *Essays: Moral, Political and Literary*, ed. Eugene F. Miller (Indianapolis: Liberty Classics, 1987), pp. 159-80.

48. David Hume, *A Treatise on Human Nature*, ed. L. A. Selby-Bigge; 2d ed., ed. P. H. Nidditch (Oxford: Clarendon Press, 1978), p. xvi.

49. As Whelan states, "Hume characteristically asks why people acknowledge and obey certain rules rather than why they ought to obey them, and his mode of presentation throughout suggests that he is presenting a body of facts concerning moral and political phenomena." See Whelan, *Order and Artifice*, p. 194.

50. This is especially important because Smith, at least, has been treated as a writer in the civic-humanist as opposed to the liberal tradition in a major revisionist work.

See Donald Winch, *Adam Smith's Politics: An Essay in Historiographic Revision* (New York: Cambridge University Press, 1978). Winch recognizes quite rightly that Smith rejects the idea of the polity as a "marketplace writ large" and that his works show a pronounced "civic dimension." He succeeds in showing that Smith's thought is distorted if read merely as a precursor to nineteenth century laissez faire capitalism. Indeed, Smith is concerned with the potential for capitalist development to undermine "men's capacity to act as citizens" (p. 174). These are, of course, only refutations of a "liberal" reading of Smith if we define liberalism as "possessive individualism," as the interpretations Winch criticizes tend to do.

51. On Hume's link to utilitarian theory, see J. L. Mackie, *Hume's Moral Theory* (Boston: Routledge and Kegan Paul, 1980), especially p. 152, and Miller, *Philosophy and Ideology*, pp. 76-77. Both come to similar conclusions to my own.

52. David Gauthier, "David Hume, Contractarian," *The Philosophical Review* 88 (January 1979): 13.

53. Hume, "Of the Original Contract," in *Political Essays*, p. 44.

54. Smith, *Moral Sentiments*, p. 158.

55. Ibid., p. 163.

56. Ibid., p. 159.

57. Ibid., pp. 515-16. For Hume's discussion of why utility pleases, see David Hume, *An Enquiry Concerning the Principles of Morals*, ed. J. B. Schneewind (Indianapolis: Hackett, 1983), pp. 38-51.

58. Hume, *Treatise*, p. 471.

59. Ibid., p. 472. See also, Hume, *Enquiry*, p. 111.

60. Flew, *David Hume*, p. 150.

61. Hume, *Enquiry*, p. 75.

62. This is an interesting argument, though, I think, a minority position among Hume scholars. See David Fate Norton, "Hume's Moral Ontology," *Hume Studies* (1985 supplement), p. 191.

63. Hume, *Enquiry*, p. 15.

64. Harrison, *Hume's Moral Epistemology*, p. 111.

65. Morton White, *Philosophy of the American Revolution* (New York: Oxford University Press, 1978), p. 99. See also May, *Enlightenment*, p. 343-46.

66. May, *Enlightenment*, p. 121.

67. Among the participants in the Constitutional Convention and ratification debates, James Wilson was most taken with Reid's work. His highly regarded lectures on law delivered in the College of Philadelphia in 1791 draw heavily on Reid, whom Wilson compared to Bacon as a scientist of the mind. See Stephen A. Conrad, "Metaphor and Imagination in James Wilson's Theory of Federal Union," *Law and Social Inquiry* 13 (1988): 22-23. On the importance of Reid in early nineteenth century American thought, see May, especially pp. 337-57.

68. Norman Daniels, *Thomas Reid's "Inquiry": The Geometry of Visibles and the Case for Realism* (New York: Burt Franklin, 1974), pp. 120-21.

69. Thomas Reid, *Inquiry into the Human Mind*, in *The Works of Thomas Reid, D.D.*, ed. Sir William Hamilton, (London: Longmans, Green, 1895), 1: 187 and 209.

70. Ibid., 1: 92.

71. Reid, *Essays on the Active Powers of Man*, in *Works*, 2: 652.

72. Reid, *Active Powers*, in *Works*, 2:654.

73. Wills the former, Adair the latter.

74. *Federalist* 31, pp. 193-94.

75. Thomas Paine, *Common Sense and Other Political Writings* (Indianapolis: Bobbs-Merrill, 1953), p. 3.

76. White, *Philosophy, "The Federalist," and the Constitution*, especially chaps. 3 and 4.

77. Hume, "Of the Original Contract," in *Political Essays*, pp. 52-53.

78. Quoted in Miller, *Philosophy and Ideology*, p. 182.

79. Hume, *Enquiry*, p. 24.

80. Ibid., p. 28.

81. Smith, *Moral Sentiments*, p. 163.

82. Ibid., p. 161.

83. Hume, "Of the Original Contract," in *Political Essays*, p. 55.

84. Hume, *Enquiry*, p. 95.

85. Ibid., p. 94.

86. See also, Hume, "Of the Origin of Justice and Property," in *Political Essays*, p. 32.

87. Hume, *Treatise*, p. 492. See also, Hume, "Of the Origin of Justice and Property," in *Political Essays*, p. 35.

88. Hume, *Treatise*, p. 499, and "Of the Origin of Justice and Property," in *Political Essays*, p. 32.

89. Hume, *Enquiry*, p. 43. See also, *Treatise*, pp. 499-500. There he argues that "self-interest is the original motive to the establishment of justice: but a sympathy with public interest is the source of the moral approbation, which attends that virtue."

90. Hume, *Enquiry*, p. 43.

91. Smith, *Moral Sentiments*, p. 167.

92. Ibid., pp. 167-68.

93. Ibid., p. 310. This is an oft-quoted criticism directed against Hume.

94. Ibid., p. 114-15.

95. Ibid., p. 126.

96. Hume, *Treatise*, p. 194.

97. Ibid., p. 198.

98. Ibid., p. 505.

99. Miller, *Philosophy and Ideology*, p. 71. Of course, superstition can also be socially useful, although Hume, like Madison, focuses more on its potentially destructive and destabilizing effects.

100. Hume, *Treatise*, p. 542.

101. Ibid., p. 556.

102. Ibid., p. 557.

103. Ibid.

104. Ibid., p. 561.

105. Ibid.

106. Ibid., p. 562.

107. Ibid., p. 556.

108. Hume, "Of the Origin of Government," in *Political Essays*, p. 40.

109. Ibid., pp. 40-41.

110. Hume, "Of the Original Contract," p. 46.

111. Hume, "Of the First Principles of Government," in *Political Essays*, p. 24.

112. Hume, *Enquiry*, p. 46.

113. Hume, "Of the First Principles of Government," in *Political Essays*, p. 24.

114. Hume, *Enquiry*, p. 81.

115. Ibid., pp. 81-82.

116. Wills, *Explaining America,* p. 268.

117. Ibid.

118. Ibid., p. 192.

119. Hume, *Treatise,* p. 492.

120. Hume, "Of the Independence of Parliament," in *Political Essays,* p. 68. Madison expresses such a similar thought in his "Vices of the Political System of the United States," that a direct Humean influence seems likely. See Marvin Meyers, ed., *The Mind of the Founder: Sources of the Political Thought of James Madison,* rev. ed. (Hanover, N.H.: University Press of New England, 1981), p. 63. The idea that restraints of character weaken in a multitude also supports Madison's assertion in *Federalist* 55 that, had every Athenian been a Socrates, the assembly would still have acted as a mob.

121. Hume, *Treatise,* p. 547.

Chapter 5

1. Jonathan Elliot, ed. *The Debates in the Several State Conventions on the Adoption of the Federal Constitution,* 5 vols. (New York: Burt Franklin, 1888), 2:320.

2. Quoted in Vernon L. Parrington, *Main Currents in American Thought,* 2 vols. (New York: Harcourt, Brace, 1954), 1: 303. For Hume's original, see "Of the Independence of Parliament," in *Political Essays,* p. 68.

3. See chapter 6, p. 101 and chapter 7, p. 150.

4. Elliot, 2: 349.

5. *Federalist,* 55, p. 346.

6. Whether there is such an inconsistency depends in how strongly the republican commitments are stated. See chapter 2.

7. Hume will loom larger in the next chapter when the latter problem is discussed. This is so largely because the language of justification of basic institutions Madison and Hamilton use is largely constructed around Lockean notions of natural rights and social contract. This is also by and large true of the Anti-Federalists I discuss in chapter 7. This Lockean language predates Hume's influence in America and was less controversial among the audience the authors of *The Federalist* wanted to reach. In addition, Madison in particular is more committed to rights-oriented defenses of free speech and religion than Hume himself would offer, though Hume, as I argued in chapter 4, can fairly be described as a liberal. The problem of allegiance to and virtue in an extended republic was, in contrast, a new one for Americans in 1787 and here Hume's political and psychological insights were more valuable. The reader will also note that I sometimes refer to the authors of *The Federalist* by their chosen nom de plume, Publius, rather than by their proper names. When I do so, one can assume that I find a confluence between the arguments used by Madison and Hamilton. Jay is more or less excluded given his rather minimal contribution to *The Federalist.* When discussing particular numbers of *The Federalist,* I refer to the proper name of the author. I do the same where I find notable differences in Madison's and Hamilton's views.

8. *Federalist* 15, p. 110.

9. Hobbes, pp. 198 and 200.

10. *Federalist* 15, p. 110.

11. Ibid.

12. *Federalist* 10, p. 78.

13. *Federalist* 51, pp. 324-25.

14. *Federalist* 45, pp. 288-89

15. *Federalist* 10, p. 79.

16. *Federalist* 46, p. 295. Edward Corwin wrote what is still among the best short treatments of the events in the states between 1776 and 1789 and their relation to the development of constitutional thought in that period. He argues that the frequent incursions of state legislatures into judicial activities were of special concern to Madison. Thus, concern over the security of private rights was one of the main impetuses, in Madison's view, for supporting a new Constitution. See Edward Corwin, "The Progress of Constitutional Theory between the Declaration of Independence and the Meeting of the Philadelphia Convention," *American Historical Review* 30 (April 1925): 511-36.

17. See, for example, Norman Jacobson, "Political Science and Political Education," *American Political Science Review* 57 (September 1963): 561-69.

18. *Federalist* 15, p. 110.

19. Meyers, *The Mind of the Founder*, p. 178.

20. *Federalist* 10, p. 78.

21. *Federalist* 55, p. 346.

22. Madison, "Vices of the Political System of the United States," in Meyers, *The Mind of the Founder*, p. 63.

23. Ibid. For Hume's original see , "Of the Independence of Parliament," in *Political Essays*, p. 68.

24. The mind, as Hume had said, is "wonderfully fortified by a unanimity of sentiments": hence our disputatious nature when confronted with contrary opinions and hence also, the propensity of religious belief to kindle into factious enthusiasms. "Of Parties in General," in *Political Essays*, p. 82.

25. Meyers, *The Mind of the Founder*, p. 64.

26. Ibid., p. 63.

27. Ibid. This argument is repeated by Madison at the Philadelphia Convention on June 6, 1787. See Farrand, ed., *Records of the Federal Convention*, 1:135. Hume's original is found in his *Enquiry Concerning the Principles of Morals*, p. 81. See chapter 4, p. 79.

28. Meyers, *The Mind of the Founder*, p. 60.

29. Ibid., p. 59.

30. *Federalist* 7, p. 61.

31. Ibid., p. 63.

32. Alexander Hamilton, *The Papers of Alexander*
Hamilton, 4 vols. ed. Harold C. Styrett, and Jacob E. Cook, (New York: Columbia University Press, 1960-1979), 2:83.

33. Ibid.

34. These are differences of degree. For Hamilton, as for Madison, "the vigor of government is essential to the security of liberty." Yet, Hamilton tends to decry the state of American politics for leading to national disgrace and failing in its promise of greatness. It is telling that he describes the stakes of the Constitutional crisis in terms of the "fate of an empire" in *Federalist* 1 (p. 1). In *Federalist* 6 he bemoans "the point of extreme depression to which our national dignity and credit have sunk," as a result of "lax and ill administration" (p. 59). Madison appears less concerned with "national dignity" or greatness and more with the pattern of rights violations he sees as emerging from dissolute government under the Articles of Confederation. See Corwin, "The Progress of Constitutional Theory."

35. Hamilton, *Papers*, 1:47.

36. For typical remarks indicating Hamilton's elitism, see Elliot, 5: 244.

37. *Federalist* 10, p. 84.

38. Meyers, *The Mind of the Founder*, p. 7.

39. Ibid., pp. 8-9, 10-11.

40. Elliot, *Debates*, 3:330.

41. Madison, it should be noted, originally opposed the inclusion of a bill of rights, although this should not be interpreted as a lack of commitment to, in this case, religious freedom. During the Virginia debates, he had followed Hume in arguing that "the multiplicity of sects which pervades America" provided a necessary and sufficient protection of religious liberty. Elliot, *Debates*, 3:330. See Hume on "factions of principle" in "Of Parties in General," *Political Essays*, pp. 77-84. Also see n. 47.

42. National Archives Manuscript Volume, "Ratification of the Constitution with copies of credentials of delegates to the Constitutional Convention." Microcopy no. T-830, Roll no. 1.

43. Meyers, *The Mind of the Founder*, p. 9.

44. There has been, of course, an extensive constitutional debate throughout our history over the relation of church and state and, more specifically, over just what the government's neutrality toward churches and sects requires. Jefferson offers one interpretation of the First Amendment's anti-establishment clause when he claims that it was intended to "erect a wall of separation between Church and State." Others have suggested that the clause forbids only giving one church an "exclusive position of power and favor over all other churches or denominations." Leonard W. Levy argues that the former construction conforms to the "founders' intents." Both, I think, point to a neutrality principle at the heart of liberal discourse in a weak and a strong form (though note understanding of neutrality offered in chapter 2). Madison's understanding of the *obligation* each person has to worship God in the manner judged most pleasing to Him, and his unwillingness to see religion used as an instrument of social policy, suggests to me that Levy is correct at least as far as Madison is concerned. See "No Establishment of Religion: The Original Understanding," in *Judgments: Essays on American Constitutional History* (Chicago: Quadrangle Books, 1972), p. 170.

45. Meyers, *The Mind of the Founder*, p. 64.

46. Ibid. The conditional "sufficiently" leaves some question about Madison's understanding of this neutrality requirement though granting clear privileges to religious sects and modes of political speech are anathema to him.

47. Meyers, *The Mind of the Founder*, p. 64.

48. This was, of course, a near paraphrase of Hume's argument in the "Idea of a Perfect Commonwealth," on the advantages of a large over a small republic. See Hume, *Political Essays*, p. 157.

49. As Herbert Storing argues, the Bill of Rights is the greatest Anti-Federalist legacy to the Constitution. See Herbert J. Storing, ed., *The Complete Anti-Federalist*, 7 vols. (Chicago: University of Chicago Press, 1981), vol. 1: *What the Anti-Federalists Were For*, by Herbert J. Storing, pp. 64-70. Neither Madison nor Hamilton thought it advisable to include a bill of rights in the Constitution prior to its ratification. Madison argues in *Federalist* 38 (p. 238) that a bill of rights is not "essential to liberty," pointing out that there was no such document under the Confederation (except, of course, in several state constitutions). Hamilton takes the stronger position that a bill of rights is an altogether ineffective instrument for protecting liberties. Discussing liberty of the press specifically, he argues in *Federalist* 84 that such a freedom "*must altogether depend* on public opinion, and on the general spirit of the people and of the government [emphasis added]" p. 514). This is a gloss on Hume's remark that it is on "opinion only that government is founded" and sustained, in "Of the First Principles of Government," in *Political Essays*, p. 24. See also Wills, *Explaining America*, pt. I, chap. 3, for Hume's

influence on this point.) This applies, for Hamilton, to such desirable practices as preserving rights of free worship as well. There were both strategic and theoretical reasons for the authors of *The Federalist* not to favor a bill of rights at this stage, although Madison later underwent an apparently sincere conversion. See chapter 6, pp. 112–15.

50. For a discussion of the understanding of freedom of the press in America in the constitutional period, see Leonard W. Levy, "Liberty of the Press from Zenger to Jefferson," in his collection, *Judgments: Essays on American Constitutional History* (Chicago: Quadrangle Books, 1972), pp. 115–58.

51. Meyers, *The Mind of the Founder*, p. 244.

52. Ibid., p. 259.

53. Ibid.

Chapter 6

1. Elliot, *Debates, 3:61.*

2. *Federalist*, 51, p. 322.

3. Elliot, *Debates*, 3:327.

4. Ibid., 3:167.

5. I will return in the next chapter to the *conception* of liberty Anti-Federalists, including Henry, see as threatened, a conception which contains positive and negative dimensions, although Henry's general theory of government seems a far cry from the more exalted versions of republicanism that call for sacrifices of self-interest for the common good.

6. Henry's objection was a common one among Anti-Federalists. Thus, Melancthon Smith argued, looking to the future that it would be "wise to multiply checks to a greater degree than the present state of things requires" And George Mason complained that there was too much overlapping of powers between the president and the Senate in foreign affairs. Such an overlap, he argues, "will destroy all balances." Quoted in Wood, *Creation*, p. 548. See also discussion of the Federal Farmer in the next chapter. The Anti-Federalists appear to be at least as committed as their rivals to the use of "mechanical devices" in government to control powers and even more skeptical of "virtue" as a restraint.

7. *Federalist* 27, p. 174. See also Elliot, *Debates*, 2:254. There Hamilton argues that the "confidence of the people will easily be gained by a good administration. This is the true touchstone."

8. *Federalist* 27, p. 176.

9. *Federalist* 45, p. 293.

10. *Federalist* 17, p. 120.

11. Ibid.

12. Madison uses this phrase in *Federalist* 46, p. 295.

13. Farrand, *Records of the Federal Convention*, 1: 285.

14. *Federalist* 46, 295.

15. *Federalist* 15, p. 112. Compare this to Hume on the ability of natural "social sympathy," to lead to injustice and political unrest in *Enquiry*, p. 46.

16. See p. 89.

17. Farrand, *Records of the Federal Convention*, 1:311.

18. *Federalist* 17, p. 119.

19. *Federalist* 9, p. 73. We know given Madison's description of the vices of small republics that he saw the ties of benevolence to be a fairly weak political bond even

over a narrow compass. As Adair noted, this line of argument is almost certainly drawn from Hume's essay "Idea of a Perfect Commonwealth." There Hume had noted both democracies tendency toward turbulence since they are susceptible to "popular tides" and "personal" factions. He went on to add that although it is harder to form a republic over a large territory, it is probably easier to maintain it. He attributes this both to the difficulties of factious majorities forming and the ability to "refine the democracy, from the lower people who may be admitted into the first elections ... to the higher magistrates who direct all the movements," Hume, *Political Essays*, pp. 157-58. See also Adair, pp. 99-100.

20. Aristotle, *Nicomachean Ethics* 1.3 and 2.1, trans. J. A. K. Thomson (Baltimore: Penguin Books, 1955), pp. 28 and 55.

21. See especially, Sunstein, "Beyond the Republican Revival," and Tushnet, *Red, White and Blue*.

22. Meyers, *The Mind of the Founder*, p. 179.

23. Ibid., p. 177.

24. Ibid., p. 178. There is here a parallel to Hume's view of the importance of custom in stabilizing property relations. See Hume, *Treatise*, pp. 501-13; and chapter 4 p. 76.

25. Ibid., p. 176.

26. *Federalist* 49, p. 314.

27. Elliot, *Debates*, 3:489.

28. Farrand, *Records of the Federal Convention*, 1:422.

29. Ibid., p. 423.

30. Meyers, *The Mind of the Founder*, p. 397.

31. It should also be noted that Madison did not find these changes to be altogether salutary. In fact, he found them a cause for regret. The point remains, however, that though these economic changes may be regrettable, they are not, for Madison, a cause for action.

32. Farrand, *Records of the Federal Convetion*, 2:203-4.

33. See Meyers, *The Mind of the Founder*, pp. 394-400.

34. Ibid., p. 400. It can be surmised that Madison sees a role for the public servant in this diffusion of a "popular sense of injustice." In this, he follows Hume, who argued that, although a sense of justice emerges in most people almost inevitably, it can be "forwarded by the artifice of politicians, who, in order to govern men more easily, and preserve peace in human society, have endeavor'd to produce an esteem for justice, and an abhorrence of injustice," *Treatise*, p. 500.

35. Meyers, *The Mind of the Founder*, p. 397.

36. Ibid., p. 398.

37. In addition to works by Barber (1977), McWilliams, and Bellah, see H. Mark Roelofs, *Ideology and Myth in American Politics* (Boston: Little, Brown, 1976), especially chap. 3.

38. Meyers, *The Mind of the Founder*, p. 169.

39. See chapter 5, pp. 197-98 n. 49.

40. *Federalist* 38, p. 238.

41. *Federalist* 84, p. 515.

42. Herbert J. Storing, "The Constitution and the Bill of Rights," in *Essays on the Constitution of the United States*, ed. M. Judd Harmon (Port Washington, N.Y.: Kennikat Press, 1978), pp. 45-46.

43. Walter Berns, "The Constitution as a Bill of Rights," in Berns, *In Defense of Liberal Democracy* (Chicago: Gateway Editions, 1984), p. 7.

44. Rawls, *Theory of Justice*, especially chap. 8.

45. See Hume, "Of the Original Contract," in *Political Essays*, especially pp. 45-47.

46. Parrington, *Main Currents*, 1: 311

47. This is a rather unsalutary example of Hume's influence. In the "Idea of a Perfect Commonwealth," Hume quotes favorably a writer who "says that all very numerous assemblies, however composed, are mere mob." Even if every individual is of "middling sense," collectively they are reduced to a rabble. See *Political Essays*, p. 153.

48. Tocqueville was to note the tendency of Americans to concern themselves almost exclusively with local political decisions. "It is difficult to force a man out of himself and get him to take an interest in the affairs of the whole state. . . . But if it is a question of taking a road past his property, he sees at once that this small public matter has a bearing on his greatest private interests." Tocqueville, *Democracy*, p. 511. Or as another great observer of American politics, Tip O'Neill put it, "all politics is local."

49. *Federalist* 63, p. 387.

50. This idea is also drawn from Hume. See "Idea of a Perfect Commonwealth," in *Political Essays*, p. 145-58.

51. Hume, "Of the Independence of Parliament," in *Political Essays*, p. 68.

52. Meyers, *The Mind of the Founder*, p. 396.

53. *Federalist* 55, p. 342.

54. *Federalist* 50, p. 319.

55. For a concise discussion of political parties in the context of late eighteenth century Anglo-American political thought, see Richard Hofstadter, *The Idea of a Party System* (Berkeley: University of California Press, 1969), especially pp. 1-39. Madison shares the view of parties as threats to national unity, that is, as factious. As Hofstadter points out, however, he follows Hume who had argued that "to abolish all distinctions of party may not be practicable, perhaps not desirable in a free government"; Hume, "Of the Coalition of Parties," in *Political Essays*, p. 93. Madison puts it more colorfully—and more strongly—when he claims that "liberty is to faction what air is to fire" *Federalist* 10, p. 78.

56. Wills, *Explaining America*, p. 187.

57. *Federalist* 76, p. 458. See also John Jay in *Federalist* 64, p. 395.

58. *Federalist* 57, p. 353.

59. Ibid., p. 350.

60. *Federalist* 51, pp. 321-22.

61. See, for example, *Federalist* 67, pp. 406-7 where the senators' motives to resist encroachments by the executive are discussed.

62. We found the same ambivalence in Hume's discussion of interest as a motive for action. Madison seems to rely on a similar distinction to the one Hume draws between long- and short-term interests.

63. Albert O. Hirschman argues that a notion of interest as a tamer of the passions is encountered with great frequency in eighteenth century political and economic thought. Interests tame passions just for this element of calculation in the former which is lacking in the latter. Albert O. Hirschman, *The Passions and the Interests* (Princeton: Princeton University Press, 1977).

64. Farrand, *Records of the Federal Conventions*, 1:422. See also *Federalist* 63, p. 371.

65. *Federalist* 35, p. 214.

66. *Federalist* 57, p. 352.

67. Hume, "Of the Rise and Progress of the Arts and Sciences," in *Political Essays*, p. 119.

68. *Federalist* 72, pp. 437-38. Hamilton makes the same point in his June 18 Philadelphia Convention speech. See Farrand, *Records of the Federal Convention*, 1:288-91.

69. *Federalist* 72, p. 438.

70. *Federalist* 75, p. 451.

71. Garry Wills misinterprets Hamilton here to be relying on "superlative virtue" as "the directing force of the republic" (*Explaining America*, p. 187). Though Hamilton has confidence that elected officials will be at least somewhat virtuous, that is hardly his point here. He is relying on an interested calculation on the part of the president regarding the risks and benefits of aggrandizement in office. This, he suggests, is a more reliable motive than is superlative virtue.

72. John Jay displays this tendency as well as Hamilton and Madison. *Federalist* 64 is a case in point. Jay defends the treaty making power granted to the president with the "advice and consent" of the Senate. Typically, he begins by stating the importance of the power and justifying its residing with the executive given the need for secrecy and dispatch in foreign affairs. He then proceeds to discuss the institutional mechanisms which prevent its abuse. Finally, he argues that *even if* opportunities for abuse were prevalent, *motives* to abuse would be lacking. "Every consideration that can influence the human mind, such as honor, oaths, reputations, conscience, the love of country, and family affections and attachments, afford security for their [i.e., the president's and senators'] fidelity"; *Federalist* 64, p. 396.

73. *Federalist* 57, pp. 351-52.

74. Ibid., p. 352.

75. Farrand, *Records of the Federal Convention*, 1:428.

76. Ibid., 1:423.

77. Meyers, *The Mind of the Founder*, p. 399.

78. John Bach McMaster and Frederick D. Stone, eds., *Pennsylvania and the Federal Constitution*, 2 vols. (N.P.: Historical Society of Pennsylvania, 1888), 1: 298.

79. Ibid., 1:297.

80. *Federalist* 62, p. 382. See also, "Vices of the Political System of the United States, in Meyers, *The Mind of the Founder*, especially p. 61.

81. See chapter 2, p. 37.

82. Elliot, *Debates*, 3:37.

Chapter 7

1. Cecilia Kenyon, ed., *The Anti-Federalists* (New York: Bobbs-Merrill, 1966), p. xcvi.

2. See Daniel J.Boorstin, *The Genius of American Politics* (Chicago: University of Chicago Press, 1953); and John P. Roche, "The Founding Fathers: A Reform Caucus in Action," *American Political Science Review* 55 (1961): 799-816.

3. See Hartz, *Liberal Tradition*; and Richard Hofstadter, *The American Political Tradition and the Men Who Made It* (New York: Vintage Books, 1973).

4. See Forrest McDonald, *We the People* (Chicago: University of Chicago Press, 1958); and Clinton Rossiter, *1787: The Grand Convention* (New York: Macmillan 1966), especially pp. 11-20.

5. Wood, *Creation*, p. 523.

6. Ibid., pp. 523, 500.

7. Ibid., p. 428.

8. Ibid., p. 547.

9. Pocock, *Machiavellian Moment*, p. 531.

10. Ibid., pp. 551-52.

11. For a good general discussion and evaluation of Anti-Federalist thought, see Storing, *Complete Anti-Federalist*, vol. 1: *What the Anti-Federalists Were For*. My criteria for selecting the Anti-Federalist texts to be analyzed in depth are purely qualitative ones. It is possible—even desirable—to restrict my focus to a few of the best pamphleteers, since doing so enables us to explore extended arguments in detail. By common consent, any short list of the best writings includes the Federal Farmer, Brutus, and Cato, all published in New York contemporaneously with the essays collected as *The Federalist*. The superiority of these works derives from their comprehensiveness—each builds from a general theory of government to a specific and salient critique of the Constitution and its "consolidation" of political power in the national government. Each also considers in some detail the view that states are better able to garner the support of their citizens than a national government could be. Their critique of consolidation is, therefore, both institutional and attitudinal. These works are better also for the specificity of their critiques, a specificity often lacking in weaker pamphlets, which turgidly repeat but do not analyze the dire consequences that will follow if the Constitution is adopted. These writers, to paraphrase Herbert Storing, who collected and edited Anti-Federalist works with diligent care, are better not because they are most directly influential (even if this could be measured) but because they dig deeper into the theoretical ground that their compatriots take for granted. Concern that my selection may be biased against a republican-revisionist thesis should be alleviated both by my focus on the issues of citizenship in all four works and by the inclusion of the essays by A Farmer.

12. Storing, *Complete Anti-Federalist*, vol. 2: *Objections of Non-Signers of the Constitution and Major Series of Essays at the Outset*, p. 373. In the following notes, I will refer to the pamphleteers by name only when it has not been specified in the text. I refer, that is, to their pseudonyms. In each case, there are doubts about authorship. On the question of authorship, see Storing 2:215-16 (on the Federal Farmer); 2:358 (on Brutus); 2:102 (on Cato); 5:5 (on A Farmer).

13. Storing, *Complete Anti-Federalist*, 2:373.

14. Ibid., 2:109-10.

15. Ibid., 2:261.

16. Wood, *Creation*, p. 499.

17. The Federal Farmer, in Storing, *Complete Anti-Federalist*, 2:232.

18. Ibid., 2:373.

19. Ibid., 5:161-62.

20. Ibid., 4:81-82. Though Agrippa's discussion of the value of unfettered commerce is unusual, it does point to the difficulties in generalizing about the Anti-Federalists, especially where their so-called "dread of modernity" is concerned. Joyce Appleby has recognized this, claiming that the Anti-Federalists were "no less concerned than the Federalists with the expanding horizons for individual self-improvement held out by commercial progress." Though she also claims that the former "did not posit a fundamental incompatibility between legislative activism and private property rights." It is impossible to evaluate this claim without discussing the sorts of specific restrictions legislatures can impose on market exchanges. It is at best speculative to claim that there

was a fundamental difference between Federalists and Anti-Federalists on this score. This difference is at least not apparent in the discussion of "first principles" currently being considered. See Joyce Appleby, "The American Heritage: The Heirs and the Disinherited," *The Journal of American History* 74 (December 1987): 806.

21. Storing, *Complete Anti-Federalist*, 4:45.

22. Ibid., 2:370-71.

23. Ibid., 2:111.

24. Ibid.

25. Ibid., 2:231.

26. Problems of scale are central to economic analyses of collective goods problems, for example. See Mancur Olson, *The Logic of Collective Action: Public Goods and the Theory of Groups* (Cambridge, Mass.: Harvard University Press, 1971), especially chap. 2. Montesquieu was the common gloss for this observation in the founding era.

27. Brutus, in Storing, *Complete Anti-Federalist*, 2:369.

28. Ibid., 2:267.

29. Ibid., 2:268.

30. Ibid., 2:267-68.

31. Ibid., 2:268. See also Cato, ibid., 2:119.

32. Lee was identified as the Federal Farmer in several contemporaneous news articles published in New England. However, recent scholars have challenged this attribution on grounds of style and substance. See note 12 above.

33. Storing, *Complete Anti-Federalist*, 5:117-18. A Farmer also expresses this antimajoritarian sentiment, observing that "the rights of individuals are frequently opposed to the apparent interests of the majority." The specific context of this claim is to argue for a bill of rights. Because of this tendency of majorities, democratic governments are *most* in need of the protections such a declaration could provide. See Storing, *Complete Anti-Federalist*, 5:15.

34. Brutus, in Storing, *Complete Anti-Federalist*, 2:380.

35. See, for example, Brutus and the Federal Farmer, ibid., 2:380 and 2:224, respectively.

36. Ibid., 2:339.

37. Ibid., 2:224, 2:234.

38. Ibid., 2:264.

39. Ibid., 2:279.

40. Ibid., 2:385.

41. Ibid., 2:384.

42. Ibid., 2:382-83.

43. Ibid., 2:385.

44. Ibid.

45. Ibid.

46. Ibid., 2:112.

47. Ibid.

48. Ibid.

49. Ibid.

50. Ibid., 2:125.

51. Ibid., 2:125, 2:117.

52. *Federalist* 55, p. 342.

53. See, for example, Brutus, in Storing, *Complete Anti-Federalist*, 2:407. Other examples are cited in the following text.

54. Ibid., 1:83n.

55. Ibid., 2:119.

56. Ibid., 2:291.

57. Ibid., 2:118.

58. Ibid., 2:291.

59. Ibid., 1:21.

60. Pocock, *Machiavellian Moment*, p. 507.

61. For the Federalists on this theme, see Hamilton, *Federalist* 28, p. 180. For the Federal Farmer's rebuke, see Storing, *Complete Anti-Federalist*, 2:180-81.

62. Storing, *Complete Anti-Federalist*, 2:260.

63. Ibid., 2:258.

64. The Federal Farmer, ibid., 2:292.

65. Ibid., 2:258.

66. See, for example, Pocock's interpretation of Jacksonian democracy in *Machiavellian Moment*, pp. 537-541.

67. Cato, in Storing, *Complete Anti-Federalist*, 2:117.

68. Ibid.

69. Ibid., 2:251-52.

70. This is not to say that early American government was strictly neutral with regard to the economy. The securities issue Beard focuses so much attention on is clearly an example of governmental decisions affecting distributions of wealth in the society. Yet the point remains that the idea that a certain pattern of economic distribution should be maintained to foster "virtue" is as foreign to the Anti-Federalists as it is to Publius.

71. Storing, *Complete Anti-Federalist*, 2:249.

72. A Farmer's essays appeared in the *Maryland Gazette*, published in Baltimore from February through April 1788. The Federalists won the ratification vote rather handily on April 28, 1788, by a 63 to 11 margin and Maryland became the seventh state to ratify. New York, in contrast, did not ratify until July of that year and by a narrow 30 to 27 vote. By this point, nine states had adopted the Constitution, which was enough to put it into effect in those states. This may have swayed New York's decision, since early indications were that the Anti-Federalists would prevail. Though I do not make any causal inference, it is at least clear that A Farmer's arguments were not terribly influential with his state's delegates to the ratifying convention.

73. Storing, *Complete Anti-Federalist*, 5:55.

74. Ibid., 5:30.

75. Ibid., 5:56.

76. A farmer in fact declares that the reasoning of this progress is inessential for his purposes. Nonetheless, he takes the cycle of decline he describes—from rule of a "few wealthy individuals" terminating in monarchy backed by a standing army—to be familiar to students of antiquity. Ibid., p. 18.

77. Ibid., 5:68.

78. Ibid., 5:36.

79. Ibid., 5:15.

80. Ibid., 5:49.

81. Ibid., 5:39.

82. As Tocqueville was to observe some forty years later, "juries invest each citizen with a sort of magisterial office; they make all men feel that they have duties toward society and that they share in its government"; Tocqueville, *Democracy*, p. 274. Jury duty is an interesting practice for testing one's views toward liberal and republican ideals. In my view, liberals can and should value it for much the reasons Tocqueville

suggests. *But* a liberal also should endorse the right of judges to overturn verdicts that are clearly at variance with the law. Here the participatory good, and right to render a verdict, must give way to the essential role of the trial: to render justice. Republicans clearly value justice as well but, I suspect, would be rather more ambivalent on this judicial right than liberals.

83. Even where elements of genuinely republican government are found, as they had been in New England's town meetings and Pennsylvania's unicameral legislature, they are quick becoming mere vestiges. Storing, *Complete Anti-Federalist*, 5:67.

84. Ibid., 5:30.

85. Ibid., 5:10, 5:35.

86. Ibid., 5:44.

87. Ibid., 5:69.

88. John Diggins provides a reading of the role of republicanism in the rhetoric of the constitutional debates. Though I see more real content to Anti-Federalist republicanism than Diggins allows, his discussion is still quite fruitful. See Diggins, *Lost Soul*, pp. 31-32.

Chapter 8

1. I am less concerned with documenting this discontent (that there is such discontent few would dispute) than with exploring the "neorepublican" solution for what we might call civic malaise. Nonetheless, a few nonscholarly examples beyond the works analyzed in detail in this chapter are in order. Public expressions of concern over apathy are especially common during presidential election years. For example, New York Times op-ed writer Anthony Lewis invokes Madison to argue that we have fallen far from the founder's vision of an active democratic citizenry: "Madison's vision was of an informed electorate 'examining public characters and measures'; the voters would be active participants in a public policy debate. Today the voters are passive figures in a process utterly removed from public policy ... " (*New York Times*, 10 November, 1988, p. A31). I do not challenge Lewis's goals of enhanced participation, although both his readings of Madison and the decline-and-fall use to which they are put are questionable. In a post-election editorial, the *New York Times* expresses regret over the 51 percent turnout. In doing so, it cites favorably the educator Robert Maynard Hutchins, who warned that "the death of democracy ... will be a slow extinction from apathy, indifference and undernourishment." (6 November, 1989, p. A24).

Public concern over the dominance of private, egoistic, goals over public ones in the "Me Decade" and beyond are rife. See, for example, Christopher Lasch, *The Culture of Narcissism* (New York: W. W. Norton, 1978). See also his op-ed article in the *New York Times* of 27 December 1989 (p. A23), "The I's Have It for Another Decade." There Lasch contends that American youth is not only bereft of civic values but is living "in an unbearable state of agony" because of it. Though Lasch is generally considered to be on the political left, his analysis bears a sharp resemblance to the kinds of complaints made by the conservative Allen Bloom in *The Closing of the American Mind* (New York: Simon and Schuster, 1987). Both contend that the incapacity of American youth to take seriously the predominant values of their culture, including political ones, leaves them falling back on a narrow hedonism ultimately not fulfilling even to themselves.

2. Robert N. Bellah, R. Madsen, A. Swindler, W. Sullivan and S. Tipton, *Habits of the Heart: Individualism and Commitment in American Life* (Berkeley: University of California Press, 1985), p. 292.

3. Tocqueville, *Democracy*, p. 245.

4. Voting is not necessarily the best indicator of civic-mindedness. In fact, there is something of a paradox in American voting behavior if it is viewed from a comparative perspective. A classic study comparing political attitudes in several western democracies (Gabriel A. Almond and Sidney Verba, *The Civic Culture*, Boston: Little, Brown, 1965) found that Americans ranked at or near the top in measures of political interest, feelings of civic duty, and feelings of political efficacy. Yet they ranked last in postwar electoral turnout. Italy, which ranked near the bottom in terms of the above attitudes had the highest voter turnout rates. See also Ivor Crewe, "Electoral Participation," in *A Comparative Study of Competitive National Elections*, eds. David Butler, Howard R. Penniman, and Austin Ranney (Washington, D.C.: American Enterprise Institute, 1981), pp. 216-63. Largely because of this paradox, political scientists have looked to other than cultural factors to explain low voter turnout in American elections. One concludes that the United States is advantaged somewhat by favorable political attitudes but strongly disadvantaged by party structure and, especially, registration laws. See G. Bingham Powell, "American Voter Turnout in Comparative Perspective," *American Political Science Review* 80 (March 1986): 17-37. Similar controversies exist in explaining voting in the United States over time. Voter turnout in American national elections has declined rather sharply from those reported in the nineteenth century. Again, it is debatable how much of this has to do with changes in attitudes and beliefs and how much with changes in the institutional and legal climate. The Australian ballot, for example, only came widely into use in the 1890s and registration laws have become more rigorous since then as well. Both events reduced voting fraud, which is believed to have been widespread throughout the nineteenth century. As there is no reliable measure of the extent of fraud, it is impossible to say whether or how much voting turnout in the nineteenth century surpassed that in the twentieth. These changes in the electoral process have been accompanied by the expansion of the electorate, including women, blacks (most of whom were effectively excluded up to the Civil Rights Act of 1964 and Voting Rights Act of 1965), and eighteen year olds. For an overview of the debate on changes in voting in the United States over time, see Richard G. Niemi and Herbert F. Weisberg, eds., *Controversies in American Voting Behavior* (San Francisco: W. H. Freeman, 1976): especially pp. 440-49. One should resist the temptation to attribute changes in political behavior to changes in attitudes reflecting deeper alterations in the ideological beliefs of the society without firm evidence.

5. Pocock, Wills, and Wood all suggest this conclusion though they differ over when the last gasp of a "virtuous politics" occurred. In Pocock's words, "the decline of virtue has its corollary in the rise of interest," in *Machiavellian Moment*, p. 521 and especially pp. 520-27; Wills, *Explaining America*, p. 268; and Wood, *The Creation*, especially pp. 606-15.

6. See p. 149.

7. Daniel Bell, "The Public Household: On 'Fiscal Sociology' and the Liberal State," in Bell, *The Cultural Contradictions of Capitalism* (New York: Basic Books, 1978), p. 256.

8. Ibid., p. 248.

9. Ibid., p. 249.

10. Bell's thesis can be challenged on this point. There is no necessary inverse correlation between even a hedonistic consumerism on the one hand and a willingness to work on the other. Though yuppie-bashing has become a popular pastime of our age largely because Yuppies are taken to represent the shallow consumerism Bell laments, one charge that will not stick concerns their commitment to a strong work ethic. (The standard office desk calendar has now extended the working day by leaving space for

writing in 7:30 A.M. appointments.) BMWs do not come cheaply. The fact that yuppies are bashed for their selfishness is a sotto voce indication of the continued strength of the Protestant ethic and of the value placed on selflessness by others.

11. Bell, *Cultural Contradictions*, pp. 244–45.

12. Samuel P. Huntington, "The United States," in *The Crisis of Democracy*, eds. Huntington, Michel J. Crozier, and Joji Watanuki (New York: New York University Press, 1975), p. 114.

13. Huntington's view is, in fact, that this ethos is largely lacking in the United States compared to other Western developed countries (and Japan) because we lack the "residual inheritances of traditional and aristocratic values" still present in these countries. Thus, though our institutions are "more open, liberal and democratic than those of any major society now or in the past," they are not perceived to be open, liberal, or democratic enough; Huntington, "The United States," p. 232. American liberal democratic values stand, for Huntington, as a perpetual indictment of its governing institutions. See also Huntington, *American Politics: The Promise of Disharmony* (Cambridge, Mass.: Harvard University Press, 1981), chap. 7, for an elaboration of this theme.

14. Benjamin R. Barber, *Strong Democracy* (Berkeley: University of California Press, 1984), pp. 24–25.

15. Sheldon Wolin, "The Idea of the State in America," in *The Problem of Authority in America*, eds. John P. Diggins and Mark Kann (Philadelphia: Temple University Press, 1981), pp. 47, and 54.

16. Ibid., p. 56.

17. Ibid., p. 57.

18. Bellah, et al., *Habits of the Heart*, p. 21.

19. Ibid., p. 287.

20. I suggested in chapter 2 that the exact nature of this claim is often left obscure. See chapter 2, p. 185, n.26.

21. There are many discussions available of these participation-oriented reforms. See, for example, Jeane J. Kirkpatrick, "Changing Patterns of Electoral Competition," in *The New American Political System*, ed. Anthony King (Washington, D.C.: American Enterprise Institute, 1978), pp. 249–85.

22. Don Herzog comes to a similar conclusion although for somewhat different reasons. See his fine piece, "Some Questions for Republicans," *Political Theory* 14 (August 1986): 473–93.

23. In fact, Barber has addressed these concerns in several essays written after *Strong Democracy*. He advocates a kind of pragmatic antiphilosophy according to which political knowledge is not so much discovered as created through a democratic praxis. See "Political Judgment: Philosophy as Practice," in *The Conquest of Politics: Liberal Philosophy in Democratic Times* (Princeton, N.J.: Princeton University Press, 1988), pp. 193–211.

24. There is a fascinating literature on this phenomenon. See, for example, Lee Sigelman, "The Nonvoting Voter in Voter Research," *American Journal of Political Science* 26 (February 1982), pp. 47–56; and Brian D. Silver, Barbara A. Anderson, and Paul R. Abramson, "Who Overreports Voting," *American Political Science Review* 80 (June 1986): 613–24. It is a rather large number of nonvoters who pay this homage to civic norms. The best surveys match reported voting against local registration and voting records. In elections studied from 1964 through 1980, roughly one-fourth of nonvoters claim to have voted, Silver et al., p. 613. Silver et al. find that most overreporting is done by educated people with a high sense of political efficacy, that is, by

the same sorts of people who also vote in greatest numbers. Nonetheless, overreporting occurs among all segments of the population to varying degrees.

25. The only way to avoid this implication would be to retreat into relativism: the political good is a good for me. This would be self-defeating, however.

26. Bellah et al., *Habits of the Heart*, p. 286. Bellah relies here on Alasdair MacIntyre's distinction between the pursuit of goods internal and external to practices. See MacIntyre, *After Virtue*, especially pp. 175-81.

27. Bellah et al., *Habits of the Heart*, p. 288.

28. See also Barber, *Strong Democracy*, pp. 254-58.

29. Ibid., pp. 273 and 308.

30. Ibid., p. 309.

31. Barber's policy recommendations are discussed in chap. 10 of *Strong Democracy* and are summarized on p. 307.

32. Ibid., p. 308.

33. For an excellent discussion on this point, see Robert Nozick, *Anarchy, State, and Utopia* (New York: Basic Books, 1974), pp. 164-66.

34. Barber, *Strong Democracy*, p. 252.

35. See chapter 2, pp. 22-24. To risk anachronism, Madison is in this sense an imperfect liberal.

36. Dworkin, "Why Liberals Should Care about Equality," in *A Matter of Principle* (Cambridge, Mass.: Harvard University Press, 1985), p. 211.

Appendix

1. Richard Ashcraft gives a particularly clear statement of this view: "A political theory is a set of structured meanings that are understandable *only in reference to a specified context*, wherein the concepts, terminology, and even internal structure of the theory itself are viewed in relation to a comprehensive ordering of the elements of social life." *Revolutionary Politics*, p. 5; emphasis added. Historical context is, of course, absolutely essential to answering the historical questions that pervade Ashcraft's study of Locke and his political milieu. That Locke practiced a radical politics, the formative role played in his thought by his political experience as Shaftesbury's aide, the reciprocal influence among Locke and his coterie of dissenters are issues he deals with skillfully. However, I am unconvinced of two points implied by Ashcraft: first, that these are the *only* sorts of questions we might want to ask of Locke, and second, that the problem with questionable interpretations of Locke has been a lack of historicity. On the latter point, Ashcraft himself demonstrates that there is a plethora of evidence in Locke's writings that should have headed off misreadings by Macpherson and others who tended to secularize Locke if they had paid heed to it. If they misinterpret Locke, it is not at all clear that their method is to be blamed for it. On the former point, there are questions *from* Locke that demand our attention and which historical context does little to illuminate. For example, contemporary liberals attracted to Locke's idea of toleration might ask whether Locke's defense of toleration is still viable if stripped of its theological underpinnings and, if not, how it can be put on firmer footing for our times. Ashcraft does not deny the validity of such questioning, but it is unclear how his method would deal with what is essentially a task in philosophical explication. I see no good reason for banishing such questions from the realm of political theory as Ashcraft's definition seems to require. For other expositions of the historical approach, see Pocock, *Politics, Language and Time*; John Dunn, *Rethinking Modern Political*

Theory: Essays 1979-1983 (New York: Cambridge University Press, 1985); Quentin Skinner, "'Social Meaning' and the Explanation of Social Action," in *Philosophy, Politics and Society*, 3d ser., eds. Peter Laslett et al. (Oxford: Basil Blackwell, 1972), pp. 136-57; and Skinner, "Some Problems in the Analysis of Political Thought and Action," *Political Theory* 2 (August 1974): 277-303.

2. I am relying here on Rawls's notion of "reflective equilibrium." See Rawls, *A Theory of Justice* (Cambridge, Mass.: Harvard University Press Belknap Press, 1971) especially pp. 48-51.

3. John Gunnell offers a cogent discussion of this point. See Gunnell, *Political Theory: Tradition and Interpretation* (Cambridge, Mass.: Winthrop Publishers, 1979), especially chap. 2.

4. I think this is certainly the case. Hobbes is widely read today, for example, not because of the historical influence of his ideas. In fact, Hobbes's defense of absolute sovereignty found far more critics than followers in succeeding generations (though an influence on future thought can be exerted negatively as well as positively). He is read because of the importance of the problems he addresses, because he provides powerful arguments for a method of reasoning about politics and because of the power of his arguments for conclusions most of us want to reject intuitively. Each of these reasons is transhistorical. The great books transcend their times. The importance of historical context depends upon the sorts of questions that interest us.

5. See Donald S. Lutz, "The Relative Influence of European Writers on Late Eighteenth-Century American Political Thought," *American Political Review* 78 (March 1984): 189-97.

6. There is a growing literature on the formation of beliefs and preferences, much of which is discussed by Jon Elster in *Sour Grapes: Studies in the Subversion of Rationality* (New York: Cambridge University Press, 1983), especially chap. 4, "Belief, Bias and Ideology," pp. 141-66.

7. Skinner, "Some Problems," p. 288.

8. Albert O. Hirschman, *The Passions and the Interests* (Princeton, NJ: Princeton University Press, 1977).

9. See, for example, Fritjof Capra, *The Tao of Physics: An Exploration of the Parallels between Modern Physics and Eastern Mysticism* (Berkeley, Cal.: Shambhala Publishing, distributed by Random House, 1975).

Index

320.51 Si67f
Sinopoli, Richard C.
The foundations of American
 citizenship